'Watson's book serves to remind us of the true purpose of education. This is a must read that forcefully puts the case for educating the young for democracy.'

Frank Furedi, Social Commentator and Author, formerly Professor of Sociology at the University of Kent, UK

'Watson draws on her considerable educational experience to encourage us to see that among the barriers to radical reform are the reliance on limited and often erroneous ideas about human nature and reality.'

Matthew Taylor, Chief Executive of the RSA, formerly Chief Adviser on Political Strategy to the Prime Minister and Director of the Institute for Public Policy Research

'This important book incisively questions the assumptions about the basis of our society that underlie much contemporary education.'

Roger Trigg, University of Oxford, Emeritus Professor of Philosophy at the University of Warwick, UK

'Watson's timely book reviews and reaffirms the crucial importance of a liberal, holistic education for all young people as we navigate a new world of artificial intelligence.'

Anthony Little, Headmaster of Eton College 2002–2015, Global Chief Education Officer of GEMS Education, and President of WLSA Shanghai Academy

'Brenda Watson's new book addresses the necessity for us to take a radical look at the way we deliver education and foster learning. This can be enabled by the massive developments currently happening in digital technology and AI. She addresses the difficult concepts of free will and consciousness and their relationships with learning, along with the huge potential for overhauling not only the system of our schools (and, incidentally, enabling teachers to deliver individualised learning rather than facts), but our political system, too. I am particularly heartened by the chapter on the curriculum. Many now mention the usefulness of music in facilitating all learning, but it is good to read a thorough analysis of its effects, ending with, 'Perhaps the chief reason for serious music education is to share the sheer joy of music'. This, the most important reason for a comprehensive musical education, is so often neglected.'

Ralph Allwood MBE DMus for 26 years director of music at Eton College where he set up the Eton Choral Courses. He conducts Inner Voices, a choir for state school children in London

'It is over one hundred years since the publication of John Dewey's Democracy and Education (1916), in which he argued that education has a crucial role in developing the personal virtues and commitments that undergird a properly functioning democratic society. That contemporary education has failed in this endeavour is painfully obvious. Brenda Watson's book looks beyond the increasingly short-lived educational initiatives that are designed to resolve the problem and identifies where the true cause of our current educational malaise truly lies, namely, in the modern mind's separation of facts from values and the moral relativism that results. It is one thing to identify the problem, it is another to resolve it. Watson does both in a book that all who support liberal education should read and act upon.'

L. Philip Barnes, Emeritus Reader in Religious and Theological Education, King's College London

'In recent times schools have been held in the grip of measurement culture. Schools are judged publicly on a certain type of academic performance. Brenda Watson's timely book reviews and reaffirms the crucial importance of a liberal, holistic education for all young people as we navigate a new world of artificial intelligence which changes the whole landscape. Watson obliges us to think afresh.'

Anthony Little, Headmaster of Eton College 2002 - 2015, Global Chief Education Officer of GEMS Education, and President of WLSA Shanghai Academy

'In the 1960s when I was studying for a Diploma in Education, questions such as those posed with such clarity and determination in Brenda Watson's timely book were peripheral at best. There is little doubt that if Dr Watson's carefully considered and keenly expressed thesis had been available, my own thoughts - and those communicated by my tutors - would have been significantly different. These questions need to be answered and this fascinating account should inspire the most serious discussion if education and democracy are to survive and prosper.'

Brian Kay, Musician, Broadcaster, Conductor and Former King's Singer

Making Education Fit for Democracy

Dewey wrote his celebrated book on *Democracy and Education* over a hundred years ago. *Making Education Fit for Democracy* asks why education has nevertheless failed to deliver such crucial support for democracy and how it should change to reflect ethical and social responsibilities. It seeks to shed light on what has gone wrong and how it can be put right.

Reforming an antiquated system of education should be a matter for public debate. This book is written not only for those currently involved in delivering education, but also for the general public. Arguing that education needs to be holistic, encouraging open-mindedness and developing a wide range of interests, it:

- Highlights the role of education in supporting democracy
- Promotes nurture in civilising values over mere information-giving
- Puts exams and accountability into perspective
- Seeks to bridge the gulf between schooling and life
- Argues for the reform of the whole system of education
- Seeks to use digital technology to personalise education

Touching upon several issues currently under debate, such as the rise of populism, the role of religion and narrow subject curriculum, this book will be of interest to all students studying education as well as those involved in teacher education.

Brenda Watson is a retired educational consultant. Her teaching in schools covered History, Music, Philosophy and Religious Studies. She became Director of the Farmington Institute in Oxford and has published both books and in academic journals.

Making Education Fit for Democracy

Closing the Gap

Brenda Watson

Routledge
Taylor & Francis Group

LONDON AND NEW YORK

First published 2021
by Routledge
2 Park Square, Milton Park, Abingdon, Oxon OX14 4RN

and by Routledge
52 Vanderbilt Avenue, New York, NY 10017

Routledge is an imprint of the Taylor & Francis Group, an informa business

© 2021 Brenda Watson

British Library Cataloguing in Publication Data
A catalogue record for this book is available from the British Library

Library of Congress Cataloging-in-Publication Data
Names: Watson, Brenda, 1935- author.
Title: Making education fit for democracy : closing the gap / Brenda Watson.
Description: Agdon, Oxon ; New York, NY : Routledge, 2020. | Includes bibliographical references and index. |
Identifiers: LCCN 2020018476 | ISBN 9780367220341 (hardback) | ISBN 9780367220372 (paperback) | ISBN 9780429270444 (ebook)
Subjects: LCSH: Democracy and education. | Educational change.
Classification: LCC LC71 .W38 2021 | DDC 379--dc23
LC record available at https://lccn.loc.gov/2020018476

ISBN: 978-0-367-22034-1 (hbk)
ISBN: 978-0-367-22037-2 (pbk)
ISBN: 978-0-429-27044-4 (ebk)

Typeset in Galliard
by Taylor & Francis Books

To Philip Barnes for his outstanding work in education

and

To Hilary Elgar for her forbearance and sympathetic presence throughout

Contents

Illustrations

Note on icons introducing the chapters

Catherine Adams, a teacher and artist who lives in the Malvern Hills, has contributed the icons around the theme of *hands* as symbols of *creative work*. This is especially appropriate for a book on the notions of *democracy* and *education*, both of which need to be seen as being of a positive and practical nature. They are not to be achieved through mechanical means, nor treated as just theory locked away from the real world. The motif continues like a thread throughout the book, highlighting what is distinctive about each chapter.

Acknowledgements

The writing of this book has been a communal effort in many ways. I received support and encouragement from so many people.

I thank Elizabeth Ashton, my discussion partner throughout and over the years, for generous comment on the whole book.

I owe a special debt of gratitude to Meriel Bennett and Stuart Freed who gave up valuable time in helping me prepare the final typescript. Meriel's enthusiasm for the project throughout and her helpful reading of the script were outstanding. Stuart's comment on the education chapters I found most stimulating.

I want to acknowledge Geoffrey Scargill for important conversations about education, which gave me the confidence to embark on writing the book, and for his interest throughout, including commenting on the education chapters.

I thank Damaris Wade for ably proof-reading the final text.

I am grateful to Ben Wakelin for undertaking at short notice the production of the figures, and to Catherine Adams for the icons representing the various chapters.

I acknowledge the help of all the following friends who read chapters for me and gave valuable comment: Dora Ainsworth, Brian Barber, Shirley Davis, Diane Featherstone, Raymond Garfoot, Henry Haslam, Shirley Karney, Vicky Lunn, Christopher Oliver, Martin Reed, Rachel Roy, Liz Russell, Derek Smith, Joan Smith, Angela Sutton, Michael Trott, David Watson and John Watson.

Introduction

The thesis I am putting forward in this book is unusual, so an introductory chapter explaining it may be helpful.

I have been involved in education all my life, whether as recipient or as provider, and have always seen the need for reform. More recently I have also become concerned about democracy. In the West democracy has mostly been assumed to be an enlightened form of government until enormous problems have shown up in the twenty-first century.

Dewey, in his book *Democracy and Education*, which was published over a hundred years ago, saw a close link between the two.[1] This suggests that current difficulties about how democracy is practised can be traced in part to failure in education. Dewey's insights into how learning happens have not been heeded in the way that education has been organised. So often, education has created problems that it then cannot resolve. Indeed, in many ways, I consider that education has actually hindered the nurture of democratic citizens.

In a democracy everyone matters. Everyone needs to be able to think wisely and be committed to use his or her particular gifts in the service of the community. Without that, democracy flounders. Education should be for the benefit of both the individual and society. The general approach to education has tended, however, to encourage conformity in thought and a strong desire for individual success. The two are clearly tied up together in the examination culture, which tests children on what they should know, namely what has been decided for them, and places them in comparison with each other. When people are treated like this over the most formative period of their lives, we should not be surprised at their lack of creative thinking or unselfish searching for the common good.

My stance in this book is different, however, from most books advocating reform in education. I have been struck by the fact that both democracy and education appear to have run aground because of some very common but misleading assumptions lying behind the intellectual life of the West. Part I exposes four of these.

I argue that these assumptions, when examined, do not hold water. Take the first assumption, which is discussed in Chapter 2, as an example. This is a narrow view of reasoning leading to what I term *a fact/opinion divide* – a general approach of over-valuing factual information and being highly suspicious of personal opinion. It assumes that knowledge must rest on empirical/scientific enquiry. Only this is considered to be objective and reliable; it produces *facts*. Anything else – values, beliefs, feelings – are only *opinions*, which are subjective and unreliable. People are always biased, so, without a proper evidence-base, what they think and feel is controversial, and there are no ways in which the truth of opinions can be publicly validated. This attitude is sometimes called *scientism*, and it has been encouraged by the philosophical school of *positivism*.

The fact/opinion divide is faulty on many grounds:

i   All civilisations have been built upon knowledge. To imagine that, without our modern scientific expertise, nothing is known goes against obvious common sense.
ii   Science itself is limited to what is physical. Note, for example, how in clinical research the possibility of placebo effects has to be guarded against. Yet, actual human life embraces much more than just the physical.
iii   Opinions concern what people think is true. So, opinions can contain facts, and almost certainly do. Equally, what are claimed as facts can be mistaken. Facts and opinions are, indeed, mostly intertwined.
iv   Reasons can be given for opinions even though they cannot be proved to be true.
v   Opinions vary as to whether they are helpful or not in their understanding of life; they can embody great insight as well as damaging oversight. They affect behaviour and decision-making, so it is important that they are as near to the truth as possible.

Overfocus on facts has emerged from a narrow view of reasoning, which sees it as being based only on logic and empirical/scientific evidence. *Empirical* relates to the evidence of the five senses; it is a kind of lowest common denominator approach to knowledge, because we all have physical bodies which see, hear, touch, etc. Beyond such everyday experience, many people now consider that scientific investigation is essential to avoid mere conjecture.

This is a reductionist view of understanding. Most of the knowledge we acquire throughout life is reached by many means other than empirical/scientific enquiry. Experience uses common sense, imagination and intuition, and it normally is built up in relationship to traditions of many kinds. The results cannot claim certainty, for we are all extremely limited in what we can know, and we can all be mistaken, but it is sufficient to live by.

To require scientific evidence before anything can be called knowledge is imperialist. It has had a major impact on the other three damaging assumptions which have been common in the West. I see these as: firstly, the poor quality of debate, which avoids rational discussion and becomes increasingly personalised and aggressive (Chapter 3); secondly, moral relativism in which the values on which civilised society depends are regarded as only opinions that cannot be adjudicated (Chapter 4); and, thirdly, negative attitudes towards religion, whereby the possibility of the existence of any transcendent dimension to the world is virtually outlawed from enquiry (Chapter 5).

I maintain that all four assumptions have had a profound effect on both democracy and education. From one point of view, they are in conflict with each other. To give overriding importance to scientifically-established facts runs counter to how most people live their lives. What, on the whole, means most to people – love of family and friends, delight in the beauty and wonder of the natural world, the joy of being creative and pursuing the arts, enjoying hobbies of many kinds, etc. – all these apparently have nothing to do with knowledge because they may be mistaken or could reflect simply personal bias.

A precise example of the incompatibility of these assumptions relates to the movement to give equality to women – an essential aspect of inclusive democracy. One of the assumptions, discussed in Chapter 4, however, relates to how the West has become afraid to talk about anything being *morally* required. Phrases preferred today mostly refer to *social* or *collaborative* or *community* grounds for action. Such words lack the force and depth of the moral appeal. This matters, because it leaves the issue of the equality of women and men (in practice still far from being reached) in a weaker position. It is easy to argue that, purely on *social* or *collaborative* grounds, segregation of the sexes in the traditional way, as practised in most societies before our own, is what works best. Women have time to look after children and the domestic aspects of life, freeing the men to organise society. It appears to be a good recipe: everyone knows where they are. Yet, this does not satisfy us today, because we see both women and men as persons to whom *morally* autonomy and freedom belong. It is not right that some people should be treated as the servants of others, however well treated. Similarly, we now view slavery as a huge *moral* offence; we no longer regard it as fine in certain cultures but not in ours, because we see it as universally immoral. So, why should we be so reticent in talking about anything being *moral*? We are undermining our own convictions.

I hope I have said enough about the confusion in thinking which lies behind so many of the problems facing the West today. The health of democracy requires these assumptions to be challenged and replaced with better ones.

The role of education

This brings me to what education should be doing about this. On the whole, instead of challenging these assumptions, education has been profoundly influenced by them. Thus, it has reinforced them by imposing them upon everyone who has been through the system. When children and young people in their most formative years constantly have these assumptions drummed into them, they find it difficult to think 'outside the box'. A vicious circle has been set up. It is as though people have been indoctrinated into accepting what they have been taught. In this way, education must take some of the blame for the problems facing democracy today in the West (see Figure 0.1).

Radical reform of how education is organised is needed. Unfortunately, the presence of the fact/opinion divide can be detected in the search for education reform itself. Talk of 'improving standards' is widespread. Yet, as Dewey noted, we can measure what is physical, but education is not a physical object; it concerns persons. Therefore, in striving to improve standards in education, we are unwittingly reinforcing what is incoherent. Yes, we can grade people, especially according to their performance on tests, but how is this related to education?

What also worries me about a lot of discussion of the impact of digital technology on education is the low vision of education on which it is based. Often education is seen simply in terms of the amount of information available. Take this comment reported of Jimmy Wales, co-founder of Wikipedia, who asks us to "Imagine a world in which every single person is given free access to the sum of all human knowledge. That's what we're doing."[2] Such a comment links up only too readily with much educational theory that sees education as being just about learning. Learning is obviously part of education, but it is only a part. What matters a great deal more is *what* is being learned, *how* it is being learned and with what judgement and understanding what is learnt is being used.

Digital technology cannot teach such valuing. Education is so much more than the amount of information which is available to people. Indeed, the problems only begin with the amount of information. We need to ask many questions about it, such as: Is this true information? How do we know it is true? Is it relevant? How is this information going to be used? Is it going to be helpful or damaging to human life?

Iain McGilchrist has written a remarkably relevant book, drawing on insights from neuroscience on the two hemispheres of the brain.[3] He argues that both the left hemisphere

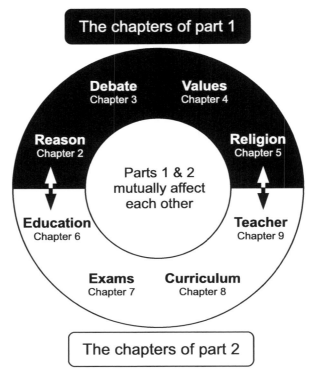

Relating parts 1 and 2

The chapters of part 1

Debate
Chapter 3

Values
Chapter 4

Reason
Chapter 2

Religion
Chapter 5

Parts 1 & 2
mutually affect
each other

Education
Chapter 6

Teacher
Chapter 9

Exams
Chapter 7

Curriculum
Chapter 8

The chapters of part 2

Figure 0.1 Relating parts 1 and 2

(LH) and the right hemisphere (RH) are needed all the time for human functioning. They work together, but they do so in crucially different ways (see Box 0.1).

This raises the question: Which should be dominant for democracy and education to flourish? McGilchrist thinks the West needs "a complete change of heart and mind", for it has allowed LH thinking to dominate and has neglected the RH. The LH, because of its focus on precision, is incapable of understanding the RH; it therefore makes a poor Master. The RH can, however, understand the LH as a good Servant, and use it accordingly. The RH therefore should be the Master. See Chapter 2 for further discussion on this.

Such a change of heart and mind cries out for education to attempt it. This is why I have written this book. I appeal to all who care for democracy as well as for education to see the urgency for such reform of the way in which education is pursued. We need to use all the new means available to us today in digital technology to rethink the system. The purpose is to enable genuine personal education to happen.

This will not mean teachers losing jobs; on the contrary, it will enable them to perform their proper role – to educate those entrusted to their care. I suspect that their status will rise as they do what no technology will ever be able to do, namely, working towards the foundational values behind any civilised society and, especially, of a democracy, namely, a concern for truth, for fairness, for compassion and for beauty. These should be at the heart of both political and educational life.

This may be regarded as hopelessly idealistic. Yet, in our complex and ever-changing world, ideals are hugely important, however much we fail to live up to them. They help us to right a capsized boat.

Box 0.1 Characteristics of the hemispheres of the brain

Left hemisphere (LH)	Right hemisphere (RH)
Is *logical*	Is *holistic*
Sees things as *definite* and straightforward	Sees *ambiguity* & need for nuanced thinking
Is articulate – *literal* use of language	Finds it hard to put into words – uses *metaphor*
Has an *either/or* mentality	Prefers *both/and* thinking
Is *critical*	Is *affirming*
Wants to *control* and manage	Wants to *collaborate* and be generous-minded
Focuses on *a part*	Focuses on *the whole*
Is *academic*	Is *embodied*
Looks for *general laws*	Accepts *uniqueness*
Ideal for finding out about *things*	Ideal for learning about *persons*

Notes

1 J. Dewey. 1916. *Democracy and Education: An Introduction to the Philosophy of Education.* Macmillan.
2 Quoted in John, P.D. & Wheeler, S. 2008. *The Digital Classroom: Harnessing Technology for the Future.* Routledge. p. 127.
3 McGilchrist, I. 2009. *The Master and His Emissary: The Divided Brain and the Making of the Western World.* Yale University Press.

Part 1

Challenging modern day assumptions

Does democracy deserve its accolade?

The case against democracy

The West has tended to regard democracy with near idolatry, putting it on a pedestal as the definitive answer to how states should be run. The word is bandied about and proudly offered to the world as a panacea for all ills. Yet a precise definition of the word *democracy* is elusive. The word itself derives from the Greek *demos*, meaning people, village, administrative unit, and *kratos*, from the Sanskrit *kratu*, denoting strength, might, dominion.[1] I accept the general sense of the word as defined by Abraham Lincoln: "government of the people, by the people, for the people." Democracy is the notion of rule by the people instead of rule by one person, one family, one group, one party – autocracy of any kind.[2]

Democracy is, however, an extraordinarily difficult form of government. It contains built-in incoherence and is ill-equipped for the decision-making needed by government in an incredibly complex world. Jason Brennan has written a carefully-considered book entitled

Against Democracy about the great problems concerning democracy. He considers that "equal, universal suffrage is in many ways on its face morally objectionable … universal suffrage incentivizes most voters to make political decisions in an ignorant and irrational way, and then impose these ignorant and irrational decisions on innocent people."[3]

Brennan develops his argument regarding American politics. He considers that citizens fall into three main groups: *hobbits* who are "mostly apathetic and ignorant about politics"; *hooligans* who are "rabid sports fans of politics with strong and largely fixed world-views" and *vulcans* who "think scientifically and rationally about politics." He considers that "most Americans are either hobbits or hooligans, or fall somewhere in the spectrum in between."[4]

His view reflects the judgment of two eminent political philosophers. Ronald Dworkin began his 2006 book *Is Democracy Possible Here?* with the words:

> American politics are in an appalling state. We disagree, fiercely, about almost everything … These are not civil disagreements: each side has no respect for the other. We are no longer partners in self-government; our politics are rather a form of war.[5]

Dworkin echoed what Jeffrey Stout said two years earlier in his book *Democracy and Tradition*: "It will take all of the intellectual and organisational creativity that the next generation of democrats can muster to sustain recognisably democratic forms of public discourse in contemporary circumstances."[6] Both were remarkably prescient regarding the way in which American politics was developing.

Brennan argues in favour of epistocracy, the rule of the knowledgeable. The notion resurrects something akin to Plato's vision of the philosopher-king shorn of its despotic associations. Plato taught that only a wise person could govern society well. If this is so, how likely is it that all those who elect a democratic government are wise? If they are not wise, is there any guarantee that those they vote for are wise? Are there not factors in democracy which actively discourage wisdom in its rulers? Recent events, such as the huge Brexit controversy in Britain, present a real challenge to democracy.

A concern for truth can easily become a casualty for several reasons, such as the following:

* Dependence on securing votes can promote easy reliance on slogans, jargon, captions and the like, which are designed to appeal quickly to people's emotions and discourage actual thinking.
* The need to convince huge numbers of people can encourage the trading of truth for influence or the promotion of bullshit, fake news and a general lack of trust – all marks of a so-called "post-truth" society (to be discussed further in Chapter 2).
* The danger of populism is ever-present. For instance, the manipulation of the masses, not just by charismatic speakers but by such elements as much-publicised opinion polls, plays on people's general wish to go along with the crowd and keep up with the *Zeitgeist*.

In more subtle ways forms of dishonesty may be built into the system. In order to establish any structure for decision-making, some form of grouping of those holding possible policies seems to be inevitable and leads to the setting up of political parties. Yet, packaging together views on a great variety of topics discourages independent, genuine thinking and makes it highly unlikely that voters who actually think for themselves will totally agree with anything that is presented to them.

Such discouragement applies with especial force to those elected. Some politicians fail to express any personal opinion. As the Gilbert & Sullivan operetta *Iolanthe* expressed so humorously, yet unfortunately still relevantly, over one hundred years ago:

When in that House M.P.s divide,
If they've a brain and cerebellum, too,
They've got to leave that brain outside,
And vote just as their leaders tell 'em to.[7]

This is bad news for the pursuit of truth upon which a flourishing democracy depends. We need politicians who think for themselves. Voting for what a person does not wholly agree with offends that person's integrity. Of course, the principle of necessary compromise comes to the rescue, but unless resorted to in an intelligent way, it also serves to discredit the idealism responsible for democracy in the first place.

Other factors discouraging responsible democratic government include:

*   The illusion of power which the right to vote gives. Voters are so remote from actually making decisions or having to be seen as being responsible for their outcomes that taking part in elections can become a low priority or seem to be a charade.
*   The ease with which voters can lose trust in politicians on the grounds that they "are just out for themselves".
*   Short-term power can promote short-term thinking, such as the idea that there is no need to bother about the effects that political decisions may have in a few years' time.
*   Needing to get elected can promote bloated egoism, especially if the individual is successful. Egotism, in turn, can lead to irresponsibility in making judgements or decisions, which is in direct contrast with Edmund Burke's ideal: "Your representative owes you, not his industry only, but his judgment; and he betrays, instead of serving you, if he sacrifices it to your opinion".[8]
*   The danger of tyranny by the majority, whereby minorities are trampled upon or oppressed.

The problems facing any kind of meaningful democracy are immense. The political scientist James Fishkin summarises the reality well: "We live in a world of relentless advocacy, massive financing of the persuasion industry, the viral spread of fake news, social media discussions among the like-minded, and the pressures of political competition built into our practices of democracy."[9]

What can democratic government offer to counteract these threats and difficulties? Fishkin quotes E. E. Schattschneider's short, widely-read book, *The Semisovereign People*: "The people are a sovereign whose vocabulary is limited to two words, 'Yes' and 'No'. This sovereign moreover can speak only when spoken to."[10] Schattschneider argued that, as generally practised, democracy is far from being universal in scope; it is unbalanced in favour of a fraction of a minority.

Fishkin expresses the problem clearly:

If elites or other political actors manipulate public opinion or mass political behaviour, then even if the public appears to be exercising popular control, it is not. It is not in control of itself. Someone is pulling the strings. Furthermore, if manipulation works, then there will be incentive for political actors to engage in it, whether they are candidates, parties, or political operatives with partisan or interest group leanings. After all, the incentives within competitive democracy are all about winning, and not much about truth-telling.[11]

Why democracy deserves to be affirmed

These are grave problems. Nevertheless, democracy remains a noble ideal. It has two major advantages over other forms of government.

1 A built-in means of safeguarding against tyranny

Democracy can lay claim to being the most effective way, as yet experimented with, of being able to safeguard against tyranny. Following a conference on democracy at Yale University in 1997, Ian Shapiro and Casiano Hacker-Cordón quoted the political scientist Adam Przeworski, who grew up in Communist Poland:

> The miracle of democracy is that conflicting political forces obey the results of voting. People who have guns obey those without them. Incumbents risk their control of government offices by holding elections. Losers wait for their chance to win office. Conflicts are regulated, processed according to rules, and thus limited. This is not consensus, yet not mayhem either. Just limited conflict: conflict without killing. Ballots are "paper stones" as Engels once observed.[12]

They further comment: "To those who reject this view as too minimal to be worth valuing, [Przeworski's] answer is straightforward: tell that to the billions in the world who currently live without it."[13]

Even Brennan concedes as much: "The only thing that could justify unrestricted, universal suffrage would be that we cannot produce a better-performing system. ... In general, the best places to live right now are liberal democracies, not dictatorships, one-party governments, oligarchies, or real monarchies."[14] Democracy has built into it opportunity for criticism and renewal, even though both are difficult to achieve. Its structure, however varied, contains the need for ongoing criticism, accountability and reform, which helps to prevent the accumulation of absolute power which, as Lord Acton famously remarked, "corrupts absolutely."

2 Democracy embodies the moral insight of the equality of every person

Democracy's embodiment of moral equality is an ethically mature notion which strikes a universal chord. As Brennan notes, "most philosophers think that we should value democracy the way we value a painting or a person. They claim that democracy uniquely expresses the idea that all people have equal worth and value."[15]

Equality is an insight of which the West can be proud – one almost unknown in earlier civilisations. Throughout human history there has been enormous resistance to the notion of power-sharing. For the most part it has been simply taken for granted that the role of women in society is a domestic one with no direct say in government. Moreover, societies dependent on manpower for their economic success, even if not reliant on slavery, have had large populations of working-class people accorded less status and dignity in society than the smaller populations responsible for managing labour. Those with wealth and influence have seen it as appropriate to lord it over everyone else. This is a common situation. Indeed, it is largely the norm. The concept of every single human being's dignity represents a revolutionary break with the past. It has given rise, for example, to the human rights movement which, however differently understood in different parts of the world and despite its imperfections, still embraces this notion of equality and has had an enormously beneficial effect on the quality of life of billions of people throughout the world.

We may agree, therefore, with Churchill's famous comment about democracy being the worst form of government except for all the rest. Yet, it remains an incredibly difficult and sophisticated way of organising decision-making in society. It should not be idolised. Rather, it should be valued as a means of government which can help guard against the misuse of power. It is a system that allows change and revision of policy.

Brennan may be right to see democracy in instrumentalist terms, likening it to a hammer for doing a job of work and nothing more. Thus he claims that giving everyone an equal share of political power is not inherently just, even as other forms of government are not inherently unjust. He admits that morally arbitrary, repugnant or evil reasons have distributed political power unequally for most of civilised history by forbidding power-sharing by those who were black, Catholic, Irish, Jewish or female. It does not follow, however, that political inequality is inherently unjust, because there could be good reasons for excluding some.

> In comparison, we should not exclude citizens from driving because they are atheists, gay or Dalits. Yet that does not mean that all restrictions on the legal right to drive are unjust. There might be just reasons to forbid some people from driving, such as they are incompetent drivers who impose too much risk on others when they drive.[16]

Brennan's perspective on democracy in more lowly terms is, nevertheless, itself dependent on the view that every human being, of whatever class, ability, economic background, health, age, race or gender, is to be respected as themselves, and individuals are not to be used just as a means to further someone else's purpose. Democracy incorporates both a self-critical capacity and high moral intention. In this way we can promote it realistically without undue expectations of what it can achieve.

These twin insights behind democracy should be supported by education (see Figure 1.1).

What is fundamentally needed to make democracy work?

In this book I cannot be concerned with the mechanics of how people can share power. As Fishkin notes, there are four conceptions of democratic practice, namely: competitive democracy, participatory democracy, deliberative democracy and avoiding tyranny by the majority.[17] Discussing the merits and demerits of different forms of democracy is an immensely important topic, but it is beyond the range of what I can tackle in this book.

However, I would like to draw attention to Fishkin's highly positive and optimistic thesis on the possibilities of deliberative democracy and how modern technology can help to make it a reality. He offers a way to take government by "the will of the people" seriously and constructively based on the development in classical Athens of a Council of 500, which was drawn by lot and discussed major legislation.[18] The Council was intended to act as a democratic brake on the power of charismatic orators, who might have swayed the Assembly

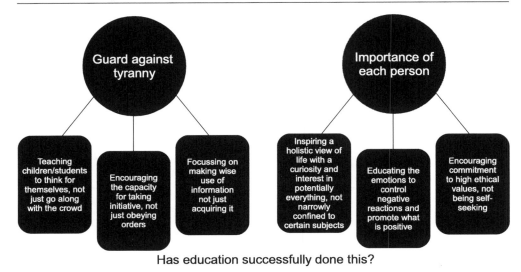

Figure 1.1 The twin insights of democracy should be supported by education

of eligible citizens into making dangerous and foolish decisions. Further detail of this will be given in Chapter 3.

Fishkin's book has been hailed as being capable of changing the face of democracy. According to Jane Mansbridge, the Adams Professor of Political Leadership and Democratic Values at Harvard University's Kennedy School of Government, who is quoted on the cover, "Case upon case – from California, Texas, Mongolia, Uganda, China, Japan, Macau, Australia, the UK, and Europe – [the book] breaks new ground in the growing global movement to harness, for legitimacy and good outcomes, the deliberative intelligence of citizens drawn by lot," i.e., individuals randomly selected through the use of statistical expertise.

My focus is on what is needed to make any form of democracy work well, namely, the underlying beliefs and values to be nurtured in all. The rest of Part I looks at the question of values and beliefs in detail. Here I want to note two qualities badly needed for the reasoned debate which is the life-blood of democracy. Firstly, there needs to be strong emphasis on the desire to achieve a common mindset as the basis for accepting diversity, which involves taking care to avoid splintering the basic liberal democratic ideal into rival interpretations. Secondly, there should be a real effort to educate people's emotions, especially anger, so as not to promote "them-and-us" attitudes.

I The importance of concern for what is held in common

Democracy is inevitably concerned with diversity, which it has to turn into community. Strong emphasis on what is held in common is therefore crucial. Diversity can only be contained in a civilised manner if certain values and attitudes and dispositions are potentially agreed by all. Yet, the West has been weak on this aspect of nurture. Stout argues that "We are not used to discussing what, if anything, links us together."[19] What democracy needs is genuine conversation and debate which is generous and affirming. It needs to bring people with different views together in a constructive enterprise valuing a common mind. As Stout asserts, "Part of the democratic program is to involve strangers and enemies, as well as fellow citizens, in the verbal process of holding one another responsible."[20]

Without courteous and rational debate, politics, whether American or not, is in a poor state. The lack of concern for seeking a common way of thinking is at the root of the absence of dialogue noted by Dworkin. He does see, however, a realistic way forward for a liberal democracy, because he considers that both sides in the American divide, Republicans and Democrats, share fundamental values:

> [I]t would be silly to expect that Americans will cease to disagree radically about politics any time soon. It would nevertheless be a great improvement if they came to see their continuing disagreements as controversies about the best interpretation of fundamental values they all share rather than simply as confrontations between two divergent worldviews neither of which is comprehensible to the other.[21]

The term *liberal democracy* suffers from slipperiness of the meaning of the word *liberal*, however.[22] Can liberalism be genuinely inclusive? Dworkin thinks that it is possible to express an understanding of liberalism which can admit *liberal* or *conservative* interpretation based on principles we all share. He sees what is held in common as two-fold: the principle of intrinsic value to be accorded to every human life, and the principle of personal responsibility for how that life is lived. The first principle relates to equality; the second to liberty.[23] These principles form the basis for human dignity. They attach importance to individuals one by one, but the principles are not individualistic in the sense of not caring about shared tradition. Equality includes concern for liberty and the struggle to attain liberty and discover in what liberty consists. It is more than freedom from constraint which necessarily is impossible; it concerns inner liberty from enslaving passions and from false values. So he sees these virtues as compatible, as indeed an aspect of each other.

The tribute paid to the American Republican politician John McCain on his death in 2018 provides a relevant example of such a democratic spirit at work. According to *The Times*,

> [H]is courage as a straight-shooter and a maverick in a Congress beset by venality will be his lasting legacy. Early in his senate career McCain saw how big money was eroding faith in American democracy. He set out to tame it with scant support from his own party. His chief ally was the Democrat Russ Feingold, who paid tribute to "his fundamental respect for diverging viewpoints [and] his intense desire not for political dominance but to get things done."[24]

It is to be noted that such an understanding of liberalism is very different from that denoted by the term *neo-liberalism*. This form of liberalism, dependent on economic theory, favours free-market capitalism. Colin Crouch, a leading political economist at Warwick Business School, is not alone in seeing neo-liberalism as damaging to democracy. Indeed, he believes that we now live in a post-democracy era.[25] He blames the Chicago School economists, who achieved prominence in the 1970s. Instead of insisting that efficient markets should be comprised a large number of small firms, Chicago School economists argued that the public interest could be better served by allowing a few large firms to gobble up the rest. Crouch notes that this dogma was swallowed by politicians on both the left and the right, and governments were thereby co-opted into underwriting the dominance of large firms.

Democracy was damaged in the process.[26] Chapter 6 discusses neoliberalism's particular impact on education.

2 The pervasiveness of a spirit of anger is an enemy of democracy

Reaching towards what is held in common, together with avoiding unnecessary contentiousness, has been rendered especially difficult because of the significant role emotions play in public life, especially anger. As a political movement, democracy has roots in anger. This does not augur well for the calm reliance on reason, which the movement values so highly. The contrast between the cool reasoning needed for democratic government to be efficient, and the emotional bonanza of election times constitutes a built-in incoherence. Hogarth's four prints illustrating the Election of 1754, remind us of this contradiction.[27] Similarly, current general elections display the characteristics of appeal to emotions at all costs.

Such attitudes are part and parcel of the history of democracy in the modern period. In his magisterial book on the origins of democracy, Jonathan Israel notes that the Radical Enlightenment thinkers responsible for our modern concept of democracy, who stood consistently for liberty, equality and fraternity, were angry men.[28] Anger played a huge part in their thinking and behaviour. Israel notes that this philosophical movement was marred from the outset by longstanding antipathies and personality clashes, such as Rousseau's bitter and enduring quarrel with Diderot, which began in 1757.[29]

Their intentions were high-minded. As Baron d'Holbach put it, "those who cultivate philosophy" must be

> completely honest among themselves, always calm, and must not defer to anything except reason illumined by experience which alone can show us things as they really are; philosophy must accept truth from whoever's hands it comes and reject error and prejudice no matter whose authority it rests upon.[30]

Such virtuous intentions – which we may note are in line with what Stout argues for, as discussed above – would seem to preclude the emotion of anger from playing much part. In practice, however, it was anger at the injustices caused by the *ancien regime* that propelled Enlightenment thinkers along.[31]

Radicals were a mouthpiece for social discontent, grievances and resentment against a society seen as oppressive, rapacious and fundamentally unjust.[32] They denounced the existing order more or less in toto, arguing that monarchy, aristocracy and the Church were all morally oppressive and tyrannical and, therefore, they must all go.

Disagreement with this view led to fierce disputation on the part of those who supported a moderate Enlightenment. Writers such as Voltaire and Adam Smith were more aware of the dangers of such an overthrow, and they wanted the reform of institutions instead of wholesale dismissal. Indeed, Enlightenment rulers such as Frederick the Great knew they would lose everything if the Radicals had their way. It is notable that David Hume criticised the philosophers as being too prone to exaggerate the evils of present and past society.[33]

The presence of anger can be detected especially in the failure of Moderates and Radicals to reason with each other. They all believed passionately in the power of reasoning, yet found it quite impossible to resolve their differences, as will be discussed further in Chapter 2. In the end, the ideas of the radical Enlightenment party prevailed and played a formatively crucial part in the French Revolution.[34] When ideas lead to violence, anger is a likely ingredient in their formation. Chapter 3 will discuss the emotion of anger in more detail.

The role of education in supporting democracy

Thus far the chapter has argued the case for democracy but noted the difficulty of bringing people who hold divergent views to work together. This can easily unleash emotional responses, which can embitter relationships. Can education help to resolve these problems? Indeed, can democracy exist in reality without educating people for citizenship and equipping them to be able to think rationally and become emotionally mature?

Education is often thought of in idealistic terms, similar to democracy. It is seen as providing a definitive solution for sustainable democracy. A hundred years ago John Dewey noted that "a democratic community is more interested than other communities ... in deliberate and systematic education. The devotion of democracy to education is a familiar fact." Society needs the transmission of skills and knowledge in order to survive. "Unless pains are taken to see that genuine and thorough transmission takes place, the most civilised group will relapse into barbarism and then into savagery."[35]

Dewey saw an intimate link between education and democracy. In 2017 a collection of scholarly essays inspired by his *Democracy and Education* was published to mark the book's centenary.[36] As the philosopher Bryan Magee says of him:

> He was one of the first great modernists in educational theory, and perhaps he was the best. If much of what he said is now taken for granted by many of us, that is in no small degree a measure of his success; at the time when he wrote, education was entirely different from this all over the world, including America.[37]

According to Dewey, democracy embodies two elements. Firstly, democracy breaks down barriers of class, race and nationalism by bringing people, as people, together in a shared enterprise with "not only more numerous and more varied points of shared common interest, but greater reliance upon the recognition of mutual interests as a factor in social control." Secondly, democracy enables people to grow and change through the more varied situations in which they find themselves, by meeting people different from themselves and so forth.[38]

Dewey expresses democracy's close link with education in these words:

> Since a democratic society repudiates the principle of external authority, it must find a substitute in voluntary disposition and interest; these can be created by education. But there is a deeper explanation. A democracy is more than a form of government; it is primarily a mode of associated living, of conjoint communicated experience. ... It is the aim of progressive education to take part in correcting unfair privilege and unfair deprivation, not to perpetuate them.[39]

His is a highly moral view of both education and democracy. Sidney Morgenbesser, a leading authority on Dewey, commented:

> A society of free individuals in which all, through their own work, contribute to the liberation and enrichment of the lives of others, is the only environment in which any

individual can really grow normally to his full stature. As Sidney Hook has said, this is an overstatement, but its very powerful overemphasis should indicate how important for Dewey democracy as a moral ideal is.

He considered that, for Dewey, the pursuit of efficiency in education, without this moral ideal, deprives democracy of its essential justification.[40]

Dewey's work on the theory of education was monumental. Nevertheless, Magee's view may be over-optimistic regarding Dewey's impact on the actual practice of education. Although many, perhaps most, educationalists would agree with him, in theory, little has been done to change the educational institutions which Dewey lambasted by implication, for Dewey was deeply critical of how the majority of children and students were educated.

For example, Dewey had strong views on the inappropriateness of economic utilitarianism controlling education. Yet, this has become a major factor in government educational policy, not just in America but globally. Towards the end of his book, Dewey noted the impact of such a utilitarian take-over: "At present, intellectual and emotional limitation characterises both the employing and the employed class. While the latter often have no concerns with their occupation beyond the money it brings, the former's outlook may be confined to profit and power."[41] Dewey could be talking about either 1917 or 2020!

Has education failed in its democratic nurturing? Has it even been discouraging democratic citizenship? In the Introduction to the re-print of *Democracy and Education*, Patricia Hinchey writes:

> There is much to learn about how education can be – and I would argue *is* being – used to undermine the shared values and commitments that make democracy possible. I genuinely believe that every reader who walks away from this text with a good understanding of it will be one more citizen with the insights and ideals necessary to help get American education back on track as democratic education, helping to end what many feel is a current national nightmare of divisiveness and injustice.[42]

Clearly, "American education" may be read as education in all countries which claim to be democratic.

There are weaknesses, however, in Dewey's overall understanding and advocacy of the purpose of education. Reading Dewey alone is unlikely to provide a comprehensive solution to the problem of how education can forward democracy. Indeed, Dewey has been revered by some but regarded with suspicion by many. Nell Noddings notes that Dewey has been

> hailed as the saviour of American education by those who welcome great involvement of students in their own planning and activity [but also] he has been called "worse than Hitler" by some who felt that he infected schools with epistemological and moral relativism and substituted socialisation for true education.[43]

David Bridges comments that Dewey "is probably the best-known, most widely acknowledged and also the most (unfairly) maligned philosopher of education of the twentieth century." He adds:

> [T]he continuing relevance of Dewey's writing is everywhere to be seen. But the history of the treatment or mistreatment of his philosophical and educational work indicates

that if we are to benefit from his real insights, then we need to take some trouble to understand their philosophical ground.[44]

Before taking up Bridges's point, I would like to state that Dewey's analysis of what is involved in learning was brilliant. In practice, its implementation has been impeded by the educational structures in place. What hope is there for the freedom of an individual to discover and develop natural talents and interests when he or she is required to learn alongside thirty or so others of the same age and pursue basically the same curriculum, while being denied individual attention and being tested on the results? Serious consideration of these faults in the education systems of the West as a whole forms the subject of Part II of this book, where I look in greater detail at Dewey's educational thinking.

Critique of Dewey's philosophy

From a theoretical point of view, Dewey is of less help than we might expect him to be because of his philosophy of pragmatism. Although some scholars see Dewey as "one of the most seminal and fruitful philosophers of the twentieth century," developing pragmatism in an "original and comprehensive" way, others are more cautious in their estimate of him.[45] What is beyond doubt is that Dewey was powerfully influenced by Charles Sanders Peirce, an older colleague of his and the founder of pragmatism.

The appeal of pragmatism

Pragmatism embodied a notion which was extremely congenial to Dewey, namely, that philosophy should take as its starting point how life is actually lived, and the process of thinking is generated thereby. As Peirce noted, we should not start from pure ideas but from how people converse. Pierce saw knowledge in terms of what works rather than as a search for certainty regarding the truth of beliefs. The result was, as the English philosopher Simon Blackburn says,

> the driving motivation of pragmatism is not any analysis of truth, but rather the idea that we should avoid metaphysical questions such as "what are numbers?", "what are values?", "what is truth?", "what are reasons?" in favour of asking "what are our practices of thinking in terms of numbers, values, truth, reasons ... what do they accomplish for us?"[46]

Pierce's philosophy appealed immensely to Dewey, who rebelled against the isolation of the academic world from the real world.[47] He saw education as being concerned with a constant search for growth as individuals move through life. He could not avoid metaphysical terminology altogether. He does refer to *beliefs*, but he sees these as a means to an end in the process of enquiry and actual living. Beliefs are neither true nor false in themselves. Rather, they are only effective or ineffective in being instrumental for the acquisition of knowledge – and that is knowledge to live by, not to be discussed in isolation from the real world.

Dewey never expounds on any content of those beliefs. He had an activist understanding of knowledge as process and progress achieved through experience. As Blackburn notes, "In his hands enquiry is a self-correcting process conducted in a specific historical and cultural circumstance; it requires no foundation in certainty or the 'given', and knowledge is just that which is warranted through enquiry."[48] By taking people seriously as learners in the real world, and not imprisoning enquiry within a specialised and isolated environment, Dewey overcame huge barriers to learning. His stress on practicality – learning by doing – notably appeals to a wide proportion of the population. It also promotes an understanding of knowledge as ongoing. We, both as individuals and as members of community, constantly apply ourselves in open-mindedness towards learning from fresh experiences. The experiential approach leaves behind the often highly adversarial debates of the academic world.

Drawbacks of pragmatism

Yet, pragmatism has many drawbacks. Whilst Bertrand Russell hailed Dewey as the leading philosopher in America, he criticised Dewey's philosophy as obscurantist. Russell considered Dewey's "substitution of 'inquiry' for 'truth' as the fundamental concept of logic and theory of knowledge" unacceptable.[49] The two philosophers shared much in common, including a profound interest in education.[50] However, the differences between them are striking. An absolute barrier divided them – namely, Dewey's pragmatism. Alan Ryan, author of a book on Russell's political philosophy, considers that

> [f]or Russell, at any rate, pragmatism was a sort of secular blasphemy. With God gone and most ethics shaky, all mankind had left was a concern for the truth – not a concern for what it would "pay to believe," but a concern for how things really were.[51]

Dewey speaks much about openness, the stimulus of fresh encounters, engaging the emotions and utilising imagination creatively so that the individual inwardly wants to learn and can gain ever more freedom to relate both to her/his own gifts and to the needs of others. There are, however, some serious inconsistencies in what Dewey puts forward.

Challengeable assumptions influencing attitudes towards democracy and education

The problem lies in what Dewey omits to say anything about. His omissions reflect dangerously inadequate assumptions common in the West since the Enlightenment. Such omissions have continued to disfigure the intellectual landscape of the West right up to the present time.

The weaknesses of pragmatism are the obverse of its strengths, and what it fails to address does matter. Questions of truth, values and motivations do not disappear just because we do not engage with them. The pragmatic worldview has discouraged engagement with at least four important areas:

1 A narrow view of reason based on logic and empirical/scientific evidence only

Dewey had a high regard for scientific method. Indeed, he implies that knowledge, understood in the academic sense, is reached by empirical/scientific means. "Without initiation into the scientific spirit one is not in possession of the best tools which humanity has so far devised for effectively directed reflection." His belief in science is stated even more strongly when he comments, "One who is ignorant of the history of science is ignorant of the struggles by which mankind has passed from routine and caprice, from superstitious subjection to nature, from efforts to use it magically, to intellectual self-possession."[52] Magee notes:

> Dewey was struck by the fact that the fields in which human beings have had far and away the most success in the last three or four hundred years, are those of science and technology. It is here that we have acquired the most, and most reliable, mastery of nature. And Dewey was moved to ask: What it is about scientific inquiry that gives it this marvellous success, these wonderful results? Is it something that can be adapted and applied to other fields of human activity with comparable success?[53]

Dewey did not discuss, however, the limitations of the scientific method he so revered. Thus, although he highly valued other aspects of experience, such as art, he did not show how they clearly related to the gathering of knowledge. It is a well-known criticism of Dewey that he did not clearly state how the scientific method produces knowledge. Morgenbesser notes: "some critics of Dewey argue that it is a defect of his theory that he did not stress the specific cognitive goals pursued in scientific inquiry."[54] Indeed, he seems to have assumed that the natural momentum of learning by a child was in continuity with the advanced use of scientific method in all branches of scientific specialism.

This omission serves to reinforce an assumption of the supremacy of scientific method over other ways of seeking knowledge. For example, if any link between aesthetic awareness and the acquisition of wisdom is not made clear, then by implication knowledge becomes associated only with what can be grounded scientifically. It gives way to what I term a fact/opinion divide, which will be discussed in Chapter 2.

2 An aggressive approach towards debate and the handling of disagreement in a diverse society

The low level of political debate already discussed is not only paralleled by much academic practice but also in much everyday conversation, or the lack of it. Democracy must take account of the plain fact that people disagree, often on very important matters. For democracy to work well, high quality critical, but courteous, engagement with controversial subjects is necessary to foster healthy debate between diverse views, which is utterly essential. Nurture in values of respect for opponents is a much needed but neglected aspect of education for democracy.

Democracy requires quality of thinking in everyone. It needs to enable all children to learn to think for themselves, so far as possible. It needs to distinguish between degrees of truth as well as the importance or appropriateness of beliefs, values and opinions. The anti-metaphysical bent of pragmatism, however, is unhelpful here. It stresses the intimate link between belief and action, seeing belief as functional in propelling forward fresh problem-solving. So, whilst Dewey acknowledges the importance of thought and the need to widen horizons in the ongoing growth which constitutes education, he does not wrestle with the real-life problem of what to do about disagreement. Chapter 3 discusses this problem in some detail.

3 Implied values and moral relativism

Dewey tends to assume that the beliefs and values behind everyday life are primarily relative to the situations which produce them. They make up the real world in which individuals need to grow and the community of which they are a part. Such growth, facilitated by habits arising from precise situations, is the purpose of life. The question of truth is unimportant, for we can have no absolute certainty in knowledge anyway: it is always evolving. What matters, therefore, is the transient usefulness of beliefs, values and habits in leading to fresh experience, which is never-ending.

Yet, may not these values and beliefs be prone to the whims of the moment? Hume notes that actual practice in living is driven by emotions.[55] Can emotions be trusted to be sound? Dewey acknowledges the importance of a cultivated imagination capable of intelligent sympathy and goodwill. However, he offers little help with regard to which values, especially ethical values, need to be nurtured for a flourishing democracy. He tends to presume that the individual will, if her/his abilities are properly engaged, find her/his own place in society and become engaged as a fair-minded citizen. Dewey's optimistic view of human nature received some battering after he witnessed shortcomings in some of the progressive schools intended to embody his teaching. He did not, however, discuss how emotions may be educated to function in a constructive a way so as to deter negative outcomes.

Moreover, his prominent use of the word *social*, as meaning more or less the same as *moral*, robs the latter of much of its efficacy. Thus, he does not discuss what ethical values are essential for civilised society and democracy to set ethical values and beliefs alight in the hearts and minds of people, a subject I shall return to in Chapter 4.

4 The marginalisation of religion in any form

Today it is common knowledge that acknowledged authority is under stress, which stems from a mistrust of tradition in general. The safe running of a democracy is destabilised when the religious commitments of many of its members are regarded as irrelevant. The implication is that religion is something dangerous, and it must be removed from the public arena as far as possible.

Dewey does not help here at all. His work is remarkable for its omission of anything about religion. He manages to ignore completely the Judeo-Christian tradition out of which the schools and universities of the West emerged and, moreover, from which the democracy he so highly valued eventually developed. He devotes space, for example, to considering the educational achievements of Plato, the eighteenth-century Enlightenment, and Prussia in the early nineteenth century, but says nothing about religious-inspired liberal education that was, and still is, found in many British schools. As Tony Little, writing as headmaster of Eton, put it: "The British tradition of holistic, liberal education has been one of the glories of our development as a society – and we must reclaim it."[56]

Democracies must cater for all, including religious as well as non-religious people. As such, ignoring the impact of religion is serious. American political experience shows the significance and influence of religious populations. Despite the presumption that religion is separate from law-making and education, religion nevertheless constitutes an important factor in politics. It has been suggested, for example, that Donald Trump would not have been elected as President of the USA in 2016 without the fundamentalist Christian vote.[57] Dewey never states a case against religion. He offers no help on how religion might play a proper role in supporting democracy, a subject I discuss in Chapter 5.

Concluding remarks

In many respects Dewey was but typical of the times in which he lived. He was constrained by the intellectual zeitgeist of his day. The following chapters in Part I examine some

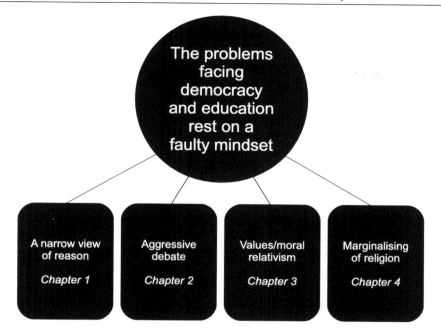

Figure 1.2 Relating democracy and education to four common but damaging assumptions

challengeable assumptions in the areas of cognitive reasoning, responsible debating, ethical valuing and realistic attitudes to religion (see Figure 1.2).

Dewey's educational insights are profound. Provided they can be dissociated from the limitations of his pragmatic worldview, which I believe they can be, his ideas shine in all their glory and point a way towards real education for democracy.

Notes

1 See, e.g., Online Etymology Dictionary. 2020. www.etymonline.com
2 For a useful summary of the origins of democracy, see, e.g., James Sickinger. 2019. "The Origins of Democracy: Democracy We Associate with the Modern West and Ancient Athens, but Little in Between." Bible Archaeological Society. https://www.biblicalarchaeology.org/daily/ancient-cul tures/daily-life-and-practice/the-origins-of-democracy
3 J. Brennan. 2016. *Against Democracy.* Princeton University Press. p. 8.
4 Ibid. p. 4f.
5 R. Dworkin. 2006. *Is Democracy Possible Here?: Principles for a New Political Debate.* Princeton University Press. p. 1.
6 J. Stout. 2004. *Democracy and Tradition.* Princeton University Press. p. 305.
7 The phrase is sung by Private Willis at the beginning of Act 2. W. S. Gilbert & A. Sullivan. *Iolanthe.* Act 2. Gilbert and Sullivan Archive. https://gsarchive.net/iolanthe/iollib.pdf
8 E. Burke. 1774. "Edmund Burke, Speech to the Electors of Bristol." *The Founder's Constitution.* Vol. 1. p. 391. http://press-pubs.uchicago.edu/founders/documents/v1ch13s7.html
9 J. Fishkin. 2018. *Democracy When the People Are Thinking: Revitalizing Our Politics Through Public Deliberation.* Oxford University Press. p. 2.
10 Quoted in Ibid. p. 35. E. E. Schattschneider. 1960. *The Semisovereign People: A Realist's View of Democracy in America.* Holt, Rinehart & Winston. p. xx.
11 Fishkin. *Democracy When the People Are Thinking.* p. 35.

12 A. Przeworski. 1999. "Minimalist Conception of Democracy: A Defense." Quoted in I. Shapiro & C. Hacker-Cordón. "Promises and Disappointments: Reconsidering Democracy's Value." In I. Shapiro & C. Hacker-Cordón (Eds.). *Democracy's Value*. pp. 1–20. Cambridge University Press. p. 5. See also A. Przeworski. 2016. "Democracy: A Never-Ending Quest." *Annual Review of Political Science* 1. pp. 1–12. https://www.annualreviews.org/doi/pdf/10.1146/annurev-polisci-021113-122919

13 I. Shapiro and C. Hacker-Cordón. 1999. "Promises and Disappointments: Reconsidering Democracy's Value." In I. Shapiro & C. Hacker-Cordón (Eds.). *Democracy's Value*. pp. 1–20. Cambridge University Press. p. 5.

14 Brennan. *Against Democracy*. p. 8.

15 Ibid. p. 10.

16 Ibid. p. 18.

17 Fishkin. *Democracy When the People are Thinking*. p. 51ff.

18 Ibid. p. 2. Drawing on Robert A. Dahl's challenge to envision institutions for an "advanced democratic society" in *Democracy and Its Critics*. 1989. Yale University Press.

19 Stout. *Democracy and Tradition*. p. 1.

20 Ibid. p. 13.

21 Dworkin. *Is Democracy Possible Here?* p. 22.

22 See, e.g., Thomas Biebricher. 2015. "Neoliberalism and Democracy." *Constellations* 22, no. 2. https://doi.org/10.1111/1467-8675.12157

23 Dworkin. *Is Democracy Possible Here?* pp. 7–11.

24 "Lion of Arizona." 2018. *The Times*. August 27.

25 C. Crouch. 2004. *Post-Democracy*. Polity Press.

26 Crouch develops the theory in *The Strange Non-death of Neoliberalism*. 2011. Polity Press.

27 The "Humours of an Election" series started as four paintings done by Hogarth in 1754–5, which were turned into engravings. They brilliantly embody Hogarth's view of party corruption and political discord.

28 J. Israel. 2010. *A Revolution of the Mind: Radical Enlightenment and the Intellectual Origins of Modern Democracy*. Princeton University Press.

29 Ibid. p. 20.

30 Ibid. p. 201f. Quoting from d'Holbach's *Essai*. p. 5.

31 Thus, for example, in 1789 Richard Price asked, "'Why are the nations of the world so patient under despotism? – Why do they crouch to tyrants, and submit to be treated as if they were a herd of cattle?' His unequivocal answer is because they lack Enlightenment. 'Ignorance,' he wrote, 'is the parent of bigotry, intolerance, persecution and slavery.'" Israel. *A Revolution of the Mind*. p. 27f. Quoting from Price's "A Discourse on the Love of Our Country." November 4, 1789.

32 Israel. *A Revolution of the Mind*. p. 32.

33 Ibid. p. 16.

34 Ibid. p. 224. Israel tends to blame the Reign of Terror on the Counter Enlightenment and Rousseau, yet it was the achievement of the Radical ideals that caused the Revolution in the first place. Voltaire predicted violence before his death.

35 J. Dewey. 2018. *Democracy and Education*. Myers Education Press. p. 6.

36 L. J. Waks and A. R. English (Eds.). 2017. *John Dewey's Democracy and Education: A Centennial Handbook*. Cambridge University Press.

37 B. Magee. 1987. *The Great Philosophers: An Introduction to Western Philosophy*. BBC Books. p. 297.

38 Dewey. *Democracy and Education*. p. 92f.

39 Ibid. p. 128.

40 S. Morgenbesser. "Dialogue 13: The American Pragmatists." In B. Magee (Ed.). 1987. *The Great Philosophers*. pp. 278–97. Oxford University Press. p. 297. Morgenbesser was the John Dewey Professor of Philosophy at Columbia University until his retirement in 1993.

41 Dewey. *Democracy and Education*. p. 337.

42 P. H. Hinchey. 2018. "Introduction." In Dewey. *Democracy and Education*. pp. xi–xxiv. Myers Education Press. p. xxiv.

43 N. Noddings. 2005. *Philosophy of Education*. 2nd ed. Westview Press. Quoted in R. Pring (Ed.). 2007. *John Dewey: A Philosopher for Our Time?* Bloomsbury. p. 3. David Bridges, in the

"Foreword" to *John Dewey: A Philosopher for Our Time?*, notes that *Democracy and Education* was once listed alongside *Mein Kampf* and *Das Capital* as being among the most dangerous books of the twentieth century. D. Bridges. 2007. "Foreword." In R. Pring (Ed.). *John Dewey: A Philosopher of Education for Our Time?* p. xi.

44 Bridges. "Foreword." pp. xii–xiii.

45 J. Gouinlock. 2000. "Dewey, John." In *Concise Routledge Encyclopaedia of Philosophy*. Routledge. p. 207. Simon Blackburn's "Pragmatism" entry in the 2005 *Oxford Dictionary of Philosophy*, 2nd ed., does not mention Dewey. Some philosophers speak a little disparagingly of Dewey as a philosopher. However, we may note that Dewey, with his wide interests, was not competing in the academic stakes but actually practising the basic tenets of pragmatism instead. Steven Levin takes Dewey as a philosopher very seriously. See, S. Levine. 2019. *Pragmatism, Objectivity and Experience*. Cambridge University Press.

46 Blackburn. "Pragmatism." p. 375.

47 As Gouinlock comments, "The tendency of thinkers is to become bewitched by inherited philosophic puzzles, when the persistence of a puzzle is a consequence of failing to consider the assumptions that created it." Gouinlock. "Dewey, John." p. 207.

48 Blackburn. "Dewey, John." p. 132.

49 B. Russell. 1946. *History of Western Philosophy*. Allen & Unwin. p. 774.

50 According to Tim Madigan, "The two men shared many philosophical traits: an internationalist outlook, a high regard for the scientific method, a concern for social matters, and a suspicion of dogma, especially religious dogma." T. Madigan. 2016. "Russell and Dewey on Education: Similarities and Differences." In T. Madigan & P. Stone (Eds.). *Bertrand Russell: Public Intellectual.* pp. 51–60. Tiger Bark Press. https://fisherpub.sjfc.edu/philosophy_facpub/4

51 A. Ryan. 1990. "Dewey and Russell." *The Wilson Quarterly* 14, no. 1. p. 141.

52 Dewey. *Democracy and Education*. pp. 202, 243.

53 Magee. *The Great Philosophers*. p. 291.

54 Morgenbesser. "Dialogue 13." 296.

55 See E. S. Radcliffe. 2018. *Hume, Passion, and Action*. Oxford University Press. Hume commented, "reason alone can never be a motive to action of the will," and reason alone "can never oppose passion in the direction of the will." *Treatise of Human Nature*. Book 2: Of the Passions. 413.

56 T. Little. 2015. *An Intelligent Person's Guide to Education*. Bloomsbury. p. 28.

57 Donald Trump received 81 percent of the white, evangelical vote in 2016. See E. Dias. 2016. "How Evangelicals Helped Donald Trump Win." *Time*. November 9. https://time.com/4565010/donald-trump-evangelicals-win

Chapter 2

What do we mean by reason?

We live in a world in which the capacity to reason wisely is urgently needed. The Enlightenment heralded reason, which took the place of religion in sustaining civilisation. It saw reason as the means whereby society could be efficiently organised, enabling sensible decisions to be made. By applying reason, the rule of law could provide the necessary bulwark against antisocial behaviour.

The endangered role of reason

Many still believe in the importance of reason, but the very capacity for reasoning has come under siege. The distinguished lawyer Philip Allott comments:

> The most troubling aspect of the state of the human world in the twenty-first century is a collapse in the higher levels of intellectual life and a collapse in the theory and practice of education at all levels. We have disempowered ourselves spiritually and intellectually in empowering ourselves practically.[1]

He implies that the technological revolution distracted people to the extent that the world of the mind was neglected. The problem of distraction is compounded by the impact of social media, in particular, which reduces communication to brevity and is designed most of all to influence people.

Indeed, we now live in an era dubbed by some as "post-truth."[2] The Oxford Dictionaries selected "post-truth" as their 2016 Word of the Year, defining it as shorthand for "circumstances in which objective facts are less influential in shaping public opinion than appeals to emotion and personal belief."[3] It is, however, more than that. In her book entitled *The Death of Truth*, Michiko Kakutani notes: "For decades now, objectivity – or even the idea that people can aspire toward ascertaining the best available truth – has been falling out of favour."[4]

When concern for truth becomes downgraded, then anything goes, and "bullshit" can reign supreme. The American philosopher H. G. Frankfurt, whose book *On Bullshit* became a bestseller in 2005, argues that the

> bullshitter does not reject the authority of the truth, as the liar does, and oppose himself to it. He pays no attention to it at all. By virtue of this, bullshit is a greater enemy of the truth than lies are.[5]

The propensity for bullshit comes uncomfortably close to receiving academic approval in Hugo Mercier and Dan Sperber's interesting study of reasoning, which they claim as scientific. They argue that

> reason has two main functions: that of producing reasons for justifying oneself, and that of arguments to convince others ... When we speak to others, it is often in our interest to mislead them, not necessarily through straightforward lies but by at least distorting, omitting, or exaggerating information so as better to influence them in their opinions and in their actions.[6]

Disdain for truth has even reached science and its understanding. Mike Hulme, who according to Reuters was the tenth most cited author in the world in the field of climate change between 1999 and 2009, drew on the concept of post-normal science in responding to a book by Singer and Avery, wherein they put forward scientific evidence against Anthropological Global Warming (AGW).[7] Instead of debating the evidence, Hulme moved the debate to issues of values. He used the interesting phrase: "scientists – and politicians – must trade (normal) truth for influence."[8] He noted that Singer and Avery presented science as "the process of developing theories and testing them against observations until they are proven true or false." However, Hulme continues:

> Self-evidently dangerous climate change will not emerge from a normal scientific process of truth-seeking ... The danger of a "normal" reading of science is that it assumes science can first find truth, then speak truth to power, and that truth-based policy will then follow. Singer has this view of science.[9]

Whatever political allegiance one has, whether one supports AGW or not, it should be clear that this approach of post-normal science is dangerous. It is obfuscating and dishonest. The whole AGW movement is built on the presumed scientific evidence that human-induced carbon emissions are endangering the planet. However, not only did Hulme not debate the scientific evidence put forward by Singer and Avery, he implied that the evidence was wrong. He later stated that the scientific method allows us to filter out hypotheses, such as those presented by Singer and Avery, as being plain wrong. In post-normal science, scientific truth changes according to social contexts. The dishonesty is compounded by Hulme's acknowledging that all science is provisional, yet he chooses to rely wholly on what some scientists say regardless of others.

The impact of postmodernism

The concept of post-normal science reflects a postmodernist perspective.[10] Postmodernism draws attention to the vulnerability of the claim to knowledge. Prophetically, *After Truth: A Post-Modern Manifesto*, published in 1986, noted:

> Our story begins with a crisis. Our most sacred values, our most certain judgments, our most solid truths have lost their value, their certainty, their truth … We have nothing left to cling on to. Religion, humanism, science are all thrown into doubt. We face a crisis of nihilism.[11]

Postmodernism has not just advocated more modesty and humility regarding what we claim to know, it questions the reality of truth. When people claim to *have* truth, they are in fact saying that they *think* they have. Therefore, in the real world there are many truths – as many as people claim. There is no notion of truth *per se* being worth seeking, even though fallible humans may not attain it. Instead, the power motive trumps concern for truth.

Such a focus helps to demote serious thinking as no more than rationalisation – emotional power-seeking dressed up as reasoning. The result is dangerous. As the *After Truth Manifesto* put it:

> We face a crisis of nihilism … We tell a tale of nihilism in two stages: relativism and reflexivity. When we consider the status of our theories and our truth we are led to relativism. Relativism, in turn, turns back on itself and disappears into the vicious spiral of reflexivity. Nothing is certain, not even this.[12]

This conclusion emerges because

> it is not just that, from one perspective, truth is relative, but "truth is relative" from all perspectives … The statement of the view contradicts itself in the very act of being stated. If it is true then it is false.[13]

Yet many intellectuals, and increasingly the public at large, are still taken in by such postmodernist thinking. John Gray sees it as "just the latest fad in anthropocentrism."[14] He may be right, but even so, we need to try to account for the phenomenon. I suggest that there are two major reasons for it.

1 The idolisation and failure of reason dependent solely on logic and empirical/scientific evidence

In his book *The Edge of Reason*, Julian Baggini argues that "[r]eason has only been knocked off its pedestal because it was raised too high."[15] He advocates the reinstatement of reason by exposing the falseness of the idolatry of it, which has prompted a swing of the pendulum to the opposite extreme.

He notes four myths. Namely, reason is considered the judge, guide, motivator and king. He summarises the four myths thus:

> [T]hat reason is purely objective and requires no subjective judgement; that it can and should take the role of our chief guide, the charioteer of the soul; that it can furnish us with the fundamental reasons for action; and that we can build society on perfectly rational principles.

He states that judgement is "philosophy's dirty secret," in that philosophers seem loathe to accept the need for so subjective a notion. Yet, "the final judge is not reason, but the reasoner, for whom rationality is a tool, not some kind of authority."[16]

The four myths mask out of consideration the holistic awareness by which we make judgements. Nor do they welcome the involvement of people's emotional capacities, which are the mainspring for action. The mistrust of emotion leads to the unsuitability of reason for driving commitment and moral awareness. Equally, it renders the search for a politically perfect state a mirage.

Thus, reliance on reason has not lived up to its promise of establishing a just society. This has been so even from the beginning of the Enlightenment movement. The historian Jonathan Israel points out the irreconcilability of what he terms the two Enlightenments: the moderate and the radical. A memorable analogy sums up the difference between the two: on the one hand

> an ambitious architect who aspires to tear down the entire existing edifice of institutions and then rebuild it from scratch on purely rational principles ... [and on the other hand] an architect retaining most of the existing foundations, walls, and roof in place at any one time, making only marginal changes without altering the building's basic shape or removing so many "of your supports at once as that the roof may fall in."[17]

The relevant point here is that both sides were entirely and passionately committed to reason, yet they could not rationally agree. Israel notes that

> the impossibility of forging any compromise between, or synthesizing, moderate and radical thought patterns was rooted, on the one hand, in the intellectual chasm separating the two, but no less importantly in social forces that exerted a continuously polarising effect.[18]

Reason proved incapable of enabling them to work together, either through resolving the intellectual disputes or controlling the social forces.

The consequences were grave. The radicals' focus on the overthrow of authority made them obsessive about their ideals. They regularly indulged in crude, irrational generalisations and failed to acknowledge the real concerns of their opponents. Anger, thus unrestrained by reason, led to the excesses and un-reason of the French Revolution. Devotees of the Temple of Reason stooped to committing gross injustices and arousing even more enmity than before, all in the name of reason, which was regarded as the guarantor of a just society.

The story has been repeated with devastating effect in the twentieth century. Presumed rational democracy permitted the rise of Hitler, who played the system to create an egotistical tsunami which swamped democracy for millions. It permitted crimes against humanity more far-reaching than those committed by the *ancien régime* of monarchy, aristocracy and church. Similarly, and perhaps even more disastrously, the Communist experiment of the twentieth century attempted to impose a rational political system.

If on its home territory in intellectual circles, reason could not adjudicate successfully between different opinions, what hope could it ever have for adjudicating them in the non-elite world? It appears, therefore, that reason is powerless precisely where and when it is most needed. Is the appeal to reason even rational?

It is important to note that the historically failed understanding of reason was restricted to logic and scientific/empirical investigation.

The limitations of logic

Logic can be an invaluable aid for working towards eradicating contradiction and incoherence. However, it can only help us to understand the real world if the assumptions underlying its premises are true, and logic by itself cannot decide that. Take, for example, the following logically correct form of an argument:

> All swans are white –
> This bird is black –
> Therefore this bird is not a swan.

The truth of the conclusion does not follow, because at least one of the premises is false: not all swans are white.

The critic and poet T. E. Hulme expressed the point thus:

> Logical reason is simply a means of passing from a certain premise to certain conclusions. It has in itself no motive power at all. It is quite impotent to deal with those first premises. It is a kind of building art; it tells you how to construct a house on a given piece of ground, but it will not choose the ground where you build. That is decided by things outside its scope altogether.[19]

Thinking has to start somewhere, and premises embody assumptions reflecting a person's wider experience of life. Such assumptions are rarely stated explicitly and, in any case, are difficult to evaluate.

The limitations of logic do not detract, however, from the very great assistance that logic can give in helping to evaluate thought – in thinking straight. It can point out, for example, logical fallacies of all kinds. Take, for example, the following false deduction on a matter of great political significance:

> X is critical of Israel –
> Criticism of Israel is antisemitic –
> Therefore X is antisemitic.

The second premise cannot stand, because it is possible to criticise Israel without being antisemitic. Israeli citizens themselves can critique how their government acts.[20]

Baggini notes that logic is "one tool rationality uses, not the essence of rationality itself."[21]

The scope and limitations of science

Baggini goes on bluntly to state, regarding the pre-eminence of science: "Honest and sincere reasoners should reject scientism, the belief that the only legitimate forms of understanding are scientific ones and anything which is not amenable to scientific methods of inquiry is baseless or meaningless."[22] We need to look into this concept of scientism in some detail, because it is a widespread danger. It is, moreover, crucial to distinguish scientism from respect for science itself.

Science carries enormous authority today. As Gray notes: "Science alone has the power to silence heretics. Today it is the only institution that can claim authority."[23] Science does appear to be able to reveal the nature of the world. The technologies science has enabled are awesome. The achievements of science have been stupendous. They have become almost the defining characteristic of the West and have enormous impact worldwide. Science has enabled a quality of life for billions beyond the wildest imagination of previous eras. It has released many from lives of servile drudgery. It has enabled the liberation of women. It has brought the benefits of clean water and sanitation. It has reduced some of the worst effects of poverty. It has advanced the boundaries of medicine. It has developed previously unbelievable forms of communication. These achievements depend upon the enormous commitment of scientists, who slowly and patiently seek the truth about the physical world and then translate it into ways of making human life safer and more enjoyable.

However, the temptation to be mesmerised by what science has achieved and what it may achieve in the future can put other aspects of knowledge in the shade. It can appear that the scientific method is the only reliable way to attain knowledge and decide whether anything is true or not. Basking in the aura of its outstanding achievements, its limitations are easily forgotten. In 2013, two books entitled *The Science Delusion* appeared. In one, Rupert Sheldrake, a practising scientist, wished the sciences would "move beyond the dogmas that restrict free enquiry and imprison imagination."[24] In the other, Curtis White sought to unfold the pretensions of neuroscience and the materialistic assumptions that guide it.[25]

The self-limitation of science

Science can make enormous strides toward attaining objective truth. It can do so, however, only by deliberately limiting its horizons and methods to the physical world. It cannot pronounce authoritatively on anything beyond that. Chris Oliver summarises the nature of science and explains why scientism constitutes abuse:

> Science owes its enormous success on restricting the field in which it claims to operate. This enables it to make some very important statements about the nature of our world, which underlies the success of our technological society. However, there are wide areas of human experience about which science has no authority to speak (by its original choice). Cultural, emotional, religious and artistic areas of humanity's experience are not describable in scientific terms. (This is not to say that accompanying brain activity is not observable. However, to go on to assert that the thoughts are *nothing but* the electrochemical changes in the brain is beyond the remit of science). This restriction in scope inherent in the scientific culture has allowed it to be so successful. One of the major dangers of a misunderstanding of the considerable success of science is that undue authority might then be given to scientists when they speak outside their speciality.[26]

An example of the limitations of science occurs in an area where its achievements appear most obvious and welcome: health. Orthodox approaches based on scientific knowledge and clinical trials tend to treat the human person like a car to be taken to the garage and repaired when it goes wrong. Yet, mechanical servicing is only part of what sustains health. Medical science ignores the uniqueness of people and the role that a person's positive notions can play in sustaining and regaining health. A positive attitude toward cancer treatment, for example, may boost the immune system. The physical is profoundly influenced by the mental/psychological.

Nevertheless, attempts by orthodox medicine to acknowledge the impact of such subjective incursions are undermined by long-standing hostility towards alternative medicine. A letter in *The Times* from the College of Medicine responded to such hostility and drew attention to the absurdity of this antagonism:

> It has been estimated that at most 25% of clinical practice in primary care has an evidence base, and that complementary therapies, that both writers ardently oppose, have yet to be finally proven or disproven ... Good science must in future explain this complexity and understand and incorporate (not reject) mind/body effects in assessment of effectiveness.[27]

The question is especially interesting because of the inbuilt incoherence of such an either/or mentality. In fact, the very need to eliminate any possible placebo effects in clinical trials acknowledges the power of subjectivity and the mind! If what a person thinks and feels about a remedy has no effect on health, there would be no need for such caution.

The philosopher Anthony O'Hear notes, "Science is a human activity, and one which deliberately abstracts from much that is real. So science should not be treated as if it is the sole arbiter of what there really is."[28] Science thus disqualifies itself from any *complete* attempt to attain knowledge. It has no basis at all, therefore, to claim that it can present the definitive understanding of the knowledge we need to live life, let alone to sustain democracy with all its necessarily subjective factors.

The role that science actually has to play can be crucially important in the search for truth, but only as regards the physical workings of the world. Therefore, reason, either in its scientific or its logical mode, cannot be sufficient by itself to create and sustain a just society.

The ubiquity of scientism, or the fact/opinion divide

Science is often treated, however, as though it and it alone can provide genuine knowledge. The term *scientism* was coined to describe the downgrading of what is not amenable to scientific validation. The seriousness of the rise of scientism is rarely appreciated because, on the whole, it has crept in unannounced. It is not something proclaimed. It happened largely unintentionally and, therefore, goes unrecognised.

While scientism is rarely acknowledged, in ordinary thinking it has taken hold in a big way. I denote this as the *fact/opinion divide* – the widely-held notion that only what rests on empirical/scientific evidence deserves to be called *knowledge*. In principle, it can be shared by all. Empirical/scientific evidence produces facts which are certain, reliable and objectively true, unlike opinions, which reflect people's subjective thinking (see Box 2.1).

The fact/opinion divide has become, for so many, a basic assumption – facts are what matter. The discussion of opinions does not lead anywhere certain. Opinion is, therefore, a matter of trying to influence people. As postmodernists would say, it is a form of power struggle.

Box 2.1 The fact/opinion divide

Fact	Opinion
Objective	Subjective
Rational	Irrational
Based on empirical/scientific evidence	Based on intuition, imagination, experience
Can be proved to be right to other people	Cannot be proved right because personal
Reliable	Unreliable because people are biased

The ubiquity of the fact/opinion divide rests on more than over-enthusiasm for the achievements of science. It owes much to long-term and influential intellectual preparation, due to the impact of the nineteenth-century philosophical school of *positivism* and its twentieth-century successor, *logical positivism*.

The impact of positivist philosophy

Following the turmoil caused by the French Revolution, two influential thinkers saw science as the positive bedrock for the renewal of society. Henri de Saint-Simon, in his book *Nouveaux Christianisme*, published in 1825, set out the tenets of virtually a new *positive* religion, that of humanity, in which in future scientists would replace priests as the spiritual leaders of society. Saint-Simon was a brilliant, yet unsystematic, thinker. His disciple, Auguste Comte, developed a precise philosophy embodying most of Saint-Simon's ideas. Both saw scientific method as the unifying feature holding the various sciences together. Comte explicitly added the science of society, or *sociology*. Comte surveyed the scope of human history, deeming it to have been organised first by religion, then by metaphysics and, finally, by science, which made the other two redundant.

Comte eventually came to adopt some of the trappings of religion himself in order to popularise his strictly scientific version of positivism, producing an atheist cult. As Gray puts it:

> It was Comte who was most successful in propagating it ... Comte's church spread from France to Britain and other European countries, then to Latin America, where it continues to exist in Brazil, while his philosophy had a profound impact on leading nineteenth-century thinkers.[29]

His positivism was widely influential, and it developed in different forms.[30] Especially notable is his influence on the twentieth-century logical positivist school of philosophy, which originated in the Vienna Circle and was popularised in Britain and the USA by A. J. Ayer. The logical positivist approach saw reason as logic, with scientific method as its handmaid. The movement was, indeed, hoisted by its own petard. Having attempted to ban metaphysics, the movement found it had to use it to defend itself against criticism. However, the defence that it came up with, termed the *verification principle*, failed. As John Cottingham summarised it: "the triumph of logical positivism ... ended up self-destructing ... when it became clear that positivism's own darling, natural science, could not pass the proposed test."[31]

Few philosophers today support such positivism. Even Ayer himself came to deny it.[32] Its influence, however, is still powerfully at work behind the scenes in the search for what is objectively certain. Paul Strathern's book, *Hume in 90 Minutes*, boldly stated: "Hume is the only philosopher whose ideas remain plausible to us today."[33] Yet, Hume was an early positivist. His famous injunction to get rid of all academic clutter that could not be empirically proved is often quoted:

> If we take in our hand any volume of divinity or school metaphysics, for instance, let us ask, Does it contain any abstract reasoning concerning quantity or number? No. Does it contain any experimental reasoning concerning matter of fact and existence? No. Commit it then to the flames: for it can contain nothing but sophistry and illusion.[34]

Similarly, the impact of Comte's positivist cult is still at work. Gray notes, "The cult he established has been almost forgotten. Yet it formed the template for the secular humanism that all evangelical atheists promote today ... It continues to have a pervasive though unrecognised influence today."[35] Brian Leiter, writing in 2004, spoke of "the naturalistic revolution which has swept anglophone philosophy over the last three decades." It was inspired by the vision that philosophers should either "adopt and emulate the method of successful sciences or ... operate in tandem with the sciences, as their abstract and reflective branch."[36]

The fact/opinion divide, which reflects scientism and positivism, forms the background to how so many judge the validity of what is presented to them. It is like the air they breathe, of which, as Hulme noted, we only become conscious when we breathe something that is not air. Wittgenstein supplies a reason: "the aspect of things that are most important for us are hidden because of their simplicity and familiarity. (One is unable to notice something because it is always before one's eyes)."[37]

Consciousness, the fact/opinion divide and education

The clear embodiment of positivism today appears in attempts to explain consciousness and personhood, as well as appreciation of the arts and other achievements of human culture, solely in terms of neuroscience and its ongoing discoveries. In her book *Are You An Illusion?*, Mary Midgley noted that, apparently in the name of science, many

> believe themselves, and indeed their readers, not to exist, selves having apparently been replaced by arrangement of brain cells ... a necessary pillar of their faith in science: a vindication of the material world; a crucial prop for the certainty that, in today's widespread disorder, we so badly need.[38]

Discussion of consciousness provides a close link with education. Anthony Seldon, in his book *The Fourth Education Revolution*, considers that the new era should give more attention to consciousness. He acknowledges Guy Claxton's argument that "thinking or mental intelligence is highly important, but not all-important."[39] Seldon comments,

> We would go further than Claxton and assert that more attention in the fourth education era needs to be given to consciousness, and less just to cognitive thinking, which so dominated the first three eras, and which struggles to answer the question *Why?* Or, to translate Descartes' maxim differently, "I am, whatever I think."[40]

The problem is, as he later states, "We are least clear of all about consciousness, despite sixty years and more of intensive scientific research and many centuries of philosophical speculation."[41] Of course, Seldon's comment itself reflects scientism, as though consciousness *should* be able to reveal its secrets to scientific enquiry. He goes on to discuss different theories of consciousness. Yet, if consciousness is so important for life and for education, and if we are unsure whether it even exists, then we are not in a good position to develop it. I shall return to this point in Chapter 10.

The pull of scientism and positivism is extraordinary considering that, as Cottingham notes,

> there are vast swathes of human life where understanding and enrichment does not come through the methods of science; these include not just poetry, music, novels, theatre, and all the arts, but the entire domain of human emotions and human relationships as they are experienced in the inner life of each of us, and in our complex interaction with our fellows.[42]

A major factor for the ubiquity of the fact/opinion divide, however, lies in the impact it has had on education, which has, in turn, re-bounded back on all who have been through the educational system (see Figure 2.1).

2 Concern for certainty which is objective

My enemy in this chapter, therefore, is emphatically *not* science but scientism – the imperialist claim that science provides the royal road to knowledge, ousting all others. So long as people

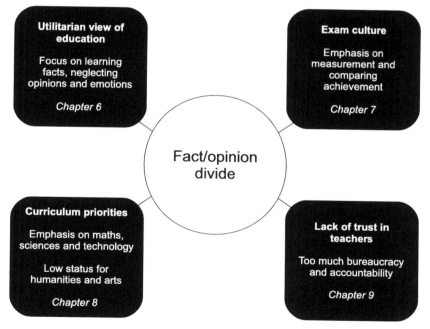

Figure 2.1 Impact of the fact/opinion divide on education

value certainty, however, the claims of scientism are likely to be taken seriously. Compared to other ways of knowing, such as common sense, imagination, and intuition, science offers a seemingly more reliable approach to the search to discover truth. Even the work of Dewey, polymath as he was, offers weak resistance to the development of scientism. See Chapter 1 for my discussion of Dewey's understanding of scientific method. When speaking of knowledge, he clearly had science in mind and not any other disciplines. Thus, he wrote:

> Science represents the fruition of the cognitive factors in experience. Instead of contenting itself with a mere statement of what commends itself to personal or customary experience, it aims to be a statement which will reveal the sources, grounds, and consequences of a belief.[43]

The quest for certainty which is utterly reliable is what has produced a narrow view of reason. An example of this is the celebrated dictum of W. K. Clifford: "It is wrong always, everywhere, and for anyone to believe anything on insufficient evidence."[44] Such a view results in the assumption that what cannot be established publicly as true knowledge is regarded as mere opinion. It is the very embodiment of an unbridgeable either/or binary split between objectivity and subjectivity.

By contrast, the twentieth-century scientist Michael Polanyi saw this as

> a rejection of the very things which scientific discovery required to be tacitly held ... Explicit knowledge is only to be had as it is rooted in a far wider expanse of tacit awareness, utilizing tacit powers of intuition, imagination, and confirmation in our search for reality.

He fulminated against, as Esther Meek puts it, "the very false ideal of objectivism, the deeply ensconced fact-value, reason-faith, divorces, which he laboured to defeat."[45] She quotes from *Personal Knowledge* Polyani's goal "to achieve a frame of mind in which I may hold firmly to what I believe to be true, even though I know that it might conceivably be false."[46] Polanyi's approach reflects the famous adage of Aristotle: "It is the mark of the trained mind never to expect more precision in the treatment of any subject than the nature of that subject permits."[47] It is a principle that deserves to be kept steadily in mind. Indeed, academic science always sees itself as unfinished business. Hypotheses can only claim to be true provided further evidence does not question or call them into doubt. So, to claim that science gives us absolutely reliable certainty is mistaken.

The need for certainty which is partial and provisional (see Figure 2.2)

The levels of certainty to which we should aspire is a fundamental question. In daily life, and in the life of the mind, it is unavoidable that we operate with some things taken for granted and some things we presume are certain. No decisions can be made without some presumption of certainty regarding what is necessary and what outcomes are possible. Otherwise, there is constant dithering and thought merely floats at the mercy of whatever currents there happen to be. Similarly, thinking cannot get going at all without some starting point, which is itself not being questioned at the moment of beginning.

Yet, just as we arrange an event, an outing or a holiday feeling certain that a significant number of factors, such as the weather, health, and transport, will make it possible,

Four possible approaches

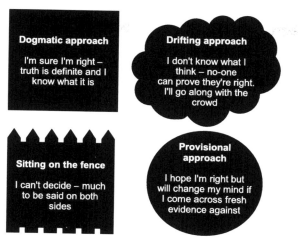

Dogmatic approach

I'm sure I'm right – truth is definite and I know what it is

Drifting approach

I don't know what I think – no-one can prove they're right. I'll go along with the crowd

Sitting on the fence

I can't decide – much to be said on both sides

Provisional approach

I hope I'm right but will change my mind if I come across fresh evidence against

Which approach do you favour?

Figure 2.2 Certainty and conviction

worthwhile or enjoyable, it must be acknowledged that we may be mistaken. We may have functional certainty that all will be well, but we know from experience that circumstances may not turn out as we hope. Similarly, in our thinking we start from assumptions which enable us to use our reasoning powers, but we ought to acknowledge that those assumptions could be wrong, and, therefore, the line of thought following from them could be wrong. On the whole we are not good at acknowledging this. Instead, we tend to get excited and emotionally involved in our convictions. We fail to contemplate that they may be mistaken, as this may weaken resolve. What we need, to quote Edward Hulmes, is a:

> commitment which is firm, but provisional, or partial. That is to say it reflects the dynamic inner quality of the individual engaged in a searching progression through life ... the search may discover fresh evidence in the light of which the commitment is to be modified.[48]

Acceptance of a degree of uncertainty relates to the persons we actually are. Better by far to accept that we cannot have incorrigible certainty and seek to embrace all the clues we find as to what the world really is like, what knowledge is and how reasoning, as such, can contribute to the quest for truth without dominating it. A certain uncertainty in knowledge and understanding is just part of life; to pretend otherwise is to fall into a positivist trap.

A scientist friend of mine notes:

> Scientists need to be aware that there is a wholly different dimension to life, based upon experience, imagination, empathy, tradition (that works!) and intuition. Meaningful life requires us to inhabit both dimensions. It may be conceded that scientific method is the

sole route to *reliable* knowledge, reliable being defined as that which can be repeatedly verified objectively, but this does not mean that knowledge reached by other means is unreliable; it is just *not precisely verifiable*. [49]

This distinction is crucial. The search for objective certainty is a search for what can be proved to be the case, not for what actually is the case so far as we can judge. For the latter enterprise, we need to use all of the means for striving towards knowledge that are open to us. Common sense, imagination and intuition need to be regarded as partners. Life, after all, was held together before the rise of science – and today most of the time outside actual academic study and reflection – by knowledge achieved by other means.

Ways of seeking knowledge which lie beyond scientific method

Common sense is often derided as uncommon or, where present, as fuzzy and unreliable. By itself, a lack of precision or reliability provides no reason to dismiss common sense, for reason itself, as we have seen, cannot guarantee rectitude either. In real life common sense is what may save the day, because it is not narrowly confined and can quickly respond to the changing circumstances of the moment. Thus, we speak of *common sense* as the product of experience both at a personal and communal level. It does not supply proof of correctness, but it enables life to continue in a more or less stable way, both today as well as in the past.

Imagination tends to be distrusted because of an overemphasis on what is purely imaginary – what is not real. Imagination, however, does not need to be so sceptically regarded, for it is a major faculty. It allows what is absent to current sensory experience to be glimpsed. Although it is highly subjective, imagination is needed, nevertheless, in the search for scientific knowledge. Indeed, Einstein's axiom, "Imagination is more important than knowledge," is often quoted.[50] A lack of imagination makes people blind to possibilities. The dangerous ubiquity, for example, of either/or thinking, which promotes ill-advised combativeness, instead of both/and thinking, is symptomatic of a lack of imagination for conceiving alternatives. Through imagination we can enter into what is real but unavailable directly to us in any other way. We can never, for example, literally enter into someone else's life and feelings, but imagination can help us get some idea of what it is like to be another person.

Intuition supplies the lifeblood of action. The world views we choose to espouse, as compared with those we are conditioned into without thought, are based on our intuitive sense of what is meaningful and true. We cannot believe what we consider not to be true. Intuition is the resolutely personal and ultimately subjective factor that we each utilise for our views, great and small. Obviously, the products of intuition cannot be proved to others, for they are inherently personal. But, this does not mean that they are therefore false. If Sharon intuits that Brian loves her, that can be true, even if it is not demonstrable to others. *Intuition* is also a vital component of the scientific method, since it assists hypothesis (conjecture), which is a major step in that method.

Such ways of knowing combine to create judgement, which is what John Henry Newman called the *Illative Sense*, beyond which there is no appeal. His philosophical work, *A Grammar of Assent*, published in 1870, is remarkably pertinent regarding the place of doubt and how to seek right reasoning. According to Newman,

> Errors in reasoning are lessons and warnings, not to give up reasoning, but to reason with greater caution. It is absurd to break up the whole structure of our knowledge,

which is the glory of the human intellect, because the intellect is not infallible in its conclusions.

Reasoning, which is verbal, depends on what lies deeper, the Illative Sense, which "has its function in the beginning, middle and end of all verbal discussion and inquiry, and in every step of the process."[51] Such certainty is the fruit of persistent reasoning, in contrast to prejudice, which is assent given before rational inquiry.

Putting the search for objectivity into perspective

Newman contrasts certitude with prejudice. People are wayward. They choose to pay attention to this and ignore that if it does not suit the whim of the moment or their own self-centred needs and interests. In almost everyone egoism plays an enormous role, promoting bias and prejudice, which is clearly an enemy of truth-seeking. We cannot believe someone just because they say that such-and-such is so. They may not be deliberately deceiving us, but sincerity can be mistaken. It is understandable, therefore, that objectivity appears to be so desirable. Mitchell saw the chief merit of the stress on objectivity as seeking to combat a "native vice":

> We are by nature intellectually lazy. Left to ourselves, we find it comfortable to be ruled by prejudice or by prevailing fashions ... To combat this native vice requires an early and insistent emphasis upon rigour; upon clarity of expression, upon recognition of and search for unwelcome facts, and upon the use of any methods that will correct individual bias.[52]

The virtues of attempted objectivity are obvious, yet there is no way we can reach objective certainty about judgement. Baggini tries to relate judgement to objective reasoning. He considers: "A rational argument is one which gives objective reasons for belief." Yet, this introduces an incoherence, because he readily acknowledges the problem concerning who decides what is objective: "No reasons are perfectly objective. Rather, our understanding becomes more objective the less it depends on idiosyncratic features of our viewpoint, reasoning, conceptual framework and senses."[53]

Baggini's comment implies a continuum, where objective (A) is at one pole, and subjective (B) is at the other pole. His view is close to Thomas Nagel's, which he quotes: "knowledge does not divide neatly between the either/or of 'objective' and 'subjective'. Rather there is a spectrum, with absolute objectivity and subjectivity at opposite ends, and degrees of each in between."[54]

This view does indeed, avoid the idiocy of the fact/opinion divide, but it still generates a worry. The price to be paid for being absolutely sure we are not mistaken might be to attend only to what we can lay claim to as being publicly reliable. Anyone inclined towards scientism will see it as desirable to be as close as possible to (A). This collides with any notion of relative importance. What may be crucial for the safe running of society, for example, can appear unsupported and close to (B), whilst what is relatively mundane and trivial can be close to (A). We can be absolutely sure that the human foot normally has five toes. However, the mindset of an Islamist terrorist is difficult to be certain of, yet political decisions of enormous import are based on such understanding or misunderstanding. If (A) is strongly valued, it discourages proper scholarly attention to (B). Indeed, this is what has happened, especially in education, as will be discussed at length in Part II of this book.

Therefore, the danger of over-concentration on what we can be certain of needs to be tackled head on. Whether we like it or not, the difficult wrestling with ideas close to (B) matters. Is it not better to accept subjectivity and look for ways in which reasoning can evaluate and safeguard it against abuse rather than trying to chase objectivity? We have to continue being persons, living in the world, relating to others, etc. Why should these experiences not be embraced within a real search for knowledge? Why not see subjectivity – educated subjectivity – as a strength rather than a weakness?

I do not mean that we can just think what we like, that anything goes, that some judgements are not better than others or more likely to be true than others. For some judgements, we can draw on much better reasons than we can for other judgments. We cannot claim absolutely certain knowledge; neither can we claim absolutely certain ignorance. We need knowledge, not ignorance, to live at all. If I am ignorant of what a poisonous toadstool looks like and I mistake it for a mushroom, I may die if I eat it. Knowledge is *that* important. Such knowledge is built up communally as well as individually. The question of certainty is, in a sense, irrelevant. I may not be able to identify conclusively a particular mushroom as a toadstool, but reason would dictate caution and not eating it in case that it is.

For the life of the mind, we need to approach assumptions in the same way as we approach practical day-to-day living. We need to identify reasons, as far as we can, and ask how far they are justified. Our beliefs and values cannot ever be proved, to ourselves or anyone else, to be utterly reliable. Yet, we cannot operate at all without such beliefs and values and the assumptions on which they are based. As Mitchell says:

> Insofar as our actions have to be consistent, our choices need to be consistent too, that is to say they have to be based on some more or less coherent view of the world. Our choice of such a view of the world determines not only what we do, but also to a large extent, who we are.[55]

A broader understanding of reason that embraces subjectivity

Baggini argues:

> We need a more expansive notion of what it means to be rational, one which includes all the elements that are left out when we focus only on the strictly formal and empirical ones. At the heart of this notion we need to place judgement.[56]

The education of judgement is crucial, therefore, for "accepting the role of judgement is not the same as saying anything goes and that no reasoned arguments can have any force in a debate."[57] Baggini sees the possibility for such educated judgment, and his book culminates in a 52-point "user's guide to reason."[58]

Criteria for discernment

The reasoning now needed must embrace subjectivity instead of seeking at all costs to avoid it. There are in fact important criteria upon which to draw in exercising judgement.[59] Baggini suggests the following: "Objective reasons must be 'comprehensible, assessable, defeasible, interest-neutral, concerned with practical rationality – what we ought to believe – and compelling.'"[60] Three of the six criteria he suggests are problematic, however.

Problematic criteria 1: Assessable

Baggini notes, "Unless others can judge the truth of what is claimed, it remains in the domain of the subjective." Evaluation is what the criteria are about, so this cannot be one of them! It would make sense if *assessable* referred to *measurement*, but, as already conceded, measurement is not possible beyond the domains of logic and scientific investigation.

Problematic criteria 2: Interest-neutral

In relating to the real world, when decisions must be made, people's experiences and commitments are resources upon which to draw, not things to be deliberately excluded in the interests of neutrality – even if it were possible to exclude them, which in practice it is not. What is needed for rational debate is not neutrality but impartiality, a subject addressed in greater detail in Chapter 3.

Moreover, to have a personal viewpoint is not necessarily to be biased or idiosyncratic. To assume that private judgement is bound to be wayward is unjustified. It is parallel to the false assumption that everyone is biased because they can be. They may be correct. It is unfair to call a person's judgment biased if the person's subjective viewpoint is based on experience and the person does not assume that "only my experience counts" or that anyone who had a different experience misunderstood or misinterpreted it.

Problematic criteria 3: Compelling

The unavoidable challengeability of reason means that any expectation of agreement by all is not possible. The whole history of philosophy argues against it, because philosophers are excellent at perceiving objections to anything said.

While three of Baggini's criteria are problematic, the other three are essential.

Essential criteria 1: Comprehensible

Clarity and accuracy in understanding what is being debated is definitely crucial. We need to establish *what* is under discussion. It is clear that if the point under discussion is not understood, then there is no rational way forward.

Understanding what is at stake is far from easy, however. Reason has to use words to communicate, and words are notoriously slippery and difficult to handle. They have a strange and far from obvious relationship with the reality they purport to describe. Words are only signs that point to something and, as such, are not an aspect of that reality. Words can mean so many different things to different people depending on experience, which is varied. As such, comprehensibility is something that cannot be taken for granted. It needs work.

Essential criteria 2: Defeasible, i.e., non-dogmatic and prepared to seek fresh understanding

Here we are on very firm ground. Anything does *not* go. If a claim is made that a belief, proposition, view or opinion is definitive, then there is no more to be said on the matter, for it is an absolutely dogmatic stance which prevents further debate. The criterion of defeasibility specifically admits the possibility of revision. It implies that knowledge is partial and provisional. See the discussion above on certainty and the importance of non-dogmatism.

Essential criteria 3: Practical rationality – what works

Practical rationality relates to the need to overcome artificial boundaries between thinking and the real world, as discussed above. It is a hugely important matter. It draws on a pragmatic attitude to life, involving common sense, imagination and intuition to deal with the unexpected, and it implies a hope for benevolent consequences. As a total philosophy, pragmatism may be wanting, as discussed in Chapter 1 regarding Dewey's acceptance of it. The possibility of practical application, however, remains important as one criterion for judging how sensible a theoretical idea is.

I would like to add two further criteria to Baggini's three essential ones:

Essential criteria 4: In line with moral awareness

This criterion is closely related to practical rationality. It is associated with benevolent consequences and draws on compassion and moral awareness in the judgment-making process, so that decision-making and actions promote the common good. If an opinion fails to cohere with moral awareness, then it is questionable. By contrast, an opinion which encourages virtuous character and morally beneficial consequences should be taken seriously.

While it is closely related to practical rationality, the criterion of moral awareness deserves to stand on its own because it does not necessarily refer to *practical* decision-making. It is grounded in moral awareness – something deeply embedded in almost everyone and foundational for any sustainable society. The concept of moral awareness is discussed in detail in Chapter 4. Generally, if an opinion is morally suspect, that is a powerful reason for denying or rejecting it.[61]

Essential criteria 5: What is as comprehensive as possible

Anything does *not* go, which may give the overall impression of a comprehensive understanding but may ignore what is relevant. This is incoherent. Holistic understanding is essential for actual living, and verbalisation should reflect that. It may immediately be objected that such comprehensiveness is impossible. Yes it is, but the search for it – the desire to be as fair as possible to all possible perspectives and not to omit from discussion what may be significant – is the mark of the fair-minded thinker.

This criterion draws on the sophisticated awareness of the manner in which what we say both reveals and conceals at the same time. As McGilchrist notes, "Language helps some things stand forward, but by the same token makes others recede."[62] When we state a fact about something, we cannot say everything that there is to be said about it, even if it is a simple thing, like a potato, a hammer, a rose. We choose to say what we consider interesting and relevant. The question always remains: may we be leaving out more that is relevant than we are taking into account? Does Paul's speech about Peter say more about Paul than about Peter? Our utterances can mislead because of what we fail to draw attention to, thereby implying irrelevance or falsity. In education, for example, what has been termed the *null curriculum* may have as powerful an effect as the explicit curriculum, which I discuss further in Chapter 8.

A holistic use of reason seeks to garner insight from everywhere and anywhere. It acknowledges that contradictions in experience may well be apparent only because they are tied to inadequate concepts. Often only limited experience sees inconsistency. The holistic thinker searches for what can make sense of the widest possible understanding of experience, not just of one's own experiences, but also the experiences of others.

It may help to consider an example (see Box 2.2). Can the essential criteria suggest that a viewpoint, such as antisemitism, is mistaken?

Box 2.2 Why is antisemitism wrong?

Criteria 1: <u>Comprehensible</u> – Careful consideration of what antisemitism consists of, and how it came about, is needed. For example, envy of the wealth of many Jews is one likely reason. Thus, Hitler hated the Jewish philosopher Wittgenstein for his privileged financial and cultural background. This provides a weak reason for antisemitism, because there are and always have been many financially poor Jews. This is the logical fallacy of implying "all" in generalisations when only "some" is true.

Criteria 2: <u>Defeasible</u> – Antisemitism fails this test because it is definite and dogmatic, leaving no room for further exploration.

Criteria 3: <u>Practical rationality</u> – The existence of so many Jews, and the need to replace their contributions to society, constitutes a major reason against antisemitism. Only the ruthless, immoral use of power has ever enabled the extermination or removal of large numbers of people.

Criteria 4: <u>In line with moral awareness</u> – Antisemitism can easily lead to hatred and evil consequences. Auschwitz, as a supreme offense against humanity, stands as a permanent reminder of this.

Criteria 5: <u>What is as comprehensive as possible</u> – Antisemitism is one-sided. It exaggerates certain presumed characteristics, such as wealth and influence, but ignores others, such as Jewish people's contributions to the arts. Moreover, it fails to consider the most obvious point of all, their humanity. As Shakespeare put in the mouth of Shylock, "If you prick us, do we not bleed?"

Applying the five criteria to the truth or falsity of antisemitism comes up with a clear view that antisemitism is false.

The above criteria are all challengeable, but not negligible. None of the criteria is foolproof. All can be abused. Yet, they become stronger as they interact with each other, like interlocking links. Their cumulative force serves to point out weaknesses, both in the content of belief and in how it is expressed. They identify weaknesses in a way that can helpfully foster discussion with other people. The difficulty of applying them does not exonerate serious thinkers from trying to do so. Their very determination to utilise the five criteria to attempt to get an all-round view of a subject reflects their usefulness.

We should be able to gain, therefore, a more hopeful and optimistic view of subjectivity, welcoming it instead of trying to distance it. Ongoing experience of life can correct and amend subjectivity, allowing it to blossom into what we might call, using a classical but now largely ignored term, *wisdom*. T. S. Eliot famously asked, "Where is the wisdom we have lost in knowledge? Where is the knowledge we have lost in information?" Abandoning the narrow view of reason, which has so dominated thinking in the West, may enable us to regain what has been lost.

Notes

1 P. Allott. 2016. *Eutopia*. Edward Elgar Publishing. p. viii.
2 M. D'Ancona. 2017. *Post Truth and How to Fight Back*. Ebury Press. p. 8f.
3 "Word of the Year 2016." 2016. Oxford Languages. https://languages.oup.com/word-of-the-year/2016
4 M. Kakutani. 2018. *The Death of Truth*. William Collins. p. 17.
5 H. G. Frankfurt. 2005. *On Bullshit*. Princeton University Press. p. 56.
6 H. Mercier & D. Sperber. 2017. *The Enigma of Reason: A New Theory of Human Understanding*. Allen Lane. p. 8.
7 F. Singer & A. Avery. 2006. *Unstoppable Global Warming: Every 1,500 Years*. Rowman & Littlefield. For information on Mike Hulme and his citation history, see M. Hulme. 2019. "About Me." Mike Hulme: Professor Mike Hulme's Site. https://mikehulme.org/about-me
8 M. Hulme. 2007. "The Appliance of Science." *The Guardian*. March 14. https://www.theguardian.com/society/2007/mar/14/scienceofclimatechange.climatechange
9 Ibid. Mike Hulme was Professor of Climate Change at the University of East Anglia and is now Professor of Human Geography at Cambridge University.
10 For a useful overview of postmodernism, see "Postmodernism." 2020. All About Philosophy. https://www.allaboutphilosophy.org/postmodernism.htm
11 Second of January Group. 1986. *After Truth: A Post-Modern Manifesto*. Inventions Press. p. 4.
12 Ibid. p. 4.
13 Ibid. p. 20.
14 J. Gray. 2002. *Straw Dogs: Thoughts on Humans and Other Animals*. Granta Books. p. 55.
15 J. Baggini. 2016. *The Edge of Reason*. Yale University Press. p. 7.
16 Ibid. pp. 6, 61, & 12.
17 J. Israel. 2010. *A Revolution of the Mind: Radical Enlightenment and the Intellectual Origins of Modern Democracy*. Princeton University Press. p. 17. Quoting Adam Ferguson, the Scottish Enlightenment figure.
18 Ibid. p. 238.
19 P. McGuiness (Ed.). 2003. *T. E. Hulme: Selected Writings*. Fyfield Books. p. 164.
20 A classic work on the value of awareness of logical fallacies is R. H. Thouless. 1930. *Straight and Crooked Thinking*. A number of books seek to make these better known, e.g., A. Almossawi. 2014. *Illustrated Book of Bad Arguments: Learn the Lost Art of Making Sense*. Scribe. J. Baggini lists ten Common fallacies in 2012. *Philosophy – All That Matters*. Hodder Education. p. 142f.
21 Baggini. *Philosophy – All that Matters*. p. 69.
22 Ibid. p. 242, point 25.
23 Gray. *Straw Dogs*. p. 19. Commenting on the religion it has replaced, he adds: "For us, science is a refuge from uncertainty, promising – and in some measure delivering – the miracle of freedom from thought; while churches have become sanctuaries for doubt."
24 R. Sheldrake. 2013. *The Science Delusion*. Coronet. p. 4.
25 C. White. 2013. *The Science Delusion: Asking the Big Questions in a Culture of Easy Answers*. Melville House.
26 An eminent scientist in correspondence with me. Christopher John Oliver, BA, PhD, CBE. Before retirement was an Individual Merit Deputy Chief Scientific Officer at DERA, Malvern, also Fellow of Institute of Physics and Visiting Professor at King's College, London, University College, London and La Sapienza, University of Rome.
27 D. Michael Dixon. 2012. "Patients' Beliefs and Good Medicine." *The Times*. May 30. Dixon is Chair of Council and George Lewith Vice-Chair at the College of Medicine.
28 A. O'Hear. 2001. *Philosophy in the New Century*. Continuum. p. 119.
29 J. Gray. 2018. *Seven Types of Atheism*. Allen Lane. pp. 10f.
30 See, e.g., Herbert Spencer's evolutionary positivism or Richard Avenarius and Ernst Mach's philosophy of science.
31 J. Cottingham. 2005. *The Spiritual Dimension: Religion, Philosophy and Human Value*. Cambridge University Press.
32 See, e.g., A. J. Ayer. 1959. *Logical Positivism*. Allen & Unwin. p. 9f.
33 P. Strathern. 1996. *Hume in 90 Minutes*. Constable. p. 11.

34 D. Hume. 1777. *An Enquiry Concerning Human Understanding*. p. 166.
35 Gray. *Seven Types of Atheism*. p. 10f.
36 B. Leiter (Ed.). 2004. *The Future of Philosophy*. Clarendon Press.
37 L. Wittgenstein. 1953. *Philosophical Investigations*. Trans. G. E. M. Anscombe. Basil Blackwell. p. 50, point 129.
38 M. Midgley. 2014. *Are You An Illusion?* Acumen.
39 See G. Claxton. 2017. *Stronger Than We Realised*. Yale University Press. Quoted in A. Seldon. 2018. *The Fourth Education Revolution: Will Artificial Intelligence Liberate or Infantilise Humanity*. University of Buckingham Press. p. 98.
40 Seldon. *The Fourth Education Revolution*. p. 97f.
41 Ibid. p. 280.
42 Cottingham. *The Spiritual Dimension*. p. viii.
43 J. Dewey. 2018. *Democracy and Education*. Myers Education Press. p. 144f.
44 W. K. Clifford. 1886. *Lectures and Essays*. Macmillan. p. 346.
45 E. L. Meek. 2012. "Michael Polanyi: Unknown and Untapped." *Comment Magazine*. p. 41.
46 Ibid. p. 119.
47 Baggini refers to the phrase as "Aristotle's immortal adage." Baggini. *The Edge of Reason*. p. 119.
48 See E. Hulmes. 1979. *Commitment and Neutrality*. Geoffrey Chapman.
49 In conversation with Michael Trott, BSc (physics) and MSc (aeronautical engineering). Trott comments that his view is formulated upon one percent of the BSc and 99 percent of the half-century since the BSc.
50 See, e.g., G. S. Viereck. 1929. "What Life Means to Einstein: An Interview by George Sylvester Viereck." *Saturday Evening Post*. 26 October. p. 117.
51 J. H. Newman. 1979. A *Grammar of Assent*. University of Notre Dame Press. pp. 187, 283, & 207. Newman has a high view of the notion of such rational inquiry and the courage and persistence needed to support it: "It … attends upon the whole course of thought from antecedents to consequents, with a minute diligence and unwearied presence, which is impossible to a cumbrous apparatus of verbal reasoning, though, in communicating with others, words are the only instrument we possess, and a serviceable, though imperfect instrument." Ibid. p. 283.
52 B. Mitchell. 1985. "Certainty, Commitment and the Academic Vocation." In V. Hornby-Northcote (Ed.). *Confidence and Certainty in Matters of Religion*. pp. 59–67. Farmington Institute for Christian Studies. p. 59f.
53 Baggini. *The Edge of Reason*. p. 240f, points 11 & 12.
54 Ibid. p. 113.
55 B. Mitchell. 1994. *Faith and Criticism*. Oxford University Press. p. 37.
56 Baggini. *The Edge of Reason*. p. 55.
57 Ibid. p. 74.
58 Ibid. pp. 239–45.
59 Eight such criteria are discussed in B. Watson & P. Thompson. 2007. *The Effective Teaching of Religious Education*. 2nd ed. Pearson Longman. pp. 143–7.
60 Baggini. *The Edge of Reason*. p. 240. In the book Baggini lists ten principles. See pp. 140–2. An interesting exercise would be to discuss their relationship with the criteria here noted.
61 See my "Religious Education and Moral Education." In L. P. Barnes (Ed.). 2018. *Learning to Teach Religious Education in the Secondary School*. 3rd ed. pp. 164–81. Routledge.
62 I. McGilchrist. 2012. *The Master and His Emissary*. Yale University Press. p. 110.

Chapter 3

Debate: Does it have to be aggressive?

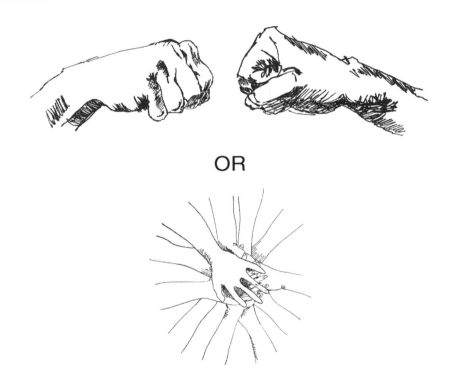

OR

The importance of debate

Debate at various levels, from the most informal conversation to dialogue at official meetings, is crucial for sustaining democracy. Discussion and exchange of reasoning enable people to relate to each other and to ideas, and they enable people to achieve projects together. Decisions have to be made. Discussion of different points of view is vital to arriving at sound policy and effective implementation. Part of being in dialogue is to explore, clarify and challenge ideas together. No one has the whole picture.

Indeed, debate is essential to the advancement of knowledge. We disagree, not arbitrarily, but because we think we are right and have reason on our side. Disagreement is unavoidable. As Keith Ward puts it:

One thing that most people would agree upon is that people are capable of disagreeing about almost everything ... When it comes to matters as abstract and complex as philosophy or religious belief, therefore, it is hardly surprising that disagreements are only to be expected. If there is to be any agreement about such matters, it is likely to be only about the most general, one might say, the most vacuous, points.[1]

We may note that political worldviews are just as complex as philosophy or religious belief.

Unwin and Yandell explain why, in view of disagreement, we need to debate intelligently and sensitively:

To dismiss those who hold different positions as simply wrong or ignorant, seems problematic to us for three distinct reasons. First, it amounts to a wilful refusal to acknowledge the simple fact that people disagree on these matters. Second, there is an irony in the use of institutional power to silence other voices: if the knowledge itself really were so powerful, why would this be necessary? Third – and most important – such a response is anti-educational: it stifles the debate that is, for us, the precondition of the advancement of knowledge.[2]

The complexity of issues and the necessity to find a *modus vivendi* for people with differing outlooks, experiences and needs calls out for debate. It needs, however, to be quality discussion in which people both say what they mean and are listened to attentively. Accepting compromise may often be necessary, yet only necessary compromise, which can be reached after listening responsibly to what opponents have to say. Disagreement is unavoidable. It needs to be handled intelligently and without ridicule, one-upmanship, name-calling or inferences that may be personal but not part of the argument.

The metaphors with which we operate are important. For many, debate has become an arena for aggression – for war. Instead, what is needed is a search for a meeting of minds and hearts – a concern for a just peace (see Figure 3.1).

Figure 3.1 Different metaphors for debating

Poor quality of public debate

Unfortunately, the West is generally suffering from a debasement of public discourse. It is as though people have lost faith in the power of reasoning. Dworkin, whose comment on the poor state of American politics was mentioned in Chapter 1, was especially worried that, typically, neither side makes any proper effort to find the common ground. He astutely commented:

> [Democracy] can be healthy even if there is no consensus if it does have a culture of argument. But it cannot remain healthy with deep and bitter divisions and no real argument, because it then becomes a tyranny of numbers.[3]

Two years earlier in Britain, Frank Furedi made similar stringent comments:

> The prevailing level of education, culture and intellectual debate is important for the flourishing of a democratic ethos. Intellectuals in different guises play a crucial role in initiating debate and engaging the curiosity and passion of the public. Today that engagement is conspicuously feeble.[4]

This is borne out by a letter in *The Times* by Max Hastings, who noted:

> It is terrifying to behold universities in general, and Oxford in particular amid its British Empire controversy, cowering before student mobs which demand that unwelcome points of view should not even be articulated … At our peril do we yield to exponents of ignorance and stranglers of debate, above all in universities.[5]

The precise example from Cambridge University deserves quoting because it constitutes such a serious indictment of what universities are supposed to stand for. Nigel Biggar's "Ethics and Empire" project provoked a mass online denunciation led by Priyamvada Gopal, Reader in Cambridge's English Faculty and Fellow of Churchill College. In a letter to *The Times*, Biggar wrote: "Her earliest tweet, 'OMG. This is serious shit. We need to SHUT THIS DOWN.' was followed by others describing my scholarship as 'supremacist shit' and me as a 'racist and a bigot.'" When Biggar appealed to two authorities in Cambridge, they showed relative indifference: "Neither touched the issue of a teacher's responsibility to model behaviour; both upheld Gopal's legal right to 'freedom within the law.'"[6]

We may note the incoherence of an understanding of any claim to inclusiveness which excludes contrary opinions. It is also worth remembering David Hume's comment regarding the nature of democratic government: "The governors have nothing to support them but opinion, It is, therefore, on opinion only that government is founded."[7]

Analysis of why debate has become debased: three considerations

1 The impact of political correctness

The intrusion of certain political agendas has had the effect of unintentionally, but nevertheless really, shutting down debate. Furedi specifically draws attention to the anti-elitist agenda and the subsequent therapeutic turn in education. People have become afraid to speak out for high standards – intellectual and artistic – instead of, as Furedi puts it, "flattering" the public. "Unsurprisingly, the cultural elites' cynicism towards knowledge and truth has been transmitted to the people through educational and cultural institutions and the media."[8] Even reference to the word *beauty* in discussion of the arts has been virtually banned as denoting unacceptable class elitism. A similar thing has happened to aspects of the word *truth*. Furedi drew attention to the danger: "Those who insist on undertaking a genuine journey of intellectual discovery risk being labelled as elitist and irrelevant."[9] Furedi sees responsibility for this state of affairs as lying more with intellectuals, both inside and outside the university, and their colleagues in the world of culture and the arts, rather than with politicians. "What is worrying is not the role of the political class so much as the compliance of the world of art and education with a philistine social engineering agenda."[10]

Anti-elitism is a manifestation of what has for many decades been termed *political correctness*. By trying to enforce tolerance through controlling speech, political correctness has discouraged people from saying what they think. Instead, people have been taught to conform, at least outwardly, so as to not get into trouble. The sheer incoherence between, on the one hand, insisting that free speech is a human right for all and, on the other hand, policing speech and disallowing the expression of certain opinions, appears not to have been acknowledged.

Typical is a recent incident involving the BBC programme *Thought for the Day*, which the former Chief Rabbi, Lord Sacks, described as "one of the last remaining places in the public square where religious communities are given a voice in Britain" – itself a particularly damning comment regarding the level of openness in the country.[11] When Lord Singh of Wimbledon complained to the BBC Director-General about being forbidden to use certain expressions or to refer to events because they might cause offence to Muslims, the complaint was not upheld. Any interest in or concern for the truth, or otherwise, of what is said was sidestepped because of an obsession with the notion that some groups of people must not be offended – whilst implying that it is perfectly all right to offend others!

So powerful has been the impact of political correctness that it is worth analysing why it has been detrimental to the open and honest expression of opinions for debate. Two major difficulties present themselves:

(i) Problems with the values chosen

Let me discuss two values that are constantly assumed to be central: tolerance and freedom of speech.

TOLERANCE

Tolerance of those who are intolerant of others or those who wish to harm others is clearly illogical and dangerous. Constant appeal to tolerance thus throws up a host of questions. Should we tolerate bad behaviour, hate speech, injustice or, indeed, intolerance? If so, does tolerance refer to allowing other people to have space but not allowing them to have their beliefs, actions or words? Yet, can we separate people – the person from the person's basic views about life – in this way? So, what exactly is tolerance?

Moreover, emphasis on tolerance can easily convey the impression of relativism. In his book *On Tolerance*, Furedi noted that if non-judgementalism is always appropriate, then "anything goes."[12] In this case, whether something is true, meaningful or helpful becomes irrelevant, because all that matters is self-expression and other people's tolerance of it.

This is not really what people generally mean when they say they value tolerance, but it is what can happen unless special safeguards are in place. Thus, the Liberal Democrat politician Nick Clegg has noted:

> the core of liberalism for me is tolerance, and I mean real tolerance – a profound antagonism to prejudice of all sorts. Of course there are limits to tolerance, absolutely. When I say "tolerance", I don't mean relativism ... a sort of moral free-for-all.[13]

This comment cries out for further clarification. What *are* the limits of tolerance? How can the siren voices of relativism be overcome?

The need for tolerance in so many situations, where real despotism is at work, is huge and exceedingly important. Insistence on tolerance is the product of the long fight against tyranny, which has afflicted history in various forms and still does today. Where dogmatism and the potential for violent conflict flourish, tolerance, and the non-judgementalism it implies, are crucial values. They are not, however, absolute ones to be called on in all situations. To argue that it is never the case that tolerance is a wrong response to a situation is actually to tie up critical faculties in a spirit of anything goes. Yet the call for tolerance arose as a critical response to prejudice and injustice. So tolerance is not a universal, absolute moral value, but one which may be mostly appropriate, but not always.

FREEDOM OF SPEECH

Freedom of speech is not a universal, absolute moral principle either, even though Timothy Garton Ash argues that "this principle is first not just in order but in importance."[14] As with tolerance, we can agree that freedom of speech is crucial if by that we mean not being punished, or even executed, for what we say. Freedom of speech is rightly an essential safeguard against despotic government, as we know from so many devastating examples from around the world today. Freedom of speech is also needed as a safeguard against many forms of indoctrination and judgmental blanketing of people who think differently from the norm, whether this happens by the state, by the media, through education, through religion or through any other source.

The problem with making freedom of speech an absolute value in this way, however, is that it is dangerously underdetermined. Like tolerance, freedom of speech is not strictly fundamental because of the possibility of incitement to hatred, unfair defamation of character, manipulation of crowds by a charismatic dictator, etc. These are occasions when freedom of speech can be, and is, damaging. Anthony Lester makes the point clearly:

> We all cherish the right to free speech. Or rather, we cherish our *own* right to communicate freely. But what about the right of other people to free speech – those who maliciously attack our reputation, or who invade our lives to sell newspapers?[15]

Even in relatively innocent situations, such as everyday contact and relationships, constant hogging of the conversation by someone ought to be challenged. Should not that person's freedom of speech be momentarily curtailed in the interests of other people's freedom of speech?

In practice there are enormous unavoidable constraints on freedom of speech. To treat it as the highest value, as in the reaction to the Charlie Hebdo atrocity in 2015, involves dangerous incoherence.[16] Insistence on free speech at all costs has been put on a pedestal it does not deserve because, like its twin cry for tolerance, it arose out of a special situation.

In fact, all life involves necessarily compromise between my freedom and that of others, between expressing myself and fitting in with society. To pursue freedom as the be-all-and-end-all is impossible except in imagination. In the mind, as compared with the real world, unbounded freedom can monopolise attention. It cannot in day-to-day living, because it is hopelessly unrealistic. This is another example of the danger of the overfocus on the cognitive in education, as Anthony Seldon notes and as discussed in Chapter 2.

The perennial and deeper question is: what is freedom for? What do we do with the freedom we have? Obsessed with freedom from oppression, we forget that the crucial factor is how we live freely – freedom for what? Chapter 4 will argue on what values such positive freedom depends.

(ii) Reliance on law

The second difficulty with political correctness is its attempt to enshrine politically correct values in ever-increasing legislation and its encouragement of litigation in the pursuit of rights, which confuses principles and laws. Attempts to force people to think differently have been damaging despite high intentions.

Reliance on rules and regulations and the threat of legal penalties exacerbate the tendency towards closing down debate. Now that the West has belatedly realised that free speech can hurt, it attempts to prevent such hurt by using the law. People are free to say what they like provided that they do not give offence to anyone. In practice, however, law is impotent to prevent people saying what they like in private and, especially, via social media. Nor can law relate to all the nuances necessary for understanding any precise situation or person.

Moreover, using law in this way to insist on the equality of all people as persons is ironical. For it invades the freedom of the individual in whose name the sanctions are applied. Political correctness is a form of dictatorship, however seemingly worthy the cause, such as seeking to stop racism. The effects of this are already being felt in the attempts to close down freedom of engagement with certain ideas on university campuses in order to permit certain groups "safe space."[17] Encroachment upon the law by non-democratic authorities is why free speech historically became important. Law determined by democratic means can still have the consequence of encroaching on the liberty of the individual, however.

The book *Fundamental British Values in Education* by Lynn Revell and Hazel Bryn is a curious example of people standing up for free speech, while nevertheless objecting vehemently to attempts at legislating its enforcement. Revell and Bryan blisteringly oppose the imposition of British values on schools as making the teacher

> without agency, voiceless and without the rights or freedom to act in either the private or public spheres. Of greater concern is the possibility that these teachers who are committed to liberal values in education, who believe, passionately, that pupils should engage in free speech ... will find that all these aspirations are now forbidden to them, by the requirement to promote fundamental British values.[18]

I suspect that they are overreacting, but the warning is clear.

Trustworthiness is essential for democracy, yet the West has in many ways discouraged it through overtrusting laws, regulations and bureaucratic control. Reliance on such methods can weaken the moral sensibility upon which the safe running of democracy depends. It can discourage people from being alert to the actual situation in which they are and taking appropriate action.

Rethinking on a big scale is needed to escape this impasse. Law should be dealing primarily with protecting society from criminal behaviour. It should not be trying to police people's thoughts and conversations. Police states do that, and they are not democratic. Instead, change should be sought through nurture and education which respects people's freedom and also inspires working towards civilising values. Chapter 4 will consider this in some detail.

2 The pernicious impact of the fact/opinion divide

The reality of a fact/opinion divide on people's thinking was discussed in Chapter 2. Its impact on quality of debate is considerable.

A fact/opinion divide regards opinions as being beyond the capacity for rational discussion concerning their truth or validity. Thus, debate has tended to emphasise only what can be claimed as "evidence-based reasoning," where the word *evidence* is regularly understood to apply only to empirical or scientific findings relating to what is definite and provable to some extent, like statistical evidence. What is often disparagingly termed "anecdotal evidence" is mostly dismissed as being personal and, therefore, of no account. This is serious, because so much real conversation between people centres on what emerges from actual experience. The fact/opinion divide confines the use of reason. It holds reason in disrespect, often where it is most needed for making important decisions about the large issues in life or in politics.

Indeed, the fact/opinion divide has discouraged paying attention to the *content of what is said* in favour of *who said it*. Phrases such as "You would say that" or "Now I know where you are coming from," etc., are common. This leads to extreme difficulty in discussing ideas, because what is the point? Thus, debate has been reduced to dealing just with personalities instead of wrestling with the merits and demerits of what is said. The personalising of debate – notably, whether it may give offence – takes centre-stage. Such a withdrawal from reasoning ceases to be a verbal exchange of thought. It can easily degenerate into a mere shouting match in which logical fallacies, such as *ad hominem* attacks, can have a field day. This, in turn, can lead to a sense of victimisation, which is prominent today, and an outcry for "safe" spaces where people will not experience offence. Furedi has noted that many students now stay silent in seminars over fear they will cause offence: "They fail to distinguish between opinion and personality, so they think critiquing an argument is criticising a person."[19]

Respect should indeed include sensitivity, indeed compassion, towards opponents as persons. What constitutes a person is discussed below. But respect is distinct from the search for knowledge and understanding through intelligent debate with others who may think differently. Sometimes, indeed, offence needs to be given if people hold rationally and morally objectionable values. Moreover, almost all humour can be seen, from one point of view, as possibly giving offence Should we therefore try to prevent the expression of humour?

Humour can be wrongly used, of course, in which case other people may say that something is not humour. This was the case, indeed, when Warwick University suspended 11 students for writing offensive jokes about rape, racism and antisemitism in a group chat in May 2018.[20] Legitimate protest against damaging presumed humour should rely on reasoned argument. Suspending those responsible, instead of rationally confronting their views, only makes matters worse. It leaves the minds and hearts of those who delight in such things in as unenlightened a state as before. In the absence of intelligent challenge, such views will only grow and become more entrenched.

If even universities are unable to find reasons why such attitudes are wrong, then does that not fold back once again into the hold that the fact/opinion divide has had thus far, especially in education? It is notable that Charlotte Gill, who reported the incident in the *Times*, bypassed this point about the crucial nature of debate. She wrote, "Instead of being privately cautioned by friends or the university, the students' remarks were leaked to the press." Far from being *cautioned*, which implies the correctness of the political stance of the university, the opposite was needed, i.e., as much discussion and debate as possible of the offending viewpoints. The way to deal with such repugnant valuing is not by law but by debate, education and encounters in daily life. The continuing worry over antisemitism in the British Labour party, for example, is crying out for discussion of why antisemitism is wrong, not the assumption that it is, as liberals recognise, nor the dogmatic practising of it, as a minority do. See Box 2.2 at the end of Chapter 2 for the kind of reasoning that is needed.

One of the worst effects of the fact/opinion divide is the aim at an approach of neutrality in public debate, as if prior commitment to a worldview is automatically the enemy of reasoned debate. Instead of encouraging people to be who they are and speak from their experiences and traditions, individuals are supposed to keep much of what they value under wraps in the private domain of life. Public discussion is bound to suffer, as certain views are rarely represented. The ideal of neutrality from worldviews in public debate is serious enough to warrant further investigation.

3 The presumed ideal of neutrality in public debate.

Democracy has to be concerned with attempts to reach a common mind on matters, because it has to govern and make decisions. John Rawls, the influential political philosopher, considered that the way to a common mind requires neutrality in public discussion regarding worldviews. He wanted purely rational thinking in the public arena, available in principle to everyone regardless of the particular traditions to which individuals may belong.

Stout summarises the impact of this approach to how modern democracy should be seen, saying that such philosophers

> have endorsed a theory of the modern nation state as ideally neutral with respect to comprehensive conceptions of the good. Second they have proposed to establish political deliberation on a common basis of free public reason, independent of reliance on tradition.[21]

Stout attacks both of these points, which he sees as recipes for disaster. To take the second point first, Stout finds it "extremely implausible" that reasoning on important political questions must ultimately be based on principles which no reasonable citizen could reject. As already discussed in Chapter 2, reason cannot provide the clear and objective basis for decision-making which is claimed for it.

Regarding the first point, *comprehensive conceptions of the good* is what all traditions and worldviews embody. The fact/opinion divide puts these firmly on the opinion side. Yet, to require those who adhere to any one of them to adopt an attitude of neutrality in public is hardly feasible. A person's thinking and feeling does not neatly divide into public and private personas. Moreover, such a stance can have the baleful effect of shutting out from public debate that which is often most meaningful to people.

This is bound to be impoverishing. It can lead to a bogus neutrality of insisting that both sides in a debate are equally represented. It is bogus because it can easily suggest that both sets of opinions are equally valid regarding truth and feasibility, when, in fact, it should be the purpose of debate to enquire whether they are. Giving each opposing side a fair chance to speak constitutes the *beginning* of enquiry, not its conclusion.

Instead of neutrality towards such *comprehensive conceptions of the good*, Stout affirms that "central to democratic thought is the idea of a body of citizens who reason with one another about the ethical issues that divide them, especially when deliberating on the justice or decency of political arrangements." Such reasoning should be accompanied by civility, but it should not lead to superficiality: "The respect for each other that civility requires is most fully displayed in the kind of exchange where each person's deepest commitments can be recognised for what they are and analysed accordingly."[22] Stout argues, indeed, for the impartiality which Basil Mitchell notes is a fundamental academic and debating virtue. Impartiality does not mean not taking sides or sitting on a fence, as neutrality can easily come to mean.

What does impartiality involve? Mitchell describes it:

> It requires one to be scrupulous in assembling the evidence, honest in recognising arguments against one's position, fair in assessing the force of these arguments, sympathetic in representing the position of those with whom one disagrees. Academics all too often fail to satisfy these requirements, but failure nevertheless it is, and the requirements are absolute.

We can say the same about the course of debate. He goes on to say

> Impartiality does not imply neutrality. If it did, we should indeed be in a hopeless case. We should have to choose between firm convictions and fairness in debate. It is, I think, impossible to exaggerate the effects in our contemporary culture of the mistaken assumption that firm commitment is incompatible with honest recognition of difficulties.[23]

Stout is in complete agreement. He sees democracy as basically

> conversation … an exchange of views in which the respective parties express their premises in as much detail as they see fit and in whatever idiom they wish, try to make sense of each other's perspectives, and expose their own commitments to the possibility of criticism.[24]

What is appropriate to be said cannot be decided in advance. It may be noted that this is the exact opposite of the identity politics which is currently threatening the notion of freedom of speech, even on university campuses. Stout argues for "borrowing crucial insights from both sides."[25] This offers a potent way forward, to which I shall return below when discussing the notion of *critical affirmation*.

Suggestions for a way forward

In the search for common ground between controversial positions, reason needs to act as a friendly, supportive, generous-minded critic, not as a decisive judge. As such, it can be the lifeline for a democracy.

A focus on logic remains crucial. It can check for logical fallacies of all kinds, the failure to think straight and deception of an opponent. It should involve the withdrawal of any argument that fails the test of logic. Scientific evidence clearly remains hugely important if it is appropriate – but only if it is appropriate. Otherwise, the appeal to scientific evidence sinks into scientism. In addition, however, all other aspects of a well-rounded personality should be engaged, including intuition, common sense, imagination and moral sensitivity. Such reasoning, which I term *holistic*, can save us from the worst excesses of subjectivism.

The criteria for discernment discussed in Chapter 2 do not supply definitive certainty, but they can greatly aid good, positive discussion to foster decision-making. We can be enabled, therefore, to utilise reason optimistically as we search for resolutions of problems and divisive tendencies. These criteria can go far towards balancing the negativity discussed in this chapter.

I have five further specific suggestions to make: four will be addressed in this chapter and the fifth will be discussed in a chapter of its own.

I A sharper understanding of what is meant by "respect for persons"

Respect for persons needs to dominate debate. There is, however, much vagueness in what we mean by a *person*. In his book *Being Human*, Rowan Williams notes: "If there is one great intellectual challenge for our day, it is the pervasive sense that we are in danger of losing our sense of the human."[26] Individualism, which has been so prominent in the West, has tended to assume that the individual is the same as a person.

Williams first distinguishes a *person* from a machine and then distinguishes a *person* from an *individual*.[27] He explains the difference in that "a *person* acts in a mysterious, relational, conversational, environment-building manner, whilst an *individual* is simply one example of a certain kind of thing." Whilst things can potentially be investigated and understood, "there is always something about the other person that's to do with what I can't see, and that can't be mastered" (see Box 3.1).[28]

Williams makes a particular point about the power of speech, which a person uniquely has.[29] A person can change things through discussion, make a difference and create new relationships. An interesting conversation Williams had with the neuroscientist Hannah Critchlow shows how common ground can be found with those who think differently. Critchlow has this to say of her dialogue with Williams:

> I found it hugely inspiring to discuss my belief in neuroscience and biological determinism with Rowan who comes at the subject from an alternative perspective. It was also reassuring that there was overlap between new findings from neuroscience and the traditional studies of theology and philosophy … Rowan's personal belief in the vital importance of reflection, discussion and hopefulness left me feeling, well, hopeful. Perhaps we all need to be a little more like him, actively practising flexibility of thinking, compassion and curiosity.[30]

Box 3.1 What is a person?

Rowan Williams sees a person as an individual who is both conscious and self-conscious. He notes four characteristics of a person:

1   *With locality in a material world*: Consciousness is characterised by the first person singular. I can say "I am."[31]
2   *Consciousness is relational*: "I understand that while I cannot see the back of my head, you can." I am aware that there are other persons with whom to relate.[32]
3   *Consciousness is a continuous narrative*: I have a sense of continuing identity and can say "I was," "I am" and "I may be."[33]
4   *Consciousness is a shared language*: I can converse with other persons. "Speaking changes things. To say something introduces new possibilities …"[34]

Williams argues strongly against the attempt to reduce the reality of these four characteristics (see Box 3.1) to what they basically have in common:

> Reductionism is a permission to ignore certain levels or aspects of what we in fact perceive, and I would say that any intellectual strategy that gives you permission to ignore some level of legitimate description is morally deeply dangerous, as well as being philosophically odd.[35]

2 Promoting emotional maturity

Debate brings emotions to the fore. However sharp the reasoning is, there is always a thinker behind it. A thinker is a unique person, each with her/his own emotional as well as cognitive response to life. Postmodernism is correct in seeing that true impartiality is rare and, normally, will-to-power in one form or another tends to be present because most people value self-interest. The mainspring for action, indeed, lies more in the emotional capacities of people than in their cognitive capacities. We may not agree with Hume that "reason is and always ought to be the slave of passion," but it is hard to escape from acknowledging that this is usually the case.

People get excited about what they see as morally right. Emotion needs to be educated, therefore, so that it can benefit discussion instead of getting in the way. It is especially important that real points of disagreement be expressed in calm, straightforward language and eschew emotionally-charged, inflammatory language. This relates to the importance of education of emotions.

The whole gamut of emotions is huge, so I will take just two for consideration: anger, which was mentioned specifically in Chapter 1, and a spirit of forgiveness. *Anger and Forgiveness* is the title of a book by Martha Nussbaum, who considers that anger, because it is largely irrational, should have little place in public or in private.[36]

Anger is an extremely strong emotion that does not encourage calm appraisal of situations. It delights in slogans, ready-made solutions and instant reactions. It does not require people to think or reflect, so it is easy to adopt, and it makes people feel self-righteous as they can blame someone else for moral deficiencies while presuming they are morally impeccable themselves!

Nussbaum is right. Anger is a dangerous emotion. One response to the Grenfell Tower disaster in London on 14 June 2017 was shown by an angry crowd, whipped up by the Movement for Justice by Any Means Necessary. The crowd beat up a volunteer helper mistakenly identified as a responsible official.[37] Jenny McCartney saw a parallel of the attack in the Two Minutes Hate in the political novel *Nineteen Eighty-Four* by George Orwell:

> The question is not whether such a tragedy should incite anger, but what one should then do with the emotion. Controlled anger, an indignation that is tightly contained and precisely directed, can be a force for good; it flows into practical care for survivors ... That charred high-rise tomb, that blackened memorial, deserves more than a shoulder-shrug of resignation. We should be angry that the repeated warnings of residents on fire safety were blithely ignored; that they reportedly could not access legal aid to respond when threatened with solicitors' letters ... Those residents repeatedly struggled to go through the proper channels with their concerns, and the proper channels repeatedly failed them.[38]

As Nussbaum noted, anger, in particular, tends to see things in either/or categories, which is incoherent with a form of government which requires a both/and type of thinking in order to embrace diversity. Brennan, however, whose understanding of democracy was discussed in Chapter 1, makes the interesting point that "politics gives us genuine grounds to hate one another." He explains that

> the problem isn't merely that we're biased and tribalistic, that we tend to hate people who disagree with us just because they disagree. Rather, the problem is, first, that politics puts us in genuinely adversarial relationships, and second, that because most of our fellow citizens make political decisions in incompetent ways, we have reason to resent the way they treat us.[39]

Bearing in mind such an adversarial element in democracy, it is hard to avoid the conclusion that the spirit of anger needs to be watched carefully. It should be rationally-controlled anger – provided that reason itself has been understood in a holistic sense, as developed in Chapter 2.

The real antidote to anger, however, is the desire for a spirit of forgiveness. Forgiveness can turn what was negative and hurtful into something positive and creative both for the individuals concerned and for society as a whole. We constantly have to be forgiving each other over all the slights, real or imagined, which we receive. We express such forgiveness, in fact, when we continue to converse respectfully with each other.[40]

At a public, communal level, as well as at a personal level, a spirit of forgiveness is the oil that lubricates the working of daily life and of society as a whole. We need to see forgiveness as a normal and positive approach to what has been and is wrong. It is an approach which acknowledges the harm done without being chained by it.

The cult of victimisation, and concomitant concerns about giving offence, operates without any notion of forgiveness. Yet, forgiveness, if freely given, can liberate people from the chains of the past. It can empower people. Forgiveness judges and acknowledges evil, indeed, but it overcomes it with generous-mindedness. See Figure 9.1 in Chapter 9 for an example of how the importance of forgiveness can be taught.

Anger-management is not the same as forgiveness. Of course, it can help to keep society safe and improve the chances that the individual concerned is able to live a higher quality of life. But I am arguing for something much deeper and more important: the task of renewing relationships which have gone astray. On such forgiveness, in fact, the health of society depends. In practising such an attitude of forgiveness, debate with opponents can become so much more positive than when debate simply reflects anger.

3 Encourage a culture of active listening which is open i.e. affirming as well as critical

It is not impossible to teach skills of listening and speaking so as to hold to account speakers who transgress civilised ways of approaching communication. As a society we have encouraged speaking but almost completely neglected the role and responsibilities of listening. The overriding importance of individualism in the West has encouraged attention to speaking which supports the individual per se, whilst listening does not. The listener can be just one of a crowd. Moreover, because speaking is active, listening easily becomes passive. Yet, good listening is equally active. Drawing attention to active listening, therefore, could offer a way forward. We can note the temptations to which speakers are open, and we can cultivate habits of positively good listening.

Misuse of oratory in a variety of situations constitutes a major problem for democracy. Charismatic speakers tend to carry enormous weight because of the emotional charge they have – they feel something intensely and thereby are able to communicate it very effectively. Normally, such people have high levels of self-confidence or at least, as psychologists might prefer to put it, know how to overcome inner uncertainty through creating an impression of confidence. The cult of celebrity in our age only increases the power of such oratory. It is important, therefore, to guard against danger through the practice of good listening (see Box 3.2).

Box 3.2 Good listening

Good listening depends on the quality of attentiveness. This is basically an unselfish activity: paying attention to someone else's ideas.

*   Good listening requires a quality of generous expectancy, wishing the speaker well – wanting to hear what is said. A clear example is in musical performance where the active participation of the audience in listening can powerfully inspire the performers.
*   Good listening is never passive. It actively weighs up the pros and cons of what is said. It especially refuses to become inert plasticine in the speaker's hands. It notes, for example, any logical fallacies the speaker makes.
*   Good listening requires a good memory so as to properly attend to each ongoing statement yet be able to put it into the context of the speech as a whole.
*   Good listening emerges from a capacity to be silent until the right moment for speaking occurs. It is very much concerned with judging how and when to try to intervene in a constructive way, alerting speakers to faults *in order to move forward together*.
*   Good listening is realistic, aware that objecting to what a speaker says can also obscure the real issue under discussion.
*   Good listening acknowledges the limits of one's own knowledge base and engages in clarification when necessary

What might good conversation and discussion in which active listening happens look like? It tries to coax the other person into clarity regarding what exactly they think and why.

It states objections simply and without emotional undergirding. Good listening would refuse to allow logical fallacies to slip by undetected, but it would not become censorious in drawing attention to them. It might have to admit at the end, "Well, I'm afraid you still misunderstand my position, so we can't reach any agreement. Let me just once more try to make clear what I actually think, and why" (see Box 3.3).

Such a mixture of patience, determination and recognition of the inability to control how other people think is necessary for being a democratic citizen.

Box 3.3 A menu of phrases for good debate

"That's interesting. Can you tell me more about it?"

"Have I understood it right? What you mean is ..."

"Can you tell me in simple language what it is you disagree with?"

"Can you put into your own words what you think I am standing for?"

"Have you ever thought of ...?"

"I wonder why you should say ...?"

"My view is .... How does your view differ from my view?"

"Don't we need first to find points of contact – where we agree? Then we can move forward to explore our disagreement."

"I can't agree with that because ..."

"Do you mean ...?

"What matters most in the end?"

"I'm afraid that doesn't follow from what you said earlier ..."

"Mustn't we both try to avoid logical fallacies? You've just given a clear example ...."

"Can you rephrase what you mean without implying that anyone who disagrees with you must be a fool?!"

"No, that is not what I mean. Let me put it in a different way ..."

"Something doesn't become true just because it's said many times!"

"Oh, come off it! Surely you don't mean ..."

---

4 Adopt an approach of critical affirmation.

Reason tends to be associated primarily with criticism. It is rarely appreciated how serious a criticism of reason this is! Reason is good at finding fault, but poor at articulating positive commitment. It is, indeed, parasitical, because it has to have something to criticise. The values we affirm are what we live by and how we respond to events and circumstances. Affirmation, rather than criticism, is necessary for anything to be achieved. The spirit of criticism tends to operate against the affirmation upon which behaviour in the real world depends. It is easy to pull down, but hard to build up. Criticism that is too swift and unsympathetic can kill action and any further thinking.

The common adversarial attitude in which speakers seek to dominate and overwhelm those with whom they disagree does not work. Nor is it worthy of the democratic ideal. Respect for persons, therefore, needs to be upgraded into a truly generous-minded approach to people who think differently from oneself. It is an approach which affirms as well as criticises. It is also a remedy for avoiding the likelihood of giving offence.

What I have elsewhere termed *critical affirmation* offers a constructive alternative. The two words may appear to be contradictory: *critical* indicates doubt and negativity, whilst *affirmation* suggests positive approval. The paradox is deliberate, because in conversation and debate we need both aspects. *Affirmation* is particularly needed to acknowledge the other person as being worthy of respect – a person with whom it is worth disagreeing. Applying the word *critical* to the engagement signals evaluation. It is important to counteract so-called non-judgementalism. Furthermore, it is hopefully a stance in which evaluation will be fair and constructive because it is based on impartiality.

A possible misunderstanding needs to be guarded against here. I do not mean advocating a *feel-good curriculum*, which is subject, as Furedi puts it, to a political "agenda of affirmation through inclusion."[41] I agree with him about the danger of the relativism implied in non-judgementalism per se. It does not mean, however, that encouraging self-esteem does not matter. A person needs considerable confidence to accept being mistaken in something in which a good deal of emotional energy has been invested. Researchers at the University of Michigan, led by political scientist Brendan Nyhan and concerned about how "absolutely threatening" it is for people to admit that they are wrong, found an antidote in self-esteem. Respondents who felt good about themselves were consistently more willing to accept new information, whereas those who felt threatened or agitated were not.[42]

A quotation from Blaise Pascal makes this point very well:

> If we would reprove with advantage, and show another his fault we must see from what side he looks at the matter, for usually the thing is true from that point of view, and we must admit this truth, but show him the side on which it is not true. That satisfies him, for he sees that he was not wrong, and that he merely failed to see everything. But they do not like to be mistaken, and perhaps this comes from the fact that naturally man cannot see everything, and that by nature he cannot be wrong from his point of view, since what we apprehend with our senses is always true.[43]

See Figure 8.2 in Chapter 8 on the shortcomings of pre-ordained curriculum.

Rigorous debate is required in which people really listen to each other and dogmatic stances are mutually addressed. It can happen if the perspectives of other people – with their own unique experiences and insights – are acknowledged and valued. Evan Davis sees openmindedness as being clearly associated with a generous view of the contributions other people make to the debate. He asks for " a more positive view of the good sense of other people."[44] In a chapter on "the discerning listener" he notes: "I hesitate to say we get the bullshit we deserve, but there is a little truth in that … What can we do to deserve better?" His advice is:

> We need to be particularly sceptical of claims that make us feel good or satisfy our pre-existing beliefs. There is an inverse requirement too. We need to be willing to believe things which don't conform to our world-view … Embrace the fact that most arguments have two sides, and that your outrage or joyful reaction to some piece of news may simply be predicated on your unwillingness to get the full picture.[45]

Davis's view relates, indeed, to the fifth criterion that I drew attention to in Chapter 2 – concern for being comprehensive.

In an article for the philosophy journal *Think*, I summarised the advantages of an approach of *critical affirmation*:

1   Respect for others, satisfying the requirement of initial courtesy and non-judgemental-ism in order to establish contact
2   Empathy for the experience and insights of others, helping to avoid attacking Aunt Sallies, – i.e., what is not being defended – based on misunderstanding of the other's position
3   Genuineness of relationship through not hiding disagreement but allowing a situation to develop in which controversy can be fearlessly thought through *together*
4   Personal integrity, affirming oneself as well as the other person, but also seeking to learn more and widen one's experience and understanding.

I concluded the argument in this way:

Finally, it must also be noted that the notion of reciprocity is integral to an approach of critical affirmation. Criticism has to be sharp towards any failure by others to be positive towards others in the same way. It insists on treating others with the respect and fair-mindedness that avoids ridiculing, marginalising, ignoring or misrepresenting beliefs. As such, it is precisely what is needed to help avoid the poor quality of much debate which degenerates into slanging matches. It can thus afford a spectacular head-start in encouraging some change in mind and heart of erstwhile opponents. For its primary aim is not to find fault and destabilise the other, but to enable potentially mutual exchange through proper self-affirmation and considering together the probabilities of certain hypotheses, axioms and beliefs leading to a joint conclusion.[46]

The exchange between Williams and Critchlow above offers an example of the kind of creative and courteous dialogue between people who hold divergent views which really is possible.

Such an approach could be specifically related to the running of democracy by working on the notion of public deliberation put forward by Fishkin in *Democracy When the People are Thinking*, as discussed in Chapter 1. He noted that in the fourth century BCE, Athenian democracy attempted to institutionalise "deliberative democracy" in the wake of the political and military disasters, which "direct democracy" through the Assembly of all eligible citizens had failed to prevent. The idea was to have a randomly selected sample of citizens (a *nome-thetai*) who would deliberate for a day and hear arguments for and against a proposal. Its purpose was to prevent snap decisions by the Assembly.[47] Fishkin considers that reviving this notion could be invaluable for the modern era. Such a body of citizens, drawn by lot and representing the constituent members of a community as carefully as possible, could offer considered judgments after deliberative hearings *under good conditions for thinking*. Such good conditions would imply a generous-minded search for sensible, collaborative decision-making.[48]

Notes

1   K. Ward. 2019. *Religion in the Modern World: Celebrating Pluralism and Diversity.* Cambridge University Press. p. 10f.
2   A. Unwin & J. Yandell. 2016. *Rethinking Education.* New Internationalist. p. 84.

3   R. Dworkin. 2006. *Is Democracy Possible?* Princeton University Press. p. 6

4   F. Furedi. 2004. *Where Have All the Intellectuals Gone?* Continuum. p. 24.

5   M. Hastings. 2018. "We're in a Dark Age Where Hearts Rule Minds." *The Times*. October 13.

6   N. Biggar. 2019. "Cambridge has Double Standards on Free Speech." *The Times*. April 4.

7   D. J. Galligan (Ed.). 2017. *Constitution in Crisis: The New Putney Debates*. I. B. Taurus. p. 3.

8   Furedi. *Where Have All the Intellectuals Gone?* p. 24.

9   Ibid. p. 155.

10 Ibid. p. 156.

11 D. Kennedy. 2019. "Radio 4 Faith Slot 'Reduced to Platitudes.'" *The Times*. October 4.

12 F. Furedi. 2011. *On Tolerance: A Defence of Moral Independence*. Continuum. For further comment see my "The Need for Responsible Religious Education in the Light of the 'Value Free' Society." 2014. In M. Felderhof & P. Thompson. *Teaching Virtue: The Contribution of Religious Education*. pp. 29–41. Bloomsbury. p. 32.

13 S. Barrow. 2008. "Starting Afresh." *Third Way: Christian Comment on Culture* 31, no. 4. May. p. 19.

14 T. G. Ash. 2016. *Free Speech*. p. 119. Ash provides a four-fold "STGD" summary of the reasons: Self – "to realise our full individual humanity"; Truth – "it enables us to seek the truth"; Government – "it is necessary for good government"; and Diversity – "relevant to our emerging cosmopolis." He adds, "These four classic Western arguments – STGD – are combined by the former German Constitutional Court judge Dieter Grimm into a single pregnant formula: individual self-development and collective self-determination." pp. 73–9.

15 A. Lester. 2016. *Five Ideas to Fight For*. OneWorld. p. 99.

16 On January 7, 2015, 12 people were killed and 11 were injured by gunmen claiming to belong to an Islamic terrorist group. Four days later, two million people, including more than 40 world leaders, met in Paris for a rally of national unity. I develop the point, with various arguments, in my article "Belief and Evidence, and How it May Aid Reflection Concerning Charlie Hebdo." 2016. *Think* 15, no. 42. Spring. pp. 151–61. https://doi.org/10.1017/S1477175615000457

17 For a discussion of this, see F. Furedi. 2018. *How Fear Works*. Bloomsbury. pp. 228ff.

18 L. Revell & H. Bryan. 2018. *Fundamental British Values in Education: Radicalisation, National Identity, and Britishness*. Emerald Publishing. p. 105.

19 F. Ferudi quoted in R. Bennett. 2018. "Students Stay Silent in Seminars Over Fear They Will Cause Offense." *The Times*. June 14.

20 C. Gill. 2018. "Public Shaming Offensive Students is Cruel and Unjust." *The Times*. May 11.

21 J. Stout. 2004. *Democracy and Tradition*. Princeton University Press. p. 2.

22 Ibid. pp. 6 & 10.

23 B. Mitchell. 1994. *Faith and Criticism*. Clarendon Press. p. 23f.

24 Stout. *Democracy and Tradition*. p. 10f.

25 Ibid. p. 13.

26 R. Williams. 2018. *Being Human*. SPCK. pp. 25 & 44.

27 Ibid. pp. 4 & 6. Williams acknowledged the thinking of Vladimir Lossky, the Russian Orthodox theologian and philosopher, who perceived that the distinction between an individual and a person has no clear nomenclature.

28 Ibid., pp. 35 & 45.

29 Ibid., p. 32.

30 H. Critchlow. 2019. *The Science of Fate: Why Your Future is More Predictable Than You Think*. Hodder & Stoughton. pp. 156–7. She noted that Jonas suggested that free will may be an illusion, but it is probably a necessary one.

31 Ibid. p. 9. Williams quotes the philosopher Edith Stein, who called it a "zero point of orientation."

32 Ibid. pp. 11 & 13. Stein "argued with great sophistication that consciousness itself was collaborative, empathetic in the sense that to be conscious of anything, one had to have the capacity to imagine another point of view."

33 Ibid. p. 14. Williams writes that consciousness is "something that is always constructed, articulated and explored, partly in terms of where it's from. I assume continuity."

34 Ibid. p. 17. According to Williams, consciousness is "bound in with the capacity to respond to and to develop or complicate the basic information exchanges that are going on in me at every level … somebody generating signs and symbols; an agent inviting listening, interpretation, and so on."

35 Williams. *Being Human*. p. 23. Williams speaks of "emergent properties of complex systems, the fact that they're wholes whose capacities and properties are more than any of their parts, reductionism as a systemic principle is simply intellectually incoherent … It is perfectly true that a performance of Bach's solo cello suites is a set of physical operations. Catgut and string co-operate in producing certain vibrations. The usefulness of that as a description of what's going on, the usefulness of it, for example, in adjudicating between different interpretations of Paul Tortelier and Yo-Yo Ma of the Bach Cello Suites is nil. And we need to recall that what seems to be a compelling reductive version is telling you nothing, except that this is an intrinsic element in a complex reality." p. 21.

36 M. Nussbaum. 2016. *Anger and Forgiveness*. Oxford University Press.

37 An innocent person, Robert Outram, was beaten up in a case of mistaken identity. He shared the name Robert with Robert Black, the CEO of the Kensington and Chelsea Tenant Management Association. See "A Day of Rage?: There are Better Ways to Channel Our Anger." 2017. *Daily Telegraph*. June 21.

38 J. McCartney. 2017. "A Day of Rage?: There are Better Ways to Channel Our Anger." *Daily Telegraph*. June 21.

39 J. Brennan. 2016. *Against Democracy*. Princeton University Press. p. 22.

40 Nussbaum's thesis in *Anger and Forgiveness* is highly unsatisfactory, however, in that she assumes that forgiveness mostly involves resentment and what she terms "the payback wish" – quite the opposite of how a spirit of forgiveness is generally understood.

41 Furedi. *Where Have All the Intellectuals Gone?* p. 124f.

42 D. Dayden. 2010. "Exposed to Facts, the Misinformed Believe Lies More Strongly." *Shadow Proof*. July 12. https://shadowproof.com/2010/07/12/exposed-to-facts-the-misinformed-be;lie ve-lies-more-strongly

43 B. Pascal. 1905. *Pensees*. Les Editions Brunschvig. p. 684.

44 E. Davis. 2017. *Post-Truth: Why We Have Reached Peak Bullshit and What We Can Do About It*. Little Brown. p. xi.

45 Ibid. pp. 275 & 280f.

46 B. Watson. 2012. "Conversing with Those with Whom We Disagree: A Response to Aikin and Talisse's 'Argument in a Mixed Company: Mom's Maxim versus Mill's Principle.' *Think 27*". Summer. pp. 81–94.

47 J. S. Fishkin. 2018. *Democracy When the People are Thinking: Revitalising Politics Through Public Deliberation*. Oxford University Press. pp. 51ff.

48 Ibid. pp. 91ff. Fishkin gives a number of examples. For instance, in 2015 a citywide Deliberative Poll was set up in the capital city of Ulaanbaatar in Mongolia. The problem was to prioritise major proposed projects with significant financial implications. Over two days of deliberation, 317 citizens participated. As a result, the most generally favoured priorities according to general speculation were changed. Strong environmental priorities were placed at the fore. The city publicly announced that the priorities from the Deliberative Poll were included in the Action Plan for the city.

Chapter 4

Rethinking values?

We mostly believe in democracy as the best form of government possible, despite the many problems that it throws up. For it to work well, however, it depends on trusting people. Such trust, in turn, relates to character and the values, especially priorities, which people hold. Values are fundamental. They govern how we behave and act, what we say, how we think and how we react to what happens. They are shown in what we fail to do, say or think. They govern motivation, determining what we admire and what we despise. They govern the people we become, the character we have and who we are.

Reluctance to nurture values

The philosopher Roger Trigg has expressed how crucial nurture in values is: "Qualities such as a respect for human dignity and human liberty have to be fostered and passed on to future generations. They do not flourish in a philosophical vacuum, but need proper grounding."[1] Yet the West has paid too little attention to the values that need to be nurtured in everyone for democracy to work. Values have come to mean what an individual chooses. They incorporate what a person happens to think is important, and on this there are as many views as there are persons. To try to tell anyone what they should value appears to be a breach of their autonomy to decide for themselves.

This attitude has been sufficiently in place, especially in the upbringing of children in the home and in education, to have seriously weakened the notion that adults should nurture values. Over thirty years ago, Mary Warnock stated the problem and noted that a prevailing cynicism

> may have a creeping and insidious effect, and especially so in schools, where teachers may find themselves bewildered by their own half-articulate principles that they must not be dogmatic, they must not presume that there are any disinterested or unbiased arguments, and above all they must not be "judgemental."[2]

Behind the presumption that values are what people happen to choose lies the notion that values are beyond any kind of rational evaluation. Values are not objective: the fact/opinion divide, as discussed in Chapter 2, places them very definitely on the vague subjective opinion side. In an important passage, Trigg attributes this to the continuing influence of positivism, discussed in Chapter 2, even though unacknowledged:

> The attitude that lay behind verification-ism, the respect for science, and the denigration of the non-scientific, still lives on. Labelling beliefs as "values", and referring to "value-judgements" may not say they are meaningless in so many words. The underlying idea is, though, that they are somehow found wanting in comparison with facts, because they cannot be checked and verified through scientific means. They are not part of the furniture of the world. The people holding values may be real, but the values themselves are, it seems, most certainly not. They are a matter for the individuals in question, not for public discussion. They are essentially matter of private concern.[3]

Reluctance to nurture values does not mean that none are inculcated. Values are unavoidable, as is actual nurture in values, whether deliberate or by chance. Individuals do not exist on their own and are always powerfully influenced by those around them. So if no values are explicitly chosen, others will simply take over. In practice, certain values are constantly encouraged. The merest glance at newspapers, television programmes, advertising and, now importantly, social media indicates the values to which people are regularly and predominantly exposed.

This feeds back again into the problem of trustworthiness in people. If individual choice supporting personal autonomy becomes preeminent, democracy itself is in danger unless people just happen to choose the values upon which any civilisation is based. It can give rise to a situation in which the latter virtues can even be scorned. Indeed, there are worrying signs that amoralism is gaining ground. As James Wilson put it at the start of his 1993 book *The Moral Sense*, "Virtue has acquired a bad name."[4] A party was planned to reunite hundreds of former Lehman Brothers staff in London on the tenth anniversary of the Wall Street giant's collapse, regardless of the global financial crisis and decade of austerity that the crash produced. John McDonnell, a Labour politician, commented:

> People will be absolutely disgusted about this unacceptable and highly inappropriate gathering. It's particularly disgraceful in the context of all the people who lost their jobs and homes to pay for bailing out these bankers who caused the financial crash.[5]

This reaction implies that there are some values which for their validity depend not on individual choice but on whether they are morally right. In Arthur Miller's *Death of a Salesman*, which depicts the shattering of the American dream, Biff says about Willi in the Requiem: "He had the wrong dreams, all, all, wrong."[6] Willi's role model was his brother Ben, who proudly exclaims: "When I was seventeen I walked into the jungle, and when I was twenty-one I walked out. And by God I was rich."[7] Ben gloried in being a self-made adventurous youngster.

Was Biff right that some dreams are wrong? Are dreams just ephemeral and subjective? If deeper values are not nurtured, the kind of scenario in *Death of a Salesman* can result. The unregenerate human self – and not just what it does but what it fails to do – remains a problem. It has often been observed that for evil to abound, good people need to do just nothing.

Confusion between values and moral principles

The word *value* refers to at least three types of use. Firstly, values are *preferences* – what people happen to enjoy, what they like, how they feel about things. This is the arena for individual choice. No one should try to dictate to me that I should value watching rugby, shopping or a swim before breakfast. Secondly, values are *norms for living* with other people, e.g., traffic rules, etiquette, language – cultural practices which identify a particular society. Valuing belonging to a group gives me an identity, which involves valuing what others in the group do. If I choose not to accept them, then by that choice I become an outsider to the group. Thirdly, values involve *vision*, which concerns more weighty values inspiring a sense of purpose and meaning. It includes ambition, engagement on research and the desire to reach personal goals, such as climbing Everest. Such values carry their conviction within themselves.

Values need to be distinguished, however, from moral principles. The latter have a universal quality about them. When we say that torture or antisemitism is *wrong* or that risking one's life to save someone from a fire is *right*, the words *wrong* and *right* are invested with a depth which is more than the result of what someone happens to value. It is somehow appropriate to the way things *ought* to be. Stephen Pinker notes that "People feel that moral rules are universal. Injunctions against murder and rape, for example, are not matters of taste or fashion but have a transcendent and universal warrant."[8] Immanuel Kant spoke of "the moral law within" as being an aspect of reality relevant to, and accessible to, all people. There is a sense of obligation to adopt moral principles. Failure to adopt them renders someone deficient as a person. Choice is still needed, but at the root it concerns not what I like but what I *should* like (see Box 4.1).

Massive diversity regarding the mores of different cultures and societies has led to highlighting the importance of tolerance in the interests of holding society together. Customs and ways of living which may appear to us strange, but which other people find natural and sustaining, need to be appreciated. Thomas Scanlon has even suggested that instead of "In God We Trust," Americans might inscribe on their coins the words "In Tolerance We Trust"![9]

Box 4.1 Characteristics of moral principles

* Universal, transcending any and every particular culture: all people should subscribe to them and try to keep them
* Normative, operating as the basis for judging the moral worth of anything anywhere
* Of absolute importance in life, not just temporary or imagined, such that failing to see this may be said, with justification, to reflect insensitivity or immaturity
* Holistic, uniting cognitive and emotional capacities because supported by excellent reasons and by emotional satisfaction which endures and transcends moods and quick gratification
* Laying obligation on us, yet in such a way that our freedom as a person is developed, not curtailed

---

There is, however, much confusion as to what lies behind the word *moral.*

(i) Confusion between cultural and moral values

Many people see morality simply in terms of ways of behaving which are relative to a particular culture. The intensive experience of pluralism with which the West has had to contend has encouraged such confusion. Yet, cultural relativism should not have spilled over into moral relativism. Holding a knife in the right hand when eating and a fork in the left is straightforward cultural relativism, but practices such as slavery or forced marriage are not just habits – they have a moral dimension. We do judge these in a way that is inappropriate regarding culinary preferences. Yet, we have become so concerned about needing not to judge people because they are different – race, nationality, sex, gender, etc. – that we have become perilously close to the slope leading to moral relativism, namely the notion that we cannot judge moral opinions. See the discussion in Chapter 3 regarding the inadequacies of an appeal to tolerance as an overall virtue.

(ii) Confusion between moral values and law

Many people simply associate the word *moral* with commands: "thou shalt … " "thou shalt not." Whether MPs try to wriggle out of overspending their allowances or financiers refuse to acknowledge corruption or those in authority are generally unwilling to admit they have been wrong, the widespread notion is that behaviour is morally acceptable because it is within the law. A 2009 letter in *The Times* about MPs' apparent inability to distinguish between "keeping the rules" and "doing the right thing" pointed out the problem very clearly:

> Rules are the problem, not the solution. Our daily lives have been bombarded with ever-more rules … we must withdraw from our obsession with rules and get back to constructive values of moral principles – fundamental standards of behaviour. Otherwise, self-interested adherence to rules will inevitably transgress moral principle.[10]

A major reason for the overemphasis on law is the reluctance in the West to acknowledge moral awareness. Shy of proclaiming moral principles, it is necessary to regulate society in order to avoid anarchy and, for practical purposes, the appeal to the rule of law seems to be sound. Basic realism suggests that common self-centredness needs to be controlled, and there will always be a criminal element in society, which makes adherence to law essential. The barrister Helena Kennedy notes:

> Law is a cornerstone. And unless we are prepared to revert to the continuous use of force, law is the supreme regulator. Whether nationally or internationally, it is the glue that holds together the constituent parts of society, a civilising force. Law is what makes the centre hold, the mortar that fills the gaps between people and communities, creating a social bond without which the quality of our lives would be greatly undermined.[11]

The problem is that reliance on law has mushroomed out of all proportion, as Jonathan Sumption argues in his 2019 Reith Lectures.[12] The law's expanded empire has intruded into every corner of our lives.[13] He thinks it is a corroding influence in our democracy. Sumption convincingly notes:

> We cannot have more law without more State power to apply it. The great seventeenth-century political philosopher, Thomas Hobbs, believed that political communities surrendered their liberty to an absolute ruler in return for security. Hobbs has few followers today. But modern societies have gone a long way towards justifying his theories. We have made a Leviathan of the state, expanding and harnessing its power in order to reduce the risks that threaten our wellbeing. The seventeenth century may have abolished absolute monarchy. But the twentieth century created absolute democracy in its place.[14]

Nor does imposing laws readily change people's thinking; it may even have the opposite effect. Hugo Rifkind, writing in *The Times*, draws attention to the problem: "Where once we had social or moral strictures against nuisance, offensiveness, hassle or downright unpleasantness, we now expect the state, and only the state to do the heavy lifting … ."[15] Sumption notes this as a weak point in the West: "Improvements in the technical competence of humanity have given us much more influence over our own and other people's wellbeing. But they have not been matched by corresponding improvements in our moral sensibilities or our solicitude for our neighbours."

Intellectual doubt leading to moral relativism

Moral principles are to be distinguished from cultural values and from the rule of law. The word *moral* is undermined, however, by a further threat, and to that I now turn.

(i) Distinguishing between moral and socially-constructed values

There is a widespread assumption that moral values reflect what humans happen to choose to make life sustainable and more pleasant for themselves. The sociologist Immanuel Wallerstein confidently stated: "Global universal values are not given to us; they are created by us. The human enterprise of creating such values is the great moral enterprise of humanity."[16]

Such a view is strongly encouraged by the view that morality emerges naturally as a result of evolution. Many aspects of what is generally regarded as moral behaviour are apparent in the natural world: dolphins, birds, elephants and chimpanzees exhibit such features. We would not refer to their behaviour as *moral* but as *social*. The assumption of continuity between humans and the rest of the natural world means that there is no need to speak of *moral* values when the word *social* fits both and there is a scientific explanation ready to hand.[17]

Peter Singer expresses such an understanding clearly: "We can understand ethics as a natural phenomenon that arises in the course of the evolution of social, intelligent, long-lived mammals who possess the capacity to recognise each other and to remember the past behaviour of others." He considers that "Darwin was right when he argued that human ethics evolved from the social instincts that we inherited from our non-human ancestors."[18] This is a common view to be found in sociobiology and evolutionary psychology. As Mary Midgley puts it, "Serious scientific articles, as well as TV programmes about animals, now all have an obligatory section proving that the behaviour discussed … must have been selectively advantageous to the creature's ancestors."[19]

Henry Haslam, in his book *The Moral Mind*, points out the flaw in Singer's argument. Evolution can (at least in part) explain good (and bad) behaviour, but that is not the same as explaining the human capacity for moral judgement.[20] He appeals to the authority of Darwin himself to suggest that Singer's evaluation of Darwin was misplaced. In *The Descent of Man*, Darwin wrote: "I fully subscribe to the judgement of those writers who maintain that of all the differences between man and the lower animals, the moral sense or conscience is by far the most important."[21]

Haslam considers:

> The moral mind is an important part of what it is to be human. Our sense of right and wrong is deeply rooted in human nature. It is not easy to define, but we know that it exists. It comes naturally to us to consider that we, or other people, ought or ought not to have acted in a certain way, and it matters to us.[22]

He quotes distinguished zoologists, such as Konrad Lorenz and Jane Goodall:

> To read the work of these dedicated and meticulous observers is to realise how similar human behaviour is to that of other animals, in so many ways; it is therefore particularly significant that both of them should emphasise that humans are unique in their sense of right and wrong.[23]

Anthony O'Hear summarises the import of the flexibility with which matter appears to have been endowed: "Even though we and our capacities may have evolved in Darwinian ways, once evolved we and our capacities are off in quite un-Darwinian ways."[24]

(ii) The impact of positivism on intellectual moral relativism

Confusion as to the meaning of the word *moral* has been aided and abetted by much philosophical thinking. Much intellectual doubt has been voiced as to whether terms such as *good and evil* or *morally right and wrong* refer to anything specific at all. A. J. Ayer, whose positivism was discussed in Chapter 2, was especially influential in the English-speaking world after the Second World War; he was given wide publicity. Dubbed the boo-hurrah theory, his view saw moral judgements as no more than emotional responses to events as they affect oneself. Such thinking could be seen as being in line with the philosophy of Hume, who wrote concerning moral values: "Nothing remains but to feel ... some sentiment of blame or approbation, whence we pronounce the action criminal or virtuous."[25]

The irony is that Ayer himself gave this theory up, as already noted, and few philosophers would defend it now. Nevertheless, continuing intellectual doubt has seriously undermined confidence in moral values, for they appear to lack clear rational justification. Thus, Bertrand Russell worried: "I cannot see how to refute arguments for the subjectivity of moral values, but I find myself incapable of believing that all that is wrong with wanton cruelty is that I don't like it."[26]

The effects of this uncertainty have seeped into every corner of society. It has largely banished references to moral awareness from public discourse. It has become commonplace to refer, not to anything being *morally* beneficial, but to phrases such as the importance of a "sense of community," "teamwork" or "networking." Undesirable behaviour is rarely referred to as *immoral*; rather, it is described as being *anti-social*. Furedi maintains that this has led to a culture of fear:

> In today's fragile moral climate we lack a virtue that can serve as an antidote to fear. Consequently we rely on non-moral resources – psychology, therapy, expertise – to guide our responses to the threat we face. Moral confusion both sustains and reproduces the culture of fear.[27]

The reality of moral awareness

Moral awareness, nevertheless, has not disappeared. It shows itself everywhere from concern for equality and social mobility to anger at corruption and lack of transparency, and from sorrow and gratitude for those who gave their lives in World Wars I and II for freedom from aggression to recognition of the wrongness of sex abuse. Haslam considers that

> This uneasiness about moral thinking was largely confined to the realm of theory. In practice, in their daily lives, people continued to hold moral convictions and pass judgement on their own actions and those of other people – just as they always have.[28]

Christopher Bennett in *What is This Thing Called Ethics?*, his book for philosophy undergraduates, felt able to assume the reality of moral awareness for almost everyone: "We think ethically all the time, because the fabric of our lives – relationships, ambitions, projects, responsibilities, wants and needs – is constructed out of ethical materials." He helpfully elucidates the issue of how what is personal and what is objective can cohere:

> Though ethical issues seem to be in some ways a personal matter that each person should decide for himself, it is not as if this means that it doesn't matter what view we take up. We feel bad if we have done something that we later come to think was wrong.

He takes the example of women's rights. In considering

> that Western societies have made significant advances in recent decades in allowing women the freedoms previously only available to men ... They are making claims, not

just about *their* morals, but rather about *morality*. They are not just saying "This is what we do" but rather "This is what we ought to do; we are right to do this."[29]

We need to recover confidence in the reality of moral awareness and in the underlying rational support for it, provided that reasoning is seen in a properly holistic manner, as discussed in Chapter 2. Seldon quotes a 1945 report from Harvard, *On General Education in a Free Society*, which stated that education at both school and university should regard social and moral development as just as important as academic learning. The accumulation of knowledge in just one area, it said, can be "positively dangerous if it is not grounded in a broad, deep and humane understanding of the human condition and a well-grounded moral sensibility."[30]

Moral awareness and the freedom of the individual

Before leaving this theme it may be helpful to guard against a common misconception, namely that morality constricts people's freedom. Kant saw moral awareness in terms of duty – as *the categorical imperative* – but he did not see this as inhibiting personal expression and creativity. Morality should not be understood at the level of obedience to dictated rules except at the most basic, primitive level of safeguarding society against criminality. Moral awareness itself is more akin to delight in what is good and horror at what is evil. It is, indeed, more about joy. As Kant put it: "Two things fill the mind with ever-increasing wonder and awe, the more often and the more intensely the mind of thought is drawn to them: the starry heavens above and the moral law within me."[31]

Moral maturity enhances freedom, in fact. The difficulty of discerning between right and wrong is sometimes great and, therefore, requires thinking carefully for ourselves and accepting that we cannot always have certainty. Applying the moral principles does not permit easy statements of "This is right" or "That is wrong." However, it also does not mean "anything goes." The most advanced moral agents are those who appreciate the depths of the problem of how to differentiate between right and wrong, but who remain committed to those basic principles and will not let them go. For a just society to develop, this is essential.

Moreover, choice is required of us in the *application* of those fundamental moral principles of right and wrong within each unique situation. Nor is this an easy matter, for life is complex and ever-changing. Understanding each situation properly requires much sensitive awareness, and this calls for very precise use of personal freedom in reflection and reaction.

Applying moral principles, and acting on them, therefore, not only requires but develops personal freedom. The sense of *obligation* associated with moral awareness actually enhances a person's freedom, unlike the other uses of that word which imply constraint. The element of constraint present in being kind, for example, is experienced as free choice, rather than something compelled by other reasons or by people or by responding to a carrot-or-stick approach. Thus, I have freedom to defraud, but I should not do it because it is unfair. I have freedom to support tyranny, but I should not because it abuses other people. I have freedom to be kind or not, and I should choose to be kind.

The necessity, or at least the opportunity, for exercising choice here is available for everyone. In fact, it is probably present in all people, even though it can become crowded out of consideration or buried. In this sense, we may say that moral awareness is inbuilt.

The youngest child will exclaim "It's not fair!" if injustice is perceived. Nor is this just a selfish reaction, because early on children can use the word *unfair* about what happens to other people as well as to themselves.[32]

What are the foundational values upon which democracy depends?

There are many possible ways of denoting foundational values. I want to suggest that a comprehensive summary should include: *concern for truth, for fairness, for compassion, and for beauty.*

I Concern for truth

Concern for truth needs to be understood in three aspects:

(i) What is the case as opposed to falsehood

This concerns the search for *is-ness*, bridging the gap between *what is* and *what we think is*. Philosophers refer to this distinction as *ontology* (the study of what is) and *epistemology* (the study of what people think is). Concern for *what is the case* is essential for everyday living. In fact, it is assumed to be so for pragmatic reasons, such as what time the train goes or what dose of medicine to take. It is also essential for any cognitive enquiry; if no one cares about what is true, there is no point in trying to discover anything or in having any disagreement or, indeed, in bothering to hold an opinion. The fact/opinion divide is serious because truth matters. This is not just regarding whether facts actually are facts, but whether opinions are nearer or further from actual reality, for there is a great difference in the consequences of holding such opinions. Truth always matters in the real world (see Figure 4.1).

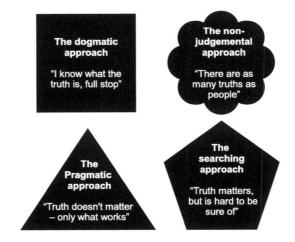

Which is your approach?

Figure 4.1 Approaches to truth

It is important to use the word *concern for truth* because of our unavoidable limitations in discovering truth and the vastness of what is to be known. Dogmatism is a form of ignorance, arrogance and limited reasoning based on a presumption of truth already and completely known. What is needed is a non-dogmatic search for truth. *Concern*, in the sense of consciously searching for truth, is the bedrock of all intellectual and practical endeavour.

(ii) Concern for honesty without intention to deceive

Trust between people depends on honesty. The search for honesty needs to be constantly encouraged, therefore, never playing fast and loose with it to achieve other ends. Talk of transparency is important. The failure to meet exacting ideals should be met with sincere apology, not with a shrug of the shoulders. There needs to be a real desire to act better in future.

Even so, it is important to note that, unlike the other two aspects of concern for truth, honesty per se is not an absolute value. There are occasions when honesty might inflict harm and jeopardise the operation of other foundational values, such as compassion. This may call for an element of pretence, such as when a teacher writing a report on a poor pupil who nevertheless tries hard puts: "Fine, she is maintaining her standard." This form of pretence is very different, however, from fraud or deliberate deception or the intentional misleading of people.

(iii) Concern for integrity as opposed to hypocrisy

Integrity concerns developing one's personal potential – being true to oneself. In *Hamlet* Shakespeare has Polonius say:

> This above all: to thine own self be true,
> And it must follow, as the night the day,
> Thou canst not then be false to any man.[33]

Polonius's speech is often quoted as a supreme maxim for an ethical life. But it raises the question: "Who am I?"

Do we not all often find ourselves in situations of pretence? Take the element of plain courtesy, which is so important for the smooth running of society. In Enid Blyton's story, "Mr. Miggles' Spectacles," when the titular character put on his glasses, he could see what people were really thinking about him, as opposed to what they said to his face.[34] It is quite a revealing point. How often have we thought, as someone approaches us, "Damn, the last person I want to meet just now!" But, we sweetly say, "Nice to see you ...." Is this deception? Is it pretence? Or, are we being true to ourselves by being polite to another person even though it may be the last thing we *feel* like doing? This is where vision overcomes mood. In trying to answer this question, I found it helpful to think of it as relating to three levels of the self (see Box 4.2).

Of course, there is a cautionary note. Courtesy must not become a habit in that one is not truly present in an encounter. There are times when people really want to know what you think about something, and it would be a failure in integrity not to tell them that you do not like something and why. Moreover, genuine debate can never happen if people never say what they really think. What is needed is care for how the disagreement is expressed. It can be done in a hurtful or in a positive and creative way, as discussed in Chapter 3.

Box 4.2 Three levels of the self

1   The self that one outwardly presents to others, which includes ordinary courtesy as well as many other motivated responses, in order to establish rapport, get things done, prevent angry engagement, provide solace for someone injured, etc.

2   What one feels like – emotions and moods, which are incredibly powerful. These moods can be affected by so many factors outside our direct control – even insomnia, indigestion, injury, bad weather, computer break-down, the annoyance of someone being late and keeping us waiting, etc.

3   Intentionality – what one holds as ideals to be sincerely worked towards. I believe that who a person really is relates to this last possibility – to what they regard as their vision, however much they may fail to realise it in practice.

Thus, I may feel a fraud in refraining from saying how much I dislike someone's new painting about which they are so pleased, but I still have integrity if the reason is according to (3) intentionality. Namely, I do not want to hurt someone over a matter involving an element of subjective taste. Again, if I am in a very bad mood, yet I respond to someone's "How are you today?" enquiry with "Fine, thank you!", I have not forfeited integrity if according to (3). I do not see why I should spill my truculent mood onto other people.

2 Concern for fairness

It is difficult to find the right word to indicate the foundational value of concern for fairness. *Justice* has too legalistic a ring. Laws can be morally bad as well as inhibitive of freedom, as discussed in Chapter 3. Moreover, obeying laws can be likened to painting by numbers. It can freeze creativity, whilst choosing to act in a spirit of fairness can unleash it. Fairness is an attribute and expression of free decision-making and is morally good.

Yet *fairness*, too, is inadequate. Stephen Asthma argues that the impartiality it implies is unworkable in practice and, indeed, undesirable, because it omits the proper sphere of preferentialism.[35] We cannot and should not have a deadpan approach to everyone ignoring ties of intimacy, companionableness and spheres of chosen loyalty to one another. I think, however, that Asthma is confusing impartiality with trying to be neutral, as discussed in Chapter 3. Impartiality does not ignore such ties. Rather, it takes them into account.

The word *goodness* actually embodies the essential substance behind both justice and fairness, but it suffers from sounding old-fashioned and moralistic. Along with the more common notion of morality, it has long been a boo-word associated with hypocrisy, imprisonment within outdated norms and presumed "worthiness." Even in popular culture the term *wicked* has become a hurrah word! Therefore, I settle for *fairness*.

3 Concern for compassion

Similarly, it is difficult to decide on a word to describe clearly the foundational value of concern for compassion. *Love* tends to be so closely associated with sexual or romantic activity that it has become far too restrictive. Also the common notion of having to like those you love makes it inevitably an exclusive matter. The words *benevolence* or *goodwill* towards other people are possibilities, in that they denote actively seeking what is helpful. They do tend, however, to have a rather cold, patronising overtone.

Often the word *empathy* is used. I agree to a large extent with the psychologist Paul Bloom, who draws a crucial distinction between empathy and compassion. He notes that they relate to different parts of the brain and summarises the distinction: "The act of feeling what you think others are feeling is different from being compassionate, from being kind, and most of all from being good. From a moral standpoint we're better off without it."[36] He gives a convincing reason: "Successful therapists and parents have a lot of cognitive empathy, but so too do successful conmen, seducers, and torturers." As an example, Bloom points to O'Brian in George Orwell's *Nineteen Eighty-Four.* [37]

So the word *compassion* seems the best term to use. It is important to note that it is compassion for all. It should not be just for family and friends, not just for neighbours, not just for those who think like we do, those whom we like and know, or those with whom we happen to sympathise anyway. It should be for all. It should not be selective. Compassion includes those with whom we disagree, even enemies. It needs to be compassion for all people as persons, even though, indeed, we shall only be in a position to show compassion to some people.

As Nussbaum said:

> It will be said, and frequently too, that the demand for love is a tall order, and unrealistic given the present state of politics in more or less every country. But think what this objection really says. The objector presumably thinks that nations need technical calculation: economic thought, military thought, good mix of computer science and technology. So, nations need these things, but they do not need the heart? They need expertise, but do not need the sort of daily emotion, the sympathy, tears and laughter that we require of ourselves as parents, lovers and friends, or the wonder with which we contemplate beauty?[38]

4 Concern for beauty

This may appear the least obvious candidate for a foundational value. A strong taboo against using the word *beauty* has been operating for a long time. Reference was made to this problem in discussing anti-elitism in Chapter 2. The historian Eric Hobsbawm comments:

> Who today still uses the word "beauty" without irony in critical discourse? Only mathematicians, chess players, sports reporters, admirers of human beauty, whether in appearance or voice, who are able without difficulty to come to a consensus on "beauty" or lack of beauty. Art critics cannot do this.[39]

Yet awareness of the beauty of nature, for example, is something which springs up naturally for most people. A sense of beauty, and the capacity to create beauty, is indeed a defining characteristic of civilisations. Works of art endure over time: the form, rhythm and harmony of the Parthenon, the Taj Mahal or Chartres Cathedral remain landmarks of human artistry. Our appreciation of them reflects the deep attraction of what is beautiful, however much individually we may prefer some exemplars over others.

O'Hear puts the case convincingly for the role of beauty in everyday life:

> Aesthetic considerations – those to do with beauty, style and taste – play a huge part in all our lives. One is tempted to say that once basic needs have been satisfied, aesthetic considerations play an increasingly predominant role in the lives of human beings. But this underestimates the need for the aesthetic. Even in the poorest of circumstances people have a yearning for order and beauty. This yearning will reveal itself in the ways they organise their shelter, prepare their meals, dress themselves and respond to natural sights and sounds.[40]

An interesting link with the management of anger, discussed in Chapter 3, is suggested by Kostas Kalintzis. He notes that "Every society, even those of social animals, must control the anger of its members lest it face dissolution." He discusses how the Greeks

> came to the conclusion that what was required was political and cultural nurturing of citizens, especially its infant citizens-to-be. Art especially was the great ally of the legislator since poetry and music could go deep into the psyche and reach the youth's impulses.[41]

In our much more scientific culture, beauty does not seem to fit in so well, for it is not scientifically measurable. Some recent research, however, is beginning to show an interest. For example, scientific studies now claim that a beautiful environment, whether in cities or in the countryside, helps to raise people's spirits: "Recently a scientific study that tracked the happiness of 15,000 people for three years found that their mood was lifted by aesthetically pleasing settings."[42]

Beauty does not need any arguments from its usefulness, however. The classical notion of the power of beauty to motivate us represents what we appreciate for its own sake, not for any utilitarian purpose.

Comment on the four-fold values

These four values – concern for truth, fairness, compassion and beauty – are fundamental, and I suspect that deep down almost everyone sees that. The enormous respect accorded to Shakespeare is a case in point. What he says seems to be true to life. His work reflects both the complexity and the variety of outward life, and the questionings and doubts of inner life. Shakespeare does not discourse about the pursuit of truth as a fundamental virtue, but it is everywhere taken for granted – the silent companion throughout. Regarding fairness, people do not generally come away from seeing or reading Shakespeare with an attitude that morally anything goes – that it does not matter how we think or behave. Shakespeare promotes moral reflection in his relentless portrayal of the consequences of character and attitudes. The same may be said of the virtue of compassion. It forms a basic attitude to the world which governs what he says and how he says it. As the Shakespearian scholar A. G. Nuttall notes, Shakespeare "is famous for being able to sympathize with anyone."[43] Concern for beauty is obviously present in Shakespeare. His genius for the use of words delivers a whole gamut of emotion and understanding.

How are such foundational values to be transmitted?

1 They need to be publicly articulated

There is something seriously wrong with a society that is ill at ease with articulating the positive values without which it cannot exist. They do need proclaiming and should be argued for explicitly. As *Guardian* columnist George Monbiot argues concerning the Statement of 16 Principles which he drew up, "They need to be expressed clearly and overtly, so that they can be explained and spread with pride and conviction."[44]

Certainly, care needs to be used in how we speak of values. Overkill can be counter-productive. Words can lose their currency value if overused. The analogy with inflation is apt, for words that are constantly repeated without being properly understood become more worthless with each repetition. Yet, aspirations need to be given voice. Overmuch cynicism is destructive. Democracy needs to embody the essential virtues and find ways of expressing them which can invite and inspire commitment by all. No society ever lives up to them. Its health, however, depends on some explicit public commitment to them as a means of righting a capsized boat.

It is difficult to talk about such foundational values without a strong impression of negativity. It can so easily sound prim, moralistic, old-fashioned, censorious, hypocritical and a host of other undesirable traits. Mary Whitehouse who complained vehemently of the increasing "blasphemy, bad language, violence and indecency" she saw on television, was in many respects right in what she said about the responsibilities of media in avoiding the promotion of unhealthy attitudes. But there was strong outrage at how she protested. Its manner made it easy for her detractors to ignore her actual message.[45]

An approach which may help is to encourage considering what the absence of the "virtues" would mean. If people do not bother about truth, there is no reason to find out about anything or disagree with anyone, because anyone can make up whatever is convenient for them. The same is true about the other values. Thus, no one can complain of unfairness without appealing to it as a moral value.

Mostly, human beings remain drawn to the love of truth, fairness, compassion and beauty. People revere these ideals deep down, which is why they are seldom talked about, yet they are apparent in much of life. They have been nurtured by civilisations since prehistoric times. Moreover, they are deeply embedded in the human psyche. A lack of permission to articulate these ideals has served, however, to push them further and further down from conscious awareness. The sneering attitude towards what is deemed "worthy" has been very damaging. It has made it seem ethically superior to have such low aspirations as to make any accusation of hypocrisy impossible! Moreover, people have been hugely distracted by the non-foundational values, such as freedom of speech and tolerance, that are constantly put across, as discussed in Chapter 3. Any new Age of Enlightenment must return to glorying in, instead of apologising for, the search for truth, fairness, compassion and beauty.

2 Impact of home background

The most successful nurture is by example and osmosis, and it is present in home life. Immersion in the values into which a child is born is hugely influential. What a tiny child absorbs normally stays, in some sense, with the child throughout her/his life. The family into which the child is born can most effectively encourage public-spirited, independent-

> **'Operation Midland' the investigation conducted by the British metropolitan police in London from November 2014 to March 2014 to March 2016 into a presumed paedophile ring**

Lack of concern for fairness

Innocent people, who included General Sir Hugh Beach. Lord Bramall, and a former MP Harvey Proctor, were publicly punished through their homes being ransacked and world-wide publicity given to the allegations against them – what in earlier days was punishment in the stocks. Helena Kennedy notes: "The criminal justice system is based on the fundamental value that it is far worse to convict an innocent person than to let a guilty one walk free."

Lack of concern for the truth

Right at the beginning of the investigation, the Detective Superintendent said that he believed the main victim of abuse "Nick" was "credible and true". Subsequently as Carl Beech, Nick was found to be a paedophile himself. The report on the operation found 43 key failings.

Lack of compassion

No thought was given during the investigation to the suffering of the wrongly and publicly accused. Lord Bramall died before his name had been cleared. Harvey Procter is still suffering from PTSD (2019)

Figure 4.2 Commitment to the foundational values can make a difference

minded, thoughtful and compassionate people. I want to give an example from a family known to me of how foundational values nurtured through generations can carry great potency in working towards a sound society.

James Denniston was a young doctor who journeyed East in 1877–78 to help Turkish victims of the war between the Russian and Ottoman empires.[46] His sensitivity and philanthropy were remarkable, as was his impact on the dynasty he founded. In the words of his biographer,

> His eldest son Alastair dedicated his life similarly to serving his country in intelligence and decryption. During WW1 he helped to found Room 40, which laid the foundations for what would, in time, become GCHQ. During WW2 he set up and headed Bletchley Park, working with mathematicians such as Alan Turing to break the Axis Enigma Code. The historical consensus is that the work in decrypting Axis communications shortened the war by two to four years. As to how many lives this foreshortening saved, the numbers are beyond counting. To this day James Denniston's descendants continue to work in medicine and charity.[47]

The link between nurture and values appears here to be crystal clear. James Denniston thought highly about the intelligence of women. Here is an extract from a letter he wrote:

> With the advance of civilisation women are now coming to the front and beginning to occupy their proper place in the social sphere – and why should not a woman be anything and do anything that she proves herself able to do? One notable obstacle to the acquisition of her proper position in life is her legal incapacity to possess a vote for the government of the country, and I propose to show that women should have the parliamentary franchise ..."[48]

Undoubtedly, his generous attitude influenced his son in employing women extensively at Bletchley Park – which was one reason for its huge success. Similarly, he had genuine respect for people as persons without dogmatic views on, for example, sexuality. This open-mindedness may have been of crucial importance in the decision to work with Alan Turing at a time when being gay entailed illegality.

3 Role of the school

Home background is crucial, but children are born into such different circumstances. Indeed, some are nurtured into the opposite of such public-spiritedness. A colleague taught for 19 years, including in a school near a socially disadvantaged housing estate in the Newcastle area which became notorious.[49] Many of the children were actually taught at home how to steal. Schools must try to make good the deficiencies of the home background. Schools, therefore, by necessity sometimes have to act *in loco parentis*. How they can do so wisely will be a major theme of Part 2.

4 Focus on the humanities and arts

Seldon writes, "The fourth education age will need to reassert a non-utilitarian vision of education, including the importance of the liberal arts, as championed in earlier ages. Education is about much more then transactional objectives and making our lives simple."[50] Nussbaum makes a passionate plea for the role of the humanities and the arts in society generally and in education:

> If the real clash for civilisations is a clash within the individual soul, as greed and narcissism contend against respect and love, all modern societies are rapidly losing the battle, as they feed the forces that lead to violence and dehumanisation and fail to feed the forces that lead to cultures of equality and respect. If we do not insist on the crucial importance of the humanities and the arts, they will drop away, because they do not make money. They only do what is much more precious than that, make a world that is worth living in, people who are able to see other human beings as full people, with thoughts and feelings of their own that deserve respect and empathy, and nations that are able to overcome fear and suspicion in favour of sympathetic and reasoned debate.[51]

Giving proper attention to the humanities and the arts is, indeed, crucial.

There is a caveat, however. We need to be aware that what counts is how the humanities and the arts are taught. Simple exposure is not necessarily helpful. Indeed, the emotional power conveyed can be used for nefarious ends. When Wilde's *The Picture of Dorian Gray* was first published, it caused a scandal. The *Daily Chronicle* believed it would "taint every young mind that comes in contact with it."[52] The theatre director Sean Aydon noted: "What really shocked people was Wilde's questioning of the basis of morality … This is not a morality tale but a tale that questions the existence of morality."[53] Such an analysis appears to take Lord Henry's utterances too seriously when he exclaims: "People have forgotten the highest of all duties: the duty that one owes to oneself."[54] Yet, in many ways, the novel is supremely moralist in showing the terrible inadequacy and dire consequences of individualism with its incapacity to control emotion. Intelligent and sympathetic discussion which highlights this latter point is needed to develop powers of interpretation, otherwise *The Picture of Dorian Gray* can seem to highlight the attractiveness of egoistic values.

Study of the humanities and arts needs to promote reflection on what is sound rather than on showering attention on what is unsound. It is important to appreciate the danger within representation: it is so much easier to capture the attention of an audience with bad characters, wrongdoing and nasty emotions than by focusing on their opposites, which can easily appear anaemic and uninteresting in comparison. Virtual reality is dangerously different from real life. Most people would not wish to consort with drug addicts, thieves, sex perverts, murderers and the like, yet they make for exciting film and TV viewing. Much thought needs to be given to the quality of discussion which study of the humanities and arts ought to engender.

Properly used, as in conjunction with the other foundational values, the arts can achieve marvels. A precise example of the amazing achievement of artistic endeavour in breaking down barriers is Daniel Barenboim's East-West Divan Orchestra, in which Israeli and Palestinian musicians share music stands. They learn to see each other as persons, no longer boxed up within an identity category. They are taken up in the service of a common cause, namely the outstanding music which they perform.[55]

Conclusion

I would like to finish this chapter with two compelling quotations. The philosopher John Cottingham has noted:

> What philosophers have come to call "normativity" is the way of referring to a remarkable feature of moral values like the wrongness of cruelty, for example, or the goodness of compassion: such values exert a demand upon us, they call forth our allegiance, irrespective of our inclinations and desires … No matter what you or I may feel about cruelty – even if we develop a taste for it – it remains wrong, wrong in all possible worlds. And no matter how disinclined you or I may be to show compassion, the goodness of compassion retains its authority over us and demands our admiration and our compliance, whether we like it or not.[56]

An impressive example of living these values is expressed by Natalia Ginzburg, widow of Leone Ginzburg, one of only ten professors out of 1,100 who refused to sign a declaration of loyalty to Mussolini, lost his job and eventually was tortured to death by the Nazis. She stated that it relates to the

> human capacity to transcend ourselves, to have imagination and empathy, to live in truth, create beauty, and do justice. This is the true greatness of honouring the dignity of every human being. This is what a democratic civilisation is all about.[57]

Notes

1 R. Trigg. 2007. *Religion in Public Life*. Oxford University Press. p. 234.
2 M. Warnock. 1988. *An Intelligent Person's Guide to Ethics*. Duckworth.
3 Trigg. *Religion in Public Life*. p. 195.
4 J. Q. Wilson. 1993. *The Moral Sense*. Simon & Schuster.
5 R. Amos. 2018. "Labour Blasts 'Sickening' Lehman Crash Reunion Party." *CityWire*. August 21. https://citywire.co.uk/wealth-manager/news/labour-blasts-sickening-lehman-crash-reunion-party/a1148215
6 A. Miller. 1949. *Death of a Salesman*. Penguin Books. p. 110.
7 Ibid. p. 37.
8 S. Pinker. 2002. *The Blank Slate: The Modern Denial of Human Nature*. Penguin.
9 Timothy Garton Ash comments that "In Tolerance We Trust" is "the best motto for the Britcoin of cosmopolis." 2016. T.G. Ash. *Free Speech: Ten Principles for a Connected World*. Yale University Press. p. 282.
10 "MPs' Rules and Moral Principles: Rules Are the Problem, Not the Solution." 2009. *The Times*. May 15.
11 H. Kennedy. 2005. *Just Law: The Changing Face of Justice – and Why It Matters to Us All*. Vintage Books. p. 9.
12 Jonathan Sumption. 2019. *Trials of State: The Law and the Decline of Politics*. Profile Books. Based on the BBC Reith Lectures. 2019. BBC Radio 4.
13 In the single year ending in May 2010, more than 700 new criminal offences were created, three-quarters of them by government regulation. In 1911 there was one solicitor in England for every 3000 inhabitants. Just over a century later, there is about one in 400 – a sevenfold increase. Sumption considers that the fundamental reason is the arrival of a broadly based democracy between the 1860s and the 1920s. Mass involvement in public affairs has inevitably led to rising demands of the State as a provider of amenities, as a guarantor of minimum standards of security and as a regulator of economic activity. He adds "Optimism about what collective action can achieve is natural to social animals. Law is the prime instrument of collective action and rising expectations of the State naturally lead to calls for legal solutions." BBC Radio 4 transcribed interview between Anita Anand and Jonathan Sumption. 2019. The Reith Lectures 2019: Law and the Decline of Politics. Lecture 1: Law's Expanding Empire. TX: 21.05.2019 0900-1000. p. 8.
14 Sumption argues: "These laws are addressed to moral issues on which people hold a variety of different views but the law regulates their choices on the principle that there ought to be only one collective moral judgment and not a multiplicity of individual ones … It marks the expansion of the public space at the expense of the private space that was once thought sacrosanct. Even where there are no compelling welfare considerations involved, we resort to law to impose uniform solutions in areas where we once contemplated a diversity of judgment and behaviour." Ibid.
15 Hugo Rifkind. 2019. "It Needs More Than a Law to Stop Up-skirting." *The Times*. June 19. He continues: "You need to grapple with porn, and tabloid culture, and communities. You need to wade deep into the sort of social battles that governments for the past two decades have used laws precisely to avoid having to fight to help men realise that, irrespective of whether snapping some woman's pants at a bus stop makes them a criminal, it very definitely makes them scum." Ibid.
16 T.G. Ash. *Free Speech*. p. 114. Quoting I. Wallerstein. 2006. *European Universalism: The Rhetoric of Power*. New Press. p. 79.
17 As Tom Chivers notes, "He makes an excellent case for the hypothesis that there is no emotion in the human psyche that we don't see in our closest relatives – and, in fact, in intelligent animals of all kinds, especially mammals and large-brained birds." T. Chivers. 2019. "*Mama's Last Hug: Animal Emotions and What They Teach Us about Ourselves* by Frans de Waal Review – They Love and Laugh Just Like Us." *The Times*. March 1.
18 P. Singer. 1994. "Introduction." In P. Singer (Ed.). *Ethics*. Oxford University Press. pp. 5 & 6.
19 H. Haslam. 2005. *The Moral Mind*. Societas. p. 35. Quoting M. Midgley. 1995. *Beast and Man*. Routledge.
20 Haslam quotes the great Darwinian defender, T. H. Huxley, on this: "Cosmic evolution may teach us how the good and evil tendencies of man may have come about; but, in itself, it is incompetent to furnish any better reason why what we call good is preferable to what we call evil than we had

before. ... Let us understand, once for all, that the ethical progress of society depends, not on imitating the cosmic process, still less in running away from it, but in combating it." p. 82f.

21 Quoted in Halsam. *The Moral Mind.* p. 1.
22 Ibid. p. 1.
23 Ibid. p. 3. Konran Lorenz studied numerous species, wild and tame. Jane Goodall's career was devoted to the study of chimpanzees in their natural habitat in Tanzania.
24 A. O'Hear. 1997. *Beyond Evolution.* Oxford University Press. p. 214.
25 The possibility that Hume was concerned with psychological description, not analytical philosophy, is a subtle point easily lost. See, e.g., A. Flew (Ed.). 1979. *A Dictionary of Philosophy.* Pan Books. p. 155.
26 B. Russell. 1960. "Notes on Philosophy, January 1960." *Philosophy* 35, no. 133. pp. 146–7.
27 F. Furedi. 2018. *How Fear Works.* Continuum. p. 32.
28 Haslam. *The Moral Mind.* p. 16.
29 C. Bennett. 2010. *What is This Thing Called Ethics?* pp. xiif, xvi, & 157.
30 A. Seldon. *The Fourth Education Revolution.* University of Buckingham Press. p. 48.
31 I. Kant. 1788. *Critique of Practical Reason.*
32 See research by O. Petrovich. 2019. *Natural-Theological Understanding from Childhood to Adulthood.* Routledge.
33 Shakespeare. *Hamlet.* Act 1, Scene 3.
34 E. Blyton. 1942. *I'll Tell You a Story.* Macmillan.
35 S. Asthma. 2013. *Against Fairness.* University of Chicago Press.
36 P. Bloom. 2016. *Against Empathy: The Case for Rational Compassion.* Penguin. p. 4.
37 Ibid. pp. 139 & 37f.
38 M. Nussbaum. 2015. *Political Emotions: Why Love Matters for Justice.* Belknap Press. p. 396f.
39 E. Hobsbawm. 2013. *Fractured Times: Culture and Society in the Twentieth Century.* Abacus. p.17.
40 A. O'Hear. 2001. *Philosophy in the New Century.* Continuum. p. 121.
41 K. Kalintzis. 2012. *Taming Anger: The Hellenic Approach to the Limitations of Reason.* British Classical Press/Bloomsbury. pp. 5 & 1.
42 R. Blakely. 2019. "Beautiful Cities Hold the Key to Happiness." *The Times.* March 15. The article reported on research published in the journal *Science Advances.*
43 G. Nuttall. 2007. *Shakespeare the Thinker.* Yale University Press. p. 276.
44 G. Monbiot. 2017. *Out of the Wreckage.* Verso. p. 10.
45 Mary Whitehouse, English social activist, became the General Secretary of the National Viewers' and Listeners' Association in 1965.
46 A. C. McKnight. 2017. *Letters from Erzurum.* Polperro Heritage Press.
47 Ibid. p. 281f. Susanna Denniston, herself a doctor, writes in the introduction of the book about her great grandfather, James Dennison, "All doctors, according to Hippocrates, need a mixture of science and art ... The science begins at medical school, but the art develops over the years. It includes expert diagnosis and an intuitive understanding of the patient's needs: physical, mental, and spiritual. Being a good listener is crucial; being alongside the patient, just being there." McKnight. *Letters from Erzurum.* p. 3.
48 James Denniston's letter is in the possession of the Denniston family.
49 Elizabeth Ashton later became Senior Lecturer at St Mary's College, University of Durham.
50 Seldon. *The Fourth Education Revolution.* p. 263.
51 M. Nussbaum. 2010. *Not For Profit.* p. 143.
52 Quoted in S. Aydon. 2019. "Director's Note." *Programme Notes: The Picture of Dorian Gray.* p. 8.
53 Sean Aydon, Director and Adaptor of the Tilted Wig Productions staging of *The Picture of Dorian Gray,* which toured in 2019.
54 O. Wilde. 2005. *The Picture of Dorian Gray.* In J. Bristow (Ed.). *The Complete Works of Oscar Wilde: Vol. 3 The Picture of Dorian Gray the 1890 and 1891 Texts.* Oxford University Press. p. 183.
55 D. Barenboim. 2009. *Everything is Connected: The Power of Music.* Phoenix.
56 J. Cottingham. 2012. "Human Nature and the Transcendent." *Royal Institute of Philosophy Supplement* 70. pp. 233–54.
57 R. Riemen. 2015. *To Fight Against This Age: on Fascism and Humanism.* W. W. Norton. p. 26.

Chapter 5

What to do about religion?

Chapters 2 and 4 noted two serious faults in thinking prevalent in the West today, namely, a narrow view of reason that promotes scientism and the drift towards moral relativism. Both might have been more effectively guarded against if serious respect had been accorded to religion. For religion places the cognitive in a larger framework which includes the personal and its subjectivity.

By religion I am meaning belief in a reality greater than, and responsible for, the physical world of which we are part. In this presumed insight, world religions can be seen as socio-logical institutions arising out of faith. The chapter is not concerned with religions as such, although for historical reasons regarding the development of the West, some reference will be made to Christianity.

Religion appeals to the heart as well as to the intellect – hence its power. Religion at its best seeks to promote sound emotions as the means of suppressing unsound ones. It does this by appealing to some reality beyond the ordinary, human-infused world in which we live – some overall spiritual reality usually referred to by a name, such as *God*. Different religions prefer different terms for denoting a sense of transcendence: *Brahman* in Hindu-ism, *nirvana* in Buddhism and so on.

As Neil MacGregor noted in his 2018 BBC TV series *Religion*, for almost every known civilisation, religion has supplied the cement, as it were, holding society together.[1] It offers a vision capable of galvanising people around an ideal, giving individuals a sense of purpose and offering a communal focus, a sense of working together inspired by what is greater than just human aspirations. The West, however, has embarked on a novel experiment. It constitutes the only attempt by a major civilisation in history to manage without religion.

Negativity towards religion

Since the Enlightenment there has been a notable suspicion of religion. Philosophers prepared to acknowledge religion in a fair-minded way have been a minority. Leading intellectuals in general have been dismissive, omitting reference to religion wherever possible and speaking of it in negative terms when discussed. It is rare, for example, for philosophy journals to take religion seriously. Again, I have been astonished, in reading about the history of education, how rarely religion is mentioned except in a slightly derogatory sense that implies indoctrination or an interest in only filling pews.

Anxiety concerning religion has seeped into society in general. Columnists in major newspapers can take it almost for granted that religion is not to be encouraged in any shape or form. An example, taken almost at random, is Janice Turner's article, "Don't Let the Religious Tide Engulf Britain." It assumes that readers do not want any public role for religion: "Don't be complacent about the encroachment of religion into the public sphere. It's occurring here too, and our leaders are doing nothing to resist it."[2]

Religion is barely mentioned in the press except for bad publicity associated with violence or transgressions of various kinds. *The Week*, which claims to provide "all you need to know about everything," comments on almost every area of human interest and experience, but features nothing on religion. In schools in many countries, religion does not feature in the charmed circle of curriculum or subjects studied. Where it does, as in Britain, its role is Cinderella-like. It has only survived through intense struggle and largely because it metamorphosed into a secularised version of religion, which is seen from the outside and discourages any attention to truth-claims. It has been treated more like an aspect of sociology, studying, for example, religious artefacts rather than discussing belief.[3]

Like everything human, religion has a long history in which it often has been abused and distorted. The West has become so highly proficient in noting this, that it is in danger of failing to see its enormous capacity for good as well as evil. The purpose and usefulness of religion have been undermined to such an extent that it seems that religion can be discarded like an old hat. This sums up fairly well the dominant attitude amongst intellectuals in the post-Enlightenment West, which has percolated down to most people via the media and education.

It is not surprising, therefore, that a public role for religion in the governing of society has been discouraged. The concept of the secular state has become all-pervasive. Whilst religion is officially tolerated, in that the right to hold whatever religious views one wants is safeguarded, religious views have been deliberately kept out of the public square, so far as possible. It has been debarred from taking much formal part, if any, in public decision-making and debate. Its vision for society has been privatised instead of being made available for all.

The level of secularisation varies from state to state, with religion retaining a more public image in some compared to others. It is practised in different degrees according to historical contexts, for example, in France, the United States or Turkey. The theory behind some forms of *laicete* – the strong form of secularisation as understood in France – argues for a safe space for all, which involves the separation of state and religious authorities. The reluctance to see much that is positive in religion in respect to the public face of democracy is prominent everywhere. It tends to be assumed that democracy is the child of the Enlightenment, and any public power wielded by religion is a real threat. It could lead to some form of theocracy, to which democracy must be opposed. This fear reflects the historical *ancien regime* in eighteenth-century France, where the overthrow of the Church's vast ecclesiastical machine was seen as necessary to deliver democracy. Today many presume that religion must never again be allowed a toehold in the running of the state. Reason serves as religion's substitute in holding society together.

How rational, however, is this attitude to religion?

The case against religion

Insistence on a secular state appears to rest on a strong case. It can seem a natural and sensible development rooted in the history of the West. I want first to examine this case.

1 Religion promotes discord not unity

The need for the secularist position is historically derived from a time when religious points of view were taken for granted and various denominations were at war with each other.[4] Moreover, as the founding of the United States demonstrated, dogmatic religious groups offered no basis for civil society, hence the perceived need to separate state and church. Political decisions must be made on rational grounds, not on religious ones. Similarly, education must not be allowed to indoctrinate students; it should be religiously neutral. Of course, people must be free to follow the religion of their choice – a major reason for the exodus to America in the first place – but they must not be allowed to force their beliefs on others.

2 Religion is responsible for much evil

Misuse of power when in political control is an even more serious charge against religion. Its propensity for violence is grave. Christendom produced bigotry, heresy-hunting and terrible abuses of human rights. Religion backed tyranny of many kinds and still does globally. Moreover, religion can easily provide a convenient banner for groups of disaffected people, even when their grievances have little to do with religion.

3 Religion is not needed for the pursuit of knowledge and human flourishing

Acquiring knowledge in science, humanities, economics, the arts or philosophy does not require belief in God. All can be studied objectively. Magnificent, real achievements resulted from focusing just on scientific/empirical evidence to produce the knowledge and technology that enables the modern world to raise the standard of living potentially for everyone.

4 Religion has many reprehensible features which the modern world should leave behind

Taking Christianity as a focal point, owing to its role in the making of the West, reprehensible features of religion include:

(I) SUBMISSIVENESS TO AUTHORITY

The hierarchical structure of Episcopalian churches promotes reverence towards those with special status. Reference to bishops with their *flocks* suggests a culture of permanent subordination for the majority. Even nonconformist services are mostly tightly organised, with people sitting in absolute quiet as they listen to a sermon telling them what to think and how to behave.

(II) GENDER STEREOTYPING

It is notable that women are still mostly denied power in religion. The Anglican Church has at last accepted women as priests but only because of intense pressure from the secularised world and insufficient vocations to the priesthood. Catholic and Orthodox Churches are still averse to the notion of gender equality. Similarly, there is still a marked lack of welcome to people who are not heterosexuals.

(III) LIVING IN THE PAST

The hold of tradition in religion is far too strong. The buildings where people meet, the vestments worn by those in authority, the words they recite – all betray a world quite different from today's. To attend a service like a Catholic Mass is like going back in time. It can be interesting and well done, just as a visit to the theatre can be, but no more.

5 A practical reason why democratic states must be secular

Religion should have no public role in the running of states because religion presumes the existence of God and not everyone in a democracy believes in God. There are two relevant points here:

(I) NON-CONTROVERSIALITY

A democracy must embrace all people in it. Therefore, it must be based on what is non-controversial or, at least, on what can be argued for by objectively drawing on reasons with which all can be expected to agree. Religion is subjective and controversial. Many people do not believe in God, so that cannot feature in the basis for democracy.

(II) PUBLIC/PRIVATE PERSONA

Democracy cannot prevent people from believing whatever they like. The state must provide a neutral arena in which people with conflicting beliefs can be free and safe to practise them away from the public eye. Thus, public concord is encouraged without robbing individuals of thinking what they like in private.

Rational grounds for challenging the case against religion

If examined closely, however, the case against religion is not as watertight as it may appear.

1 Religion promotes discord not unity

The capacity for discord comes as part of human free will and is by no means limited to religious people. The enormous tensions experienced today by states officially seeking to be democratic show how problematic managing pluralism in a positive manner is. Without any reference to religion, Ai Weiwei, a leading contemporary artist, activist and advocate of political reform in China, notes the problem:

> Human dignity is in danger. We must stand as one to survive ... A belief in ourselves and a belief in others, a trust in humanitarianism's power to do good, and an earnest recognition of the value of life – these form the foundation for all human values and all human effort.[5]

These beliefs are fragile and under threat globally today.

2 Religion is responsible for much evil

The potential for violence is endemic in being human. Its presence is everywhere. Any and all worldviews assiduously pursued can lead to violence. Simple egoism can. To regard religion as uniquely dangerous is irrational, therefore, because the possibility for the abuse of an ideal can never be eradicated. The twentieth century saw horrific examples of violence in the name of atheist worldviews, so, rationally, why should we blame violence on religion? Some non-religious people are as dangerous and anti-democratic as some religious people. Provisos against abuse should operate against all views, not just against religious views.

Blaming religion per se in this way for its violence also commits three serious faults in thinking:

(i) False generalization is a logical fallacy

The term *religion* embraces a vast area of human experience. To treat it as monolithic is as irrational as treating the term *politics* in the same way. It ignores the huge disagreements and wildly different ideals at work within it.

(ii) Obvious bias is shown in its one-sided view of religion, which presumes that nothing beneficial to human flourishing has emerged from religion

Anyone with a sense of beauty, whether in architecture or the arts, would find such an argument impossible to accept. Today, cathedrals, religious art and music sustain many people in a high quality of life regardless of any religious commitment. Whilst some religious belief has been associated with violence, often with other motives intertwined, such as power-seeking, much and arguably most religion has inspired high moral motivation. Nor is it possible for any fair-minded rational person to deny the huge input made by religious people, both in the past and today, to philanthropy. As Clare Foges put it when discussing followers of Richard Dawkins, who see religion as the source of all evil:

> Well, come with me, Dawkin-ites, to the schools, hospices and care homes where thousands of Christians do good work every day. Seek out the grittiest, grimiest edges of British life and they are there. They are helping addicts limp to liberty from drugs with infinite patience.[6]

(iii) Inattentiveness to the substance of religion fails to see that the violence for which Christianity has been vilified is, in fact, an abuse of its own teaching

Violence represents the utter failure to pursue the teachings of Jesus, whose life and death centred on love not hatred, as acknowledged by almost everyone, including atheists. There is a need to deepen understanding of what is at the heart of religion instead of attempting to eradicate religion as a whole.

3 Religion is not needed for the pursuit of knowledge and human flourishing

The reductive approach to knowledge has wrought much damage. To assume that no knowledge matters other than empirical and scientific knowhow, with its huge reliance on information and technology, is to ignore the need for wisdom. Emotional and spiritual immaturity helps no civilisation, least of all a democracy, as many are beginning to realise regarding the recent rise of populism in the West. Religion raises profound questions about the purpose and use of knowledge. It focuses on the character-development essential for democracy to flourish.

4 Religion has many reprehensible features which the modern world should leave behind

(I) SUBMISSIVENESS TO AUTHORITY

An element of submissiveness to authority has to be an essential aspect of any civilised life. If people just do what they want all the time, as extreme individualists seem to favour, the result can be anarchy. Could any of the achievements of communal human endeavour in any sphere have happened without some authority structure? Moreover, is it the case that obeying rules, following a leader, or doing what other people are doing at a particular moment is never a thing that a person freely chooses to do? Submitting to authority may be more rational than refusing to submit. No orchestral music could be played unless each individual player permitted their will to be, for the duration of the music, set aside in order to create something worthwhile together.

(II) GENDER STEREOTYPING

Treating women as equal to men is, indeed, a major insight of the modern West, even though still only partially practised everywhere. Religion is not responsible for failing to see this. Almost every known civilisation has regarded women's role as centring on the hearth and home, leaving the public organisation of society almost exclusively in the hands of men.[7] What is fascinating is to enquire whence the notion of gender equality arose. Early Christianity appears to have treated women in a markedly different way from the paternalistic attitude of the times. In a famous passage Paul of Tarsus taught that in the light of Christ all such distinctions no longer mattered because "in Christ there is neither bond nor free, male nor female, rich nor poor" for all are equal. If it be objected that the history of Christianity clearly did not embody this insight, there are many reasons why it did not. It is incredibly difficult to move against millennia of attitudes. Loving power and seeking to keep it is a fundamental weakness of all human beings. It takes great initiative and imagination to move, even in thought, beyond the boundaries of contemporary mindsets. If Christians have indeed needed a huge push from the outside to take on board in practice their own insight, reason would suggest that we still need to acknowledge the provenance of this pioneering ideal.[8]

(III) LIVING IN THE PAST

Traditionless individuals do not exist. All of us are nurtured into many traditions without which we could not develop as people. What counts is the quality of the traditions. Do they or do they not encourage quality of life, individual potential and communal achievement? A fine tradition is one which engenders both respect and the capacity for criticism.[9] By such means traditions can develop and adapt to changing situations. The fact that Christianity has managed to survive for almost two millennia and is to be found in every country in the world suggests that something in the tradition is suitably critical and adaptable. Moreover, the fact that secularism arose from within a Christian-dominated society argues that Christian tradition *has* encouraged the capacity for criticism.

5 A practical reason why democratic states must be secular

The argument for a secular state is not rationally persuasive.

(I) NON-CONTROVERSIALITY

Regarding beliefs and opinions, there are no reasons which can be expected to command everyone's agreement. All worldviews are bound to be controversial. The awareness, imagination and spirituality upon which a person's understanding of life depends cannot be objectively captured and clinically assessed. To argue that they can be is to assume a materialist worldview, which is just as controversial as any religious worldview. To keep religion out of the public square is to privilege a different controversial view. As Baggini concedes, "Secularism suits atheists more than believers. In a secular state religious vocabulary is absent from public discourse in a way that the natural lexicon of atheism is not."[10] The argument for keeping religion out of the public arena because of the need for non-controversiality thus collapses.

(II) PUBLIC/PRIVATE PERSONA

The public/private separation does not hold in reality. Character and approach to life formed by beliefs and values cannot just be donned or discarded. Clothed or unclothed, people remain the same. There is no separating what or who a person is – what they think, what they say and do, and how they react and respond to the actions and behaviour of others. Moreover, if there is no required distinction between private and public for humanists, atheists and agnostics, then religious people are not being treated as equal.

Having noted the highly challengeable nature of the case against religion, it is time to consider why democracy should show respect for religion and work with it as far as it can.

A negative attitude towards religion can inhibit the flourishing of democracy

Democracy needs all the resources it can lay hands on, rather than locking many of them away in a private cupboard, as it were. Insisting on the secular state and giving prominence

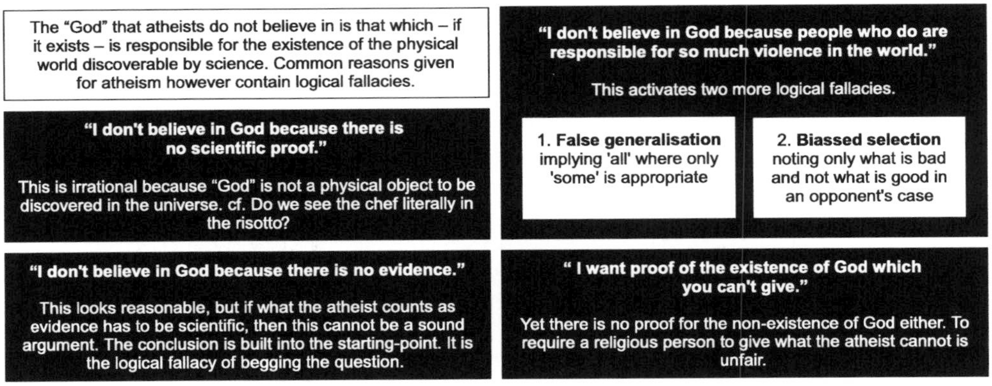

Figure 5.1 The irrationality of Atheism

to secularism fails to acknowledge the part played by religion in promoting democracy. Today's democracies tend to assume that secularism should take all the credit for democracy. Thus Jonathan Israel's book, which was discussed in Chapter 2, omits any reference to religion.[11] He firmly awards the prize for establishing democracy to the Radical Enlightenment and men like Diderot, Boulanger, Helvetius, d'Holbach, Mirabeau and their Anglo-American, Dutch and German associates. Israel claims that democratic ideals began to be expressed in the seventeenth century, especially in the work of Spinoza, who became the major fount from which subsequent democratic development grew.

Four points need to be made, however, regarding the role of religion in upholding democracy.

I Historically, the origins of inclusiveness are found in Christianity

All may concede that the notion of democracy as a form of government came from ancient Greece. What did not come from classical Athens was the notion of inclusiveness. Only around 25 percent of the population could take part – no women and no slaves. Yet, today we regard this aspect of democracy as vital. The enormous groundswell against racism, sexism, ageism, class elitism, and the failure to help and include the disabled, poor, sick and others with disadvantages insists that all human beings matter whatever their origins or abilities. Whence did this idea come?

Is it not historically the case that the Enlightenment insight which extended respect to all people emerged following the millennium in which Christianity was dominant in the West? The insight is present in the teaching of Jesus, who taught the love of God for every single person. In the parable of the sheep and the goats, those who are awarded eternal life are those who fed the hungry, clothed the naked, took care of the sick, visited those in prison – those who served the people most generally despised in society. This is because "in as much as you did it unto one of the least of these my brethren, you did it unto me."

In Israel's book on the origins of democracy there is telling evidence that the importance of inclusivity comes from Christianity. Israel sees Baruch Spinoza as the father figure of the movement towards democracy, and he notes that Spinoza revered the teaching of Jesus as the highest form of ethics.[12] It can be argued that it was from this source that Spinoza acquired his concern for equality, claiming the high moral ground throughout. Spinoza was steeped in Biblical study. Moreover, he saw that Christianity in particular had wandered far from the teaching of its founder. Thus, he was able to distinguish between the kernel at the heart of religion and the religion's failings to live up to it.

If we ask why Spinoza and those who came after him in the radical tradition never developed this connection, was it not because of the sheer anger at clericalism, which so took centre stage in the eighteenth century and gradually led them simply to equate Christianity with oppression? Israel gives no hint of critical comment concerning this. He is content to repeat what the Radicals said, adopting a simplistic anti-religious stance which, as already noted, commits the logical fallacy of false generalisation.

Israel's failure to comment on the bias of Richard Price on Methodism offers a clear example of how, by default, such false generalisations are sown. Israel records Price "fulminating against popular church movements welling up among 'the lower orders.' He considered that very many 'are sinking into a barbarism in religion lately revived by Methodism.'"[13] The story of the Methodist movement gives the lie to that. In fact, the Methodist movement was a nursery for the early trade unionists. Far from being barbaric, it was at the forefront of the move towards democracy. Price was simply wrong. The lack of any hint of this in Israel's book misleads readers. Israel's inclusion of this piece of misinformation without any critical comment has the effect of reinforcing a major controversial aspect of the Radical Enlightenment: that religion had to be opposed as an enemy of democracy.

2 Philosophically, there have been problems in grounding inclusivity in reason

Intellectuals have mostly sought to ground democracy in reasoning. A notable and highly influential attempt to base this democratic insight in reason was put forward by Rawls, who started from the self-interest he could presume in everyone. Rawls's idea relates to a long tradition of thinking in terms of a social contract, e.g., Immanuel Kant, Thomas Hobbes, John Locke, Jean Jacques Rousseau and Thomas Jefferson. Rawls presented a thought experiment in which people are required to choose the first principles to govern society from behind a "veil of ignorance," by which he means a point where they know nothing in particular about themselves or their society. They therefore cannot be sure of being among the winners, rather than the losers, once the veil of ignorance is lifted and the proposed policy is implemented. They are to choose out of self-interest, but he claims that this choice would also be in the interests of everyone. He argues that behind the veil of ignorance we would choose a "general conception" of justice that favours the interests of the least advantaged.[14]

Rawls's concept has been far from finding general agreement. There is a considerable literature critical of Rawls's theory.[15] One serious criticism is the imprecision of what such self-interest is presumed to consist. As Gray puts it:

> Followers of Rawls avoid inspecting their moral intuitions too closely. Perhaps this is just as well. If they scrutinised them, they would find they have a history – often a rather short history. Today everyone knows that inequality is wrong. A century ago everyone knew that gay sex was wrong.[16]

Rawls was assuming the spirit of the age, and that is an unreliable basis for fundamental democratic moral insight.

The key insight of inclusivity has stubbornly failed to take hold in most cultures and societies. It is something unique in the history of the world, moving far beyond the ideal of ancient Athenian democracy. Is a major reason for its slow appearance because it is not clearly supported by reason? Perception that is inspired is needed. The strongest reason for the change in attitude from exclusive notions to inclusive ones regarding who deserves respect lies in the kernel of teaching at the heart of Christianity. For, despite all of the exclusivism practised by ecclesiastical institutions, the notion of the equality of all in the eyes of God was never denied. Sometimes it was movingly realised in behaviour, such as in the life of St. Francis of Assisi.

There was need, indeed, for the ideal of inclusiveness to have a long period of gestation. It was slowly inculcated by Christianity, despite the backwardness of its official institutions in actually living up to it.[17] By masking this heritage out of consideration heritage, are we not arbitrarily curtailing understanding of democracy and its actual history?

3 Undergirding moral awareness is helpful to guard against a slide into moral relativism

Whence does the capacity for moral awareness come? The answer given in almost every civilisation known, except our own, has been some notion of the Divine – of a Transcendent order of reality. Locke wrote that the "true ground of morality … can only be the will and law of God."[18] This view has become unacceptable to the secularist and, indeed, to all who are aware that huge numbers of people in Western democracies do not believe in God.

It is possible to argue, as I do in Chapter 4, that moral awareness is found in almost everyone, despite their holding beliefs that may be contrary to it. So does the question of grounding of moral awareness actually matter? People say, for example, "you don't have to believe in religion to be good." Indeed, we may argue that many religious people are not good, whilst many non-religious people are good.

The intellectual problem remains, however. Philosophers have failed to come up with any compelling source of morality. Appeal to human decency needs underpinning with some philosophy of life, but philosophers have struggled to provide it. As already noted in Chapter 4, A. J. Ayer's famous "boo-hurrah" theory of morality is forgotten now. There is no unanimity in any theory to replace it. It clearly promotes a potentially dangerous situation for democracy if moral awareness appears not to have firm rational grounding such that all may agree.

The failure of Darwinian rationalism to combat this threat effectively is well illustrated in a revealing response by Richard Dawkins. In an interview Nick Pollard asked him, "Suppose some lads break into an old man's house and kill him … How would you show them that what they had done was wrong?" Dawkins replied, "I couldn't ultimately argue intellectually against somebody who did something I found obnoxious. I think I could finally only say, 'Well, in this society you can't get away with it and call the police.'"[19] What would this say to the criminally inclined, whether petty or not? Reason by itself appears to be impotent.

It may be argued that the concept of human rights provides reason that can be trusted. The Universal Declaration of Human Rights, which was ratified by the United Nations on 10 December 1948, is generally seen as one of the moral high points in the history of civilisation, yet does the belief that humans are created free, equal and with inherent dignity make sense without belief in some form of Transcendent Reality? Jonathan Haidt asks:

> Do people believe in human rights because such rights exist, like mathematical truths, sitting on a cosmic shelf … just waiting to be discovered by Platonic reasoners? Or do people feel revulsion and sympathy when they read accounts of torture, and then invent a story about universal rights to help justify their feelings?[20]

This is a good question. Michael Haas summarises examples of opponents of human rights. It is a formidable list.[21]

The Right To Have Rights is a recent book which raises the question of the source of human rights in a rigorous way.[22] It notes how exceedingly difficult it is to come by purely rational means to any secure grounding for human rights. It is, however, a clear example of the masking out of any reference to religion. It gives the impression that any religious view is not worth even considering. Yet, if human rights emerged from a Christian matrix and religion is totally discounted, does this not rob human rights of their validity?

As the philosopher Christopher Bennett told me, "A question philosophers ought to address: how does the humanist explain why humans should have moral capacities, if not through our having been given those capacities by God."[23] It is a real question. Presumed certainty that there is no God – no Transcendent Reality – is dangerous for any civilisation. If good and evil no longer relate to anything outside the minds of people, then the way is open for people, especially those with potentially criminal tendencies, to do whatever they wish provided they can get away with it. There is no ultimate accountability. Of course, the notion of hell can be easily ridiculed as itself an immoral delight in seeing other people punished. But people who are quite sure that there is no Reality such as God can easily think "It doesn't matter what I do." As the brutish Stanley tells his wife Stella and her sister Blanche in Tennessee Williams's play, *A Streetcar Named Desire*, "I'm king." If, on the other hand, there is some uncertainty regarding the reality or non-reality of a Higher Power which stands for goodness, then in moments of reflection the possibility of more-than-human accountability can weigh with people.

Pointedly we may ask: why should we bother about the frail, the weak, the dim, the disabled, the old, or the economically useless members of society? Reason by itself can suggest no unchallengeable arguments. Yet, is it not important that the moral insight be securely grounded?

4 The desirability of overall vision and critical respect for tradition

Belief in the reality of Transcendence can lift life above the superficiality, banality and self-centredness which threatens to engulf everyone. In the play *A Streetcar Named Desire*, Blanche eventually turns insane because she has so few spiritual resources on which to draw; her dreaming was bounded by sex, appearance, social esteem and money. By ignoring Christian heritage we are depriving people of their birthright: a sense of belonging achieved through both affirming and critiquing the tradition which they have inherited. This includes a sustaining vision that life really is worthwhile and has a wonderful purpose even in the most ordinary and difficult of circumstances. At a personal level such a lack can bring great mental and psychological suffering. At the level of society, it fails to inspire communal hope. Richard Harries's book *The Re-Enchantment of Morality: Wisdom for a Troubled World* carries an important message for sustainable democracy.[24] If people have nothing bigger than themselves in which to believe, there is loss. Why bother with so difficult an ideal as democracy?

Atheism cannot fulfil this role. As a form of faith, atheism cannot claim to be neutral or above all of the vicissitudes and problems attendant upon acknowledged religious faith. The secular state is one in which the Grand Narrative of atheism has triumphed. If the possibility of God or Transcendence with a capital *T* is hardly ever mentioned, that notion tends to go by default. Such a model cannot but privilege atheism as itself a materialist creed.

Proclaiming a Godless world trusts, unavoidably, a materialist explanation for its existence and meaning – if it has one – or meaninglessness if not. It necessarily involves the metaphysical belief that scientific discovery will eventually, in principle, explain all that exists. Common reference to evolution as an explanation of moral thinking is an example, as discussed in Chapter 4. Yet, this is faith, for there is no scientific proof to establish it.

Atheism is inadequate for sustaining a civilisation for many reasons:

(i) The concept of atheism itself is negative in form

Atheism states what is *not* believed and valued. Yet, we live by what we believe and value, not by what we do not. Indeed, a person's real beliefs and values are best understood by reference to how they behave rather than to what they say, what they pay attention to, what they ignore, or how they react to circumstances and to what others say.

(ii) Atheism relies on reason irrationally

Indeed, reason is atheism's claimed justification for opposing religion. It requires proof from religion. Yet, it cannot supply proof for its own viewpoint. As Julian Baggini, who is himself not a religious believer, notes, "Much as naturalists may dislike this … it is not a scientific claim to say that science is the only basis for justified belief … Science cannot discover that only science leads to truth."[25] Atheism, therefore, demands of religion what it cannot supply for its own belief.

(iii) Atheism cannot rationally disprove theism

Its presumed demolition of standard arguments put forward for the existence of God relies on logical fallacies. Thus, for example, if by *God* it is meant that which is responsible for the existence of the scientifically-discoverable world, then to look for proof of God's existence in the physical world is to be guilty of the logical fallacy of begging the question. For the Mind behind the universe – as Einstein put it – if existent, is not an object within it. God refers to *spiritual*, not physical, reality. People become aware of this – if they do – not by demonstrable empirical/scientific proof but by personal reflection and attentiveness.

(iv) Atheism's dogmatic denial of Transcendence in any form discourages on-going enquiry

This can shut down any questioning or debate about it. The pre-decision of a settled atheistic position is opposed to the spirit of enquiry and openness to fresh understanding. An example is the consistent opposition by atheists to education about religion in schools. For their understanding of religion, the public as a whole is left at the mercy of what they happen to pick up from the media and the people they meet. It makes for widespread ignorance concerning religion, which is a poor basis for exercising choice by individuals – something the West has rightly championed.

A potential way forward in respect and openness

If atheism will not do as the guiding worldview for democracy, neither will religious belief. Like all other human endeavours and aspirations, religion as practised has been and continues to be deeply flawed, as noted above. As a social, cultural, political phenomenon, it can provide no more guarantee of good behaviour than irreligion. As Philip Allott puts it,

> Religion is its own worst enemy in two respects (i) A particular religion may retain only its name and a bare identity over the course of time … (ii) A religion that proclaims peace and harmony may be a permanent scene of discord and conflict.

I agree with him that "To find a way to preserve the great potential benefits of religion while eliminating its very high costs is a formidable challenge standing in the way of the effort to make a better human world in the twenty-first century."[26]

May not such a way forward be found in welcoming religious voices back to the public forum on the basis, not of their having any commanding position, but as contributing alongside non-religious voices to the debate which is the lifeline for any democracy?

There are at least two principles to be kept in mind.

1 The importance of keeping alive for people the possibility that Transcendence is real

Respecting the *possibility* of both religious and non-religious viewpoints is a socially-constructive position to hold because it accommodates everyone equally. Moreover, it acknowledges the sense of Mystery which, for human-beings embodied in a physical world, is necessarily beyond what can be directly known and understood. Agnosticism holds open this possibility. It is a rationally defensible position and should be voiced openly as an alternative to religious belief. Similarly, religious faith may be truly open and non-dogmatic if it also acknowledges, as it should, a sense of uncertainty before the Mystery of that in which it believes. Belief in Transcendence cannot be demanded or required in any way, because it is reached, if at all, through personal reflection and experience. It has to be understood as what can be intuited, not intellectually grasped. It lies beyond our humanly limited and necessarily frail understanding.

2 The need for learning quality thinking, especially discernment regarding what is at the heart of religion

Understanding of religion is far from easy. All depends on people, whether religious or not, learning a quality of discernment regarding what is truly important as compared with what is peripheral, what is authentic according to its first traditions versus what has gone off at a tangent abusing its intention, what is beneficial from what is malicious, etc. In his 2017 Gifford Lectures Stout spoke of how Cicero distinguished between true religion (a moral virtue) and its counterfeits, and, similarly, Livy used a distinction between *ethical* and *unethical* religion to explain social ills. Stout developed this aspect of discernment regarding religion by noting the part that "ethical religion" has played in progressing the democratic ideal. For example, he highlights how Martin Luther King Jr. specifically drew on this distinction. Stout notes that the effects are good if the religion is good and bad if the religion is bad. An ideal of ethical religion animated the abolitionists, whom Gifford admired, and many activists since.[27]

Where discernment is absent, impoverished debate takes place. An example concerning religion is given by Allott, who argues that "Religions co-exist agonistically. They find it necessary to claim that they have exclusive access to truth, and hence that other religions are untrue."[28] There is no necessity to claim that there are no other routes to truth than one's own. This is an intellectual and psychological mistake made by committed people, religious or non-religious, when they fail to acknowledge the reality of other people's legitimate experiences of life and thought. There is need for all to develop a generous-minded spirit towards what others believe even as they may intellectually challenge them. See reference in Chapter 2 to the criterion of comprehensiveness.

It is also worth noting that failure to live up to the key beliefs of one's faith needs adding to; within religious circles there has been strong emphasis on the need for reform, interfaith dialogue, a search for ecumenism and deep research into the meaning of credal statements. So Allott's comment is giving a false impression of religion. Much depends on unravelling it, because discernment is crucial to any forward-thinking policy regarding religion or anything else.

The need for discernment applies just as much to religious people, whether the conventional masses or the seriously devout. Many fail to appreciate that God, if existent, is Mystery, and not in the pocket of any religious believer. Failure to appreciate Transcendence is what can make religion a dangerous force. A huge temptation open to religious people is to call the Will of God that which is, in fact, their own will. Tsar Nicholas II is one example out of millions that can be cited. He spent hours in prayer, yet persisted in considering that God wanted him to be an autocratic ruler turning his back on any reforms. The Islamist agenda is one of the clearest and most worrying examples today.

How can both religious and non-religious beliefs be publicly acknowledged?

Religious belief should be acknowledged properly in public so that religion is presented as a genuine option for people. We need to find a way, therefore, in which religious and non-religious views can *both* be properly expressed in public.

Public expression of such belief in situations where all citizens are assumed to be in agreement will not do, because personal integrity would be at stake. Public acts of worship, the mention of God in official statements and manifestos, prayers before meetings, compulsory assemblies for worship in schools – all might naturally follow from a religiously-controlled state, but they would not be acceptable to the non-religious.

Something much more modest is required. We need to make explicit openness to different commitments, acknowledging the possibility of both religious and non-religious viewpoints (see Box 5.1). In this way society can celebrate both agnostic and religious commitments, thus promoting the community spirit necessary for civilised society.

Box 5.1 Making explicit religious and non-religious commitments

i   The constitution could openly acknowledge the validity of a religious perspective even if not all might hold it. Words could be used such as "We hold these truths to be self-evident, which many of us see as under God."

ii   Mission statements for schools, organizations, hospitals, etc., could include a reference to the way many people see the values expressed as emanating from their religion. Thus, for example: "These are the values to which we are committed ... we see these as our duty as human beings and, for some of us, also as religious people." This is an example of the way in which religious material can be introduced in public meetings without offending against anyone's integrity because not making assumptions about people's personal commitments.

iii   Public meetings could open with a period of silence in which participants are asked to reflect upon their responsibility for a positive outcome.

iv   Religious Education in schools should be valued as an opportunity for learning how to think for oneself on the basis of understanding beliefs, especially the possibility of not just going along with the *zeitgeist*.

If the need to make religious and non-religious commitments explicit is accepted, the objections against religious faith being publicly acknowledged fall away. The element of uncertainty should be publicly displayed. It will mean that public gatherings give the opportunity for prayer and worship without making those who are not religious feel like outsiders. It should be made clear that response will always be at a personal level. Like going to the theatre, there can be no expectation of people's reactions. What is needed is to make explicit the acceptance of personal evaluation.

This does require some sophisticated thinking. It is far easier to think in terms of uniformity regarding public gatherings – even though it is in fact impossible because we are all unique as persons. Finding a way of being inclusive whilst articulating a religious position as well as a secularist position becomes possible when all acknowledge the unavoidably personal nature of all conviction. Rationally, this offers a sensible solution to the virtual apartheid practised in the West regarding secularism and religion. The practice of democracy should benefit greatly from a new spirit of partnership instead of suspicion.

Notes

1 J. Carey. 2018. "Review: *Living with the Gods: On Beliefs and Peoples* by Neil MacGregor – a Mind-Expanding History of Religion." *The Times*. September 16.

2 J. Turner. 2017. "Don't Let the Religious Tide Engulf Britain." *The Times*. Summarised in *The Week*. 2017. September 16.

3 See, e.g., L. P. Barnes. 2020. *Crisis, Controversy and the Future of Religious Education*. Routledge.

4 For example, the bitter legacy of the Wars of Religion of the sixteenth and seventeenth centuries in Europe.

5 A. Weiwei. 2019. "Human Dignity Is in Danger: In 2019 We Must Stand as One to Survive." *The Guardian*. January 1.

6 C. Foges. 2018. "The Church Should be Cherished, Not Mocked." *The Times*. December 24.

7 See, e.g., M. Beard. 2017. *Women & Power*. Profile Books.

8 Notably, Mary Beard never discusses how it was that the classical attitude towards women's rights changed. Ibid.

9 See, e.g., B. Mitchell. 1994. *Faith and Criticism*. Clarendon Press.

10 J. Baggini. 2016. *The Edge of Reason*. Yale University Press. p. 224.

11 J. Israel. 2010. *A Revolution of the Mind: Radical Enlightenment and the Intellectual Origins of Modern Democracy*. Princeton University Press.

12 Israel. *A Revolution of the Mind*. pp. 21f & 187.

13 Ibid. p. 28.

14 J. Rawls. 1971. *A Theory of Justice*. Belknap Press.

15 See, e.g., Fishkin, who offers two main reasons for questioning this thought experiment. 2018. *Democracy When The People Are Thinking*. Oxford University Press. pp. 152–4. Also see S. O. Sullivan & P. A. Pecorino. 2002. *ETHICS: An On-line Textbook*. American Public University. ch. 9. http://www2.sunysuffolk.edu/pecorip/SCCCWEB/ETEXTS/ETHICS/default.htm and C. R. Maboloc. 2015. "Difference and Inclusive Democracy: Iris Marion Young's Critique of the Rawlsian Theory of Justice." *Social Ethics Society Journal of Applied Philosophy* 1, no. 1. http://ses-journal.com/wp-content/uploads/2017/09/Iris-Marion-Youngs-Critique-of-the-Rawlsian-Theory-of-Justice-1.pdf

16 J. Gray. 2002. *Straw Dogs*. Granta Books. p. 102.

17 See, e.g., D. B. Hart. 2009. *Atheist Delusions: The Christian Revolution and Its Fashionable Enemies*. Yale University Press; L. Siedentop. 2014. *Inventing the Individual: The Origins of Western Liberalism*. Penguin; and N. Spenser. 2016. *Evolution of the West: How Christianity has Shaped Our Values*. SPCK.

18 J. Locke. 1690. *An Essay Concerning Human Understanding*. I.III.6.

19 N. Pollard. 1995. "The Simple Answer: Nick Pollard Talks to Dr. Richard Dawkins." *Third Way* 18, no. 3. pp. 15–9.

20 Haidt, J. 2012 *The Righteous Mind: Why Good People are Divided by Politics and Religion* Allen Lane p.32.

21 M. Haas. 2014. *International Human Rights: A Comprehensive Introduction*. 2nd ed. Routledge. p. 39, Table 2.4. The list includes: (1) *Traditionalism*: Wahhab. The wisdom of the ages should be respected not violated (understood as religious fundamentalism). (2) *Elitism*: Plato, Burke. Humans are born unequal – human rights are not derived from natural law. (3) *Relativism*: Von Savigny, Maine, Lee Kuan Yew. Human rights are culturally defined. (4) *Frustration-aggression theory*: Freud. Industrialisation requires repression, which leads to savagery. Hobbes, Nietzsche. Human nature is savage. (5) *Social Darwinism*: Spencer, Summer, Morgenthau. The strong should rule the weak humans. The fit survive and the weak die out. (6) *Social constructionist*: Foucault, Hume, Bourdieu. Elites establish orthodox views to justify denying human rights. "Rights " have no empirical basis.

22 S. DeGooyer, A. Hunt, L. Maxwell & S. Moyn. 2018. *The Right To Have Rights*. Verso.

23 Christopher Bennett. 2012. Letter to author. August 21.

24 R. Harries. 2008. *The Re-Enchantment of Morality: Wisdom for a Troubled World*. SPCK. Richard Harries was Bishop of Oxford 1987–2006 and is a frequent contributor to debates in the House of Lords.

25 Baggini. *The Edge of Reason*. p. 32.

26 P. Allott. 2016. *Eutopia*. pp. 180–1, 9.33 & 9.35.

27 J. Stout. 2017. "Religion Unbound: Ideals and Powers from Cicero to King." The Gifford Lectures: Over 100 Years of Lectures on Natural Theology. https://www.giffordlectures.org

28 Allott. *Eutopia*. p. 180, 9.34.

Part 2

Education: The need for reform

Chapter 6

What *is* education?

Democracy is a very difficult form of government to sustain, as discussed in Chapter 1. To flourish, therefore, it needs an education fit for purpose. It requires citizens able and willing to offer their talents and insights towards the well-being of society as a whole. Democracy implies tremendous trust in people – indeed in all people. It cannot be concerned just with the education of an elite.

Failure to educate for democracy

Are Western education systems mostly fit for purpose? I asked an experienced teacher in Britain to sum up for me how she sees the impact of education on democracy. Her response was not encouraging:

* Flawed values within the education system lead to children who are undervalued and not trusted; why then should they behave in a manner which deserves trust?
* Shockingly poor behaviour in many schools; infant, junior and senior, is created from a lack of values within society. Inability to address this behaviour effectively does not produce young people fit for a democratic society.
* The obsessive race for examination results produces meaningless league tables. It ignores the child and the values which that child can bring to democracy.
* Disappearance of the child as a young person who can explore and investigate freely. The motivated and enthusiastic youngsters who join reception classes become rapidly

downtrodden and demoralised by the rigidity and inadaptability of the education system.[1]

In many ways I share this gloomy view of the education system's failure to encourage all children to learn to think with mind and heart. It appears that not only is the education system failing to build up such trust, but worse, it is even discouraging it. Indeed, as Margaret Donaldson's seminal work on child development discovered, children enter school very enthusiastically and with curiosity, but the system extinguishes that remarkably quickly![2] It seems to produce many children who are like Brennan's *hobbits* (mentioned in Chapter 1). Specific citizenship education can only help if the deeper reasons why children are not encouraged to think for themselves and to become emotionally mature are taken seriously.

It is relevant to recall Dewey's powerful criticism of the whole system well over 80 years ago:

How many students, for example, were rendered callous to ideas, and how many lost the impetus to learn because of the way in which learning was experienced by them? How many of them acquired special skills by means of automated drill so that their power of judgment and capacity to act intelligently in new situations was limited? How many came to associate the learning process with ennui and boredom? How many found what they did learn so foreign to the situations of life outside school as to give them no power of control over the latter? How many came to associate books with dull drudgery, so that they were "conditioned" to all but flashy reading matter.[3]

Is it surprising, therefore, that Bryan Caplan can state bluntly in *The Case Against Education*:

Concisely, for all its wonder, education is grossly overrated. It's grossly overrated in the United States and around the globe. You don't have to be a professor to see it, but only a professor can credibly say it. The overrating is starkest from a social point of view. Students forget most of what they learn after the final examination because they'll never need to know it in real life.

He later adds:

Given the near-trillion dollars governments annually heap on the status quo, we're nearly immobilised. Never-ending cosmetic changes create the illusion of fluidity ... Yet no matter how many cosmetic changes accumulate, the essence of school endures: students spend over a decade learning piles of dull content they won't use after graduation.[4]

In his review of Caplan's book, Jeffrey Snyder comments:

Caplan has done us a service by compelling us to pay attention to a number of distressing facts. US adults who have gone through our public schooling system are astonishingly ignorant of basic civics, history and science. Millions of people who start college will never finish. And the pay-off for schooling is primarily about how many hours we have sat in classrooms rather than how much we have actually learned. Tick the boxes, get your degree and employers will smile on you, regardless of whether you gained any real skills and knowledge along the way.[5]

Education appears to have gone badly off the rails. Yet, this is not a new phenomenon. Dewey provided trenchant criticism of how education is mostly practised: "That education is not an affair of 'telling' and being told, but an active and constructive process, is a principle almost as generally violated in practice as conceded in theory."[6] His truly damning criticism sums up so much of what has gone wrong. For Dewey saw that learning has to have the active and passionate involvement of the learner.

The need for deep reform

The education most people seem to be receiving is not fit for purpose. Deep reform is therefore needed. Piecemeal efforts will not do, because other problems will hijack them unless they are also dealt with. Rather, fundamental reform of the whole way in which education is organised is required. The system itself creates so many of the problems encountered, such as: the boredom it produces in so many students; associated discipline troubles; frustration among teachers who have to be obedient to the system and lack the opportunity to take initiative concerning those whom they are teaching; the straitjacket of the curriculum in which, for example, creative subjects lose out; and the serious failure to educate character and communal values which encourage people to want to work towards a common purpose. These are some of the hurdles besetting schooling as it is commonly practised. How we organise education is itself the problem.

Consider four examples of the failure to help children at critical points, chosen at random out of millions that could be articulated:

i   Rosina is desperately unhappy because of her home circumstances. Her teacher wants to be able to spend at least half an hour each morning talking with Rosina and helping her become interested in doing her work. The teacher cannot, however, because there are 29 other children in the class.

ii Nicholas, another student from an extremely difficult background, cannot bear maths, but he is forced to do it for 40 minutes every morning despite the fact that his teacher knows he has a gift for writing poetry. His talent has to be ignored because it is not on the curriculum. Nicholas ends up playing truant whenever possible and finds refuge in gangs.

iii Jane is unable to concentrate one day because her much-loved grannie has just died. She flies into a temper with another child and is given a detention. She responds with a wild outburst about how unfair everyone is. But her teacher, who sees this and sympathises with Jane, has not time to give her comfort or help her sort out her complex feelings.

iv Kevin does not see the point of learning how to read. His teacher would have liked to discover why and find a way of meeting the child halfway instead of treating him as dim and making him work at boring exercises, which mean nothing to him.

These instances may seem small and unimportant, but they build into an approach to education which has ramifications throughout a person's life. The natural human responses of the teacher are blocked by how the system works: too many children in the class; a curriculum that takes precedence over a child's abilities, interests or needs; the dismissal of personal emotions aroused by events outside of school as well as in school as being unworthy of any time or attention; and unimaginative categorising of children instead of adapting the system to what each child clearly needs. Notably, in the last instance there was a happy ending. At a new school an inspired primary head noted what Kevin was interested in – growing plants. Kevin was put in charge of the school greenhouse. It was not long before Kevin was asking for help in learning to read because he saw the point of it.

Precedence is thus often given to the system, not to the persons within it. This is a strange volte-face, because the obvious purpose of education is to educate persons. The West, as a whole, gives enormous importance to the autonomy of persons, yet in its education systems children and students are treated largely as cogs in a machine or as pawns to be manoeuvred by others. Cogs and pawns do not learn how to think for themselves, nor how to empathise with others or work towards the common good. Yet, to make democracy work, these are precisely the characteristics that are urgently needed in all people.

A particular aspect of this failure to put persons at the centre of education is the assumption that people are essentially all alike, so that a uniform approach to what and how they learn is possible. As already noted, management has tended to treat children and young people somewhat like mechanical units to be managed or drilled by a common process: the same for all. Students are constantly measured against a common yardstick utilising, especially, the examination system. As Seldon puts it: "In the third education revolution model, students travel through their education journey at school as if they are on a production line." As he notes, there are, indeed, "fault lines in the very engineering of the industrial model of education."[7]

"One size fits all" wrong thinking has very serious repercussions. As Dewey put it:

> Nobody can take the principle of consideration of native powers into account without being struck by the fact that those powers differ in different individuals. The difference applies not merely to their intensity, but even more to their quality and arrangement. As Rousseau said: "Each individual is born with a *distinctive* temperament ... We indiscriminately employ children of different bents on the same exercises; their education destroys the special bent and leaves a dull uniformity. Therefore, after we have wasted our efforts stunting the true gifts of nature, we see the short-lived and illusory brilliance we have substituted die away, while the natural abilities we have crushed do not revive."[8]

Dewey makes a further important point:

> A progressive society counts individual variations as precious since it finds in them the means of its own growth. Hence a democratic society must, in consistency with its ideal, allow for intellectual freedom and the play of diverse gifts and interests in its educational measures.[9]

So the system must be taken down and reordered. The damage caused by education must be corrected by education. Many people do, indeed, see the need for educational reform, but often they set about it in a manner that reinforces so much that is already wrong. Common reactions are, for example, "Put more money into education." By itself this will achieve nothing helpful unless the money is spent in such a way that it actually improves the system and tackles the points just made about how education is failing individuals. Another common reaction is "we need more and better examinations to raise standards." Yet this ignores the fact that exam culture may be part of the problem. Another response urges getting rid of social prejudice by forcing private education to close in order to enable everyone to benefit from what hitherto was accessible to only a privileged minority.[10] Is education going to be improved by abandoning schools where it is happening effectively without considering why it happens well in those particular circumstances?

Misleading approaches to reform which should be avoided

I discuss below four ways in which such reform should *not* be approached.

1 Top-down management

Reform should not be attempted by dictating to teachers what and how they should teach. It is in the nature of governments to want to control. They imagine that they have the power to improve situations. Regarding education, however, great care is needed. It is for governments to ensure an overall framework which is as fair and useful as possible, but micromanagement should be avoided at all costs.

Such a fault has been a perennial problem, however, ever since the state took an interest in establishing schools. Nearly 50 years ago in *Pedagogy of the Oppressed*, Paulo Freire gave a withering summary of how education was often practised. Despite its political overtones, there is much truth in what he terms *banking education*, whereby pedagogies "mirror oppressive society as a whole" (see Box 6.1).

Box 6.1 Assumptions Freire saw as mirroring oppressive society

1 The teacher teaches and the students are taught
2 The teacher knows everything and the students know nothing
3 The teacher thinks and the students are thought about
4 The teacher talks and the students listen – meekly
5 The teacher disciplines and the students are disciplined
6 The teacher chooses and enforces his or her choice and the students comply
7 The teacher acts and the students have the illusion of acting through the action of the teacher
8 The teacher chooses the program content, and the students (who are not consulted) adapt to it
9 The teacher confuses the authority of knowledge with his or her own professional authority, which she or he sets in opposition to the freedom of the students
10 The teacher is the subject of the learning process, while the pupils are mere objects[11]

Much earlier, Dewey noted the absurdity of this approach to education:

> To talk about an educational aim when approximately each act of a pupil is dictated by the teacher, when the only order in the sequence of his acts is that which comes from the assignment of lessons and the giving of directions by another, is to talk nonsense.[12]

Reliance on inspection, management and accountancy culture has seriously played down the purpose of education. Endless directives to teachers as to what and how they should teach kill the spontaneity needed for real communication. Ian Burbidge, working with the RSA, noted the failure of top-down New Public Management tools, which used incentives, targets, markets and sanctions as primary levers of improvement to reform public services. According to Burbidge, the approach "left professionals disempowered, created perverse incentives as targets drove organisational focus, and crowded out creativity and innovation."[13] This has happened regarding what goes on in schools. Micromanagement fails to trust staff or pupils to act authentically and responsibly in a world of complexity and constant change.

The sheer ineptitude of government attempts to control the quality of education through inspection is shown by the bizarre case of the British Starbank School in Birmingham. The school had been gauged by Ofsted as "outstanding," yet teachers at the school went on strike in June 2019 over violence:

> Pupils as young as 11 have brought knives into school and some have threatened to stab members of staff … Teachers say that violent behaviour at the school is "out of control" and their concerns have fallen on deaf ears.[14]

The central comment has to be that a school should never be classed as "outstanding" if the vision behind education is so dimly realised. Problems such as knife crime do not suddenly emerge. They are the result of deep-seated concerns. An outstanding school would present the visitor with the sense of a basically warm and happy atmosphere in which staff respected each other and the students, and students respected each other and the staff in similar vein. Moreover, an outstanding school would be in close touch with its neighbourhood so that incipient problems, such as knife-carrying, would be identified early, and the school would add all its weight to resolving the problem instead of becoming a victim of it. It is not a question of forbidding or confiscating the carrying of knives, but of working alongside the community, alongside those who carry knives or who are tempted to and helping to lift them out of an antisocial, amoral culture by educating them into something better. All the resources of the school – time, effort and aid – should be put to this end because, by comparison, nothing else matters. Indeed, nothing can be achieved unless the situation is put right. What is the point of high reading scores or advanced mathematical/scientific understanding if students' vision for their lives is adversarial, hateful and potentially criminal? Until educationalists have learnt its lesson, the well-known comment of a Holocaust survivor deserves repetition:

> I am a survivor of a concentration camp. My eyes saw what no person should witness: gas chambers built by learned engineers. Children poisoned by educated physicians. Infants killed by trained nurses. Women and babies shot by high school and college graduates.
>
> So, I am suspicious of education.
>
> My request is this: Help your children become human. Your efforts must never produce learned monsters, skilled psychopaths or educated Eichmanns. Reading, writing and arithmetic are important only if they serve to make our children more human.[15]

2 Education being made to serve other agendas

Education must be for its own sake. It must not be allowed to become a servant for other agendas. Yet, since the nineteenth century the maintenance of an economically stable and flourishing society with sufficient employment at leadership, white-collar and blue-collar levels, has appeared to be the main desirable purpose of education. It is a utilitarian view, sometimes summed up as vocational. Young people are prepared for the world of work. It is *the* most common agenda since the state has been supporting education.

Many people – cynically perhaps, most – still see the education system more or less in such terms. As Bryan Caplan puts it:

> Our education system is supposed to be a skill factory – a place where unskilled youths go in and skilled adults come out … parents, teachers, politicians and social scientists all see schools as *the* great job training program on which our future depends.[16]

Caplan is Professor of Economics at George Mason University, Virginia, and he writes from the perspective of what is needed for a flourishing economy. He argues that the education system does not deliver what people expect of it – the training of human capital. Apart from literacy and numeracy skills, which are essential, he notes that most of the rest of the curriculum is useless, and young people simply learn how to be bored.

Dewey's vision of education was completely different: "That education is literally and all the time its own reward means that no alleged study or discipline is educative unless it is worthwhile in its own immediate having."[17] Dewey thundered against placing current learning in the context of preparation for a remote future. He makes points such as these:

* "Children proverbially live in the present; that is not only a fact not to be evaded, but it is an excellence."
* Education puts "a premium on shilly-shallying and procrastination. The future prepared for is a long way off."
* "The substitution of a conventional average standard of expectation and requirement for a standard which concerns the specific powers of the individual under instruction" is undesirable.
* "The principle of preparation makes necessary recourse on a large scale to the use of adventitious motives of pleasure and pain. The future having no stimulating and directing power when severed from the possibilities of the present, something must be hitched on to it to make it work. Promises of reward and threats of pain are employed." [18]

Dewey is careful to note: "The mistake is not in attaching importance to preparation for the future, but in making it the mainspring of present effort."[19]

He insisted that education must be for its own sake: "In education, the currency of these externally imposed aims is responsible for the emphasis put upon the notion of preparation for a remote future and for rendering the work of both teacher and pupil mechanical and slavish."[20] It more or less guarantees lack of relevance for the learner. Moreover, it has little to do with education, but much to do with training. When the activity of the immature human being is controlled in order to secure habits which are useful, Dewey considered it to be like training an animal, not educating a human being. The consequences are grave.

Other agendas less obvious than preparation for the world of work wait in the wings. Michael Young has used the term "powerful knowledge" to describe what education should be passing on. In contrast to "knowledge of the powerful" – a system of social and power relations with a particular history – "powerful knowledge" refers to the knowledge needed to address problems of the future, which include questions of justice.[21] He considers that "in the broadest sense, all education is vocational – and increasingly so as we try to prepare the new generation, whatever they are studying, for the complexities of building a safer, fairer and more sustainable world."[22]

Such a goal appears to be uncontroversial. Who could object to working towards establishing such a society? The problem is that people's views of what such a society consists and how it might be reached vary enormously. Capitalist and socialist understandings are, for example, radically different, as are their ideas about appropriate education towards such ideals. The danger lies in political overtones being brought in as part of education.

If the search for social justice is seen in terms of over-concern for accessibility and equality, for example, it can tip over into politically correct attitudes which approach the issue of social justice in a way that actually disables it. Furedi notes the damage caused by an educationally suspect philistinism which embodies a patronising approach towards what particular children like or need or are capable of. Linked with what he terms the "therapeutic turn in education," it actually has the effect of debarring many children, including those most in need of teaching, from being properly introduced to the intellectual and cultural heritage in which they could potentially thrive. See discussion in Chapter 3.

In fact, there is no need for pushing an agenda, such as social justice, if the foundational values discussed in Chapter 4 are being promoted in schools, as they should be. Social justice will emerge naturally as a concern. It does not need to be pushed in ways that may reflect political persuasions. There is huge need for discussion of politics in schools, as will be discussed in Chapter 8, but the discussion needs to be clearly educational and not in any sense indoctrinatory of particular views.

3 Not by pursuing false dichotomies

ACADEMIC VERSUS SKILLS

The history of education has seen damaging infighting between an academic and a skills or practical approach, the one side claiming to be superior to the other. The utilitarian view of education discussed above has encouraged its advocates to feel at loggerheads with those concerned with keeping the traditional curriculum based on academic study. The isolation of much academic learning from the world of work added fuel to the dispute.

Dewey did not see such isolation as educationally feasible. For him, learning must be embedded in practical application, as problems in real life are what stimulate learning anyway. He objected to the notion of disembodied skills. They are important for learning something of significance. Skills and knowledge belong together. It is impossible to think about nothing. Skills relate to content. Equally, he scrupulously avoided the view that education is about instilling facts in children's brains, the success of which could be tested: "Information severed from thoughtful action is dead, a mind-crushing load."[23]

It is interesting that this fierce divide began to give way in the last decades of the twentieth century to favouring the vocational over the academic. Paul Hirst, whose early work developed forms of theoretical knowledge as being fundamental in enabling human progress, later came to a more pragmatic view of knowledge.[24] He acknowledged that his main error was seeing theoretical knowledge as the essential basis for the development of practical knowledge, when he now considers it to be the other way round.[25]

TRADITIONAL VERSUS PROGRESSIVE

A separate but parallel dichotomy, which has split educationalists since the beginning of the twentieth century, is that between traditionalists and progressives. The latter hail Dewey as the major figure responsible for the movement. Rather than knowledge versus skills, the rift concerns how learning can happen. Traditionalists tended to see it as response to content presented by the teacher, whilst progressives emphasised the need for learners to be involved in the choice of content and the manner in which it is to be learnt. One way of encapsulating the difference is teacher talk versus discovery methods.

If seen from a basic common sense point of view, there need be no antagonism here. Pedagogy can be seen as finding a way of enabling academic learning to develop rather than as an end in itself. A former Principal of one of Newcastle's Colleges of Education, Vivienne Gibbon, regularly proclaimed in the 1970s, "We teach a child, not a subject."[26] The statement can be amended to "we teach a child through a subject." Moreover, as Ken Robinson has noted:

> In my experience, the apparently sharp divide between progressive and traditional approaches is more theoretical than real in many schools. In practice, teachers in all disciplines usually do – and should – use a wide repertory of approaches, sometimes teaching facts and information through direct instruction, sometimes facilitating exploratory group activities and projects. Getting that balance right is what the art of teaching is all about.[27]

The presumed rivalry has engendered, nevertheless, a great amount of heat. Dewey himself was much disillusioned by some of what he saw in schools that claimed to follow his principles of education. His important book *Experience and Education* was written in 1938 as a result of this experience. He noted especially the dangers of an either/or attitude. The book begins: "Mankind likes to think in terms of extreme opposites. It is given to formulating its beliefs in terms of Either-Ors."[28] He sees this at work in reaction to his ideas on education:

> There is always the danger in a new movement that in rejecting the aims and methods of that which it would supplant, it may develop its principles negatively rather than positively and constructively. Then it takes its cue in practice from that which is rejected instead of from the constructive development of its own philosophy.[29]

It is important also to note, in light of common misunderstanding of Dewey, that he equally avoided the so-called child-centred approach where children are allowed to develop just as they want: "Just because traditional education was a matter of routine in which the plans and programs were handed down from the past, it does not follow that progressive education is a matter of planless improvisation."[30] He had written earlier: "It is equally fatal to an aim to permit capricious or discontinuous action in the name of spontaneous self-expression. An aim implies an orderly and ordered activity."[31] Dewey therefore saw this major rift in educational thinking as being based on a false either/or – the word *traditional* acting like a red rag to a bull without the possibility of any differentiating between what tradition stands for.

CONSTRUCTIVISM VERSUS KNOWLEDGE

These two feuds, the academic versus vocational/practical and the traditional versus progressive; have since the 1980s been activated in a different form by the impact of postmodernist thinking.

Constructivist philosophy insists that, as knowledge is constructed, the real question is by whom. Leesa Wheelahan gives a socio-historical analysis of the "dethroning of knowledge in society and the curriculum," and she sees the influence of constructivism as crucial.[32] Knowledge thus comes to be regarded by many educationalists as being basically about power relationships. In the words of Basil Bernstein, knowledge can be treated as "no more than a ploy for power relations external to itself."[33] It has had the effect of decoupling knowledge from the way academic subjects are pursued.

Once it was assumed that conveying knowledge to the next generation is central to education. Now, however, the word *knowledge* appears to be seriously challenged. Michael Young and Johan Muller note "the increasingly widespread acceptance among educational researchers of the idea that knowledge itself has no intrinsic significance or validity." They add indeed that university colleagues visiting student teachers in their schools report something akin to a "fear of knowledge" in the schools they visit - knowledge is either not mentioned or seen as something intimidating or dominating.[34]

As Elizabeth Rata put it: "We became progressive and creative in the way we taught. By the end of the twentieth century we had become so obsessed with how to teach that we lost sight of the equally important – what to teach."[35] This has given rise to a crisis regarding the teaching of knowledge versus pedagogy.

An important book edited by Alex Standish and Alka Seghal Cuthbert challenges the undermining of the concept of knowledge. They argue that the

> knowledge, criteria and procedures entailed in disciplinary knowledge contribute to the formation of a universal, public "virtual" space where private feeling, no matter how intensely felt, can be temporarily laid aside and truth claims publicly contested ... The abstracted, theoretical ideas, and interpretative methods entailed in the study of disciplinary knowledge in all its forms, from physics to art, provide a robust resource for constructing school subjects.[36]

They conclude the chapter:

> At a time when past political markers and frameworks appear increasingly irrelevant to the public, as, arguably, does the work of much of academia, the need to reconsider disciplinary knowledge and academic school subjects could not be more pressing. Disciplinary knowledge – and its offspring, academic school subjects – presents the greatest cultural legacy from one generation to the next. Why would we want our education system to be based on anything less? ... (otherwise) we risk leaving the next generation technology-rich, but intellectually, imaginatively and spiritually impoverished.[37]

This constructivist entanglement has produced some strange results. For example, it has prompted Rata, in her efforts to restore the importance of knowledge on the curriculum, to posit a serious divide between real life and academe. Rata argues that children are to be socialised away from the sociocultural knowledge they have acquired and the identities carried with it.[38] Here she is virtually standing Dewey's educational approach on its head. He maintained that learning is a natural activity in which the child is absorbed right from the beginning. What he derides is the break that so often occurs in schooling when, instead of children pursuing knowledge with enthusiasm and interest, they are presented with knowledge irrelevant to them at that moment. The following Dewey quotations make this abundantly clear, and they point inexorably to why education seems to be failing democracy. For example, "Isolation of subject matter from a social context is the chief obstruction in current practice in securing a general training of mind."[39] Again,

> A peculiar artificiality attaches too much of what is learned in schools. It can hardly be said that many students consciously think of the subject matter as unreal, but it assuredly does not possess for them the kind of reality which the subject matter of their vital experiences possesses ... they become habituated to treating it as having reality for the purposes of recitations, lessons and examinations. That it should remain inert for the experiences of daily life is more or less a matter of course. The bad effects are twofold. Ordinary experience does not receive the enrichment which it should; it is not fertilised by school learning. And the attitudes which spring from getting used to and accepting half-understood and ill-digested material weakens vigour and efficiency of thought.[40]

Moreover, Rata's view rests on a politically motivated derision of tradition. It assumes that all tradition and culture into which children are nurtured at home can be put into a single category effectively marked *irrational power construct* from which everyone needs liberating. All cultures and traditions do, indeed, need criticism but only on the basis of their actual achievements and insights, which must first be understood and appreciated for the criticism to be valid. The rift between out-of-school experience and in-school experience is thus being celebrated, instead of decried.[41]

4 Not by trying to treat education as a science

As Hayes and Marshall note:

> At present, means of improving the authority of teachers, or the behaviour of pupils, are more commonly sought in a search that aims to emulate the language, criteria and methods borrowed from the natural sciences, and statistical analysis in particular. Statistical analysis is assumed to be a gold standard of verification.[42]

Putting a high premium on evidence-based research as a means of improving classroom practice is a particular example of scientism at work. See the discussion in Chapter 2 on this. Here I take issue with Dewey. His extremely high regard for science, as discussed in Chapter 1, led him to write:

> Every step forward in the social sciences – the studies termed history, economics, politics, sociology – shows that social questions are capable of being intelligently coped with only in the degree in which we employ the method of collecting data, formulating hypotheses, and testing them in an action which is characteristic of natural science.[43]

Reliance on evidence-based research as to best practice for the classroom may appear to be helpful and positive, but it carries a sting in its tail. Such research is not strictly scientific at all, because to be scientific the object of the investigation should be extremely clear: (i) The method of investigation has to be followed precisely and be basically repeatable to the extent that other scientists can check it; (ii) If the result proves to be unsatisfactory, the hypothesis must change.

Evidence-based research in education appears to satisfy neither of these criteria.

(i) Its object is not clear but dependent on subjective variation because people see best practice in different ways. There are a huge number of factors present in successful teaching. Almost all of these are variable, related to particular situations and persons, and incapable of being reproduced accurately; therefore deductions drawn from them are unreliable. If a major factor was the personality and experience of the teacher, how can that be replicated? The research is not repeatable.

(ii) Scientific inquiry accepts results and is open to change. See Chris Oliver's comment in Chapter 2. The application of educational research to practice is not clear, and therefore it cannot guide policy-changing as appropriate if fresh evidence emerges. Scientific hypotheses last only as long as evidence against them has not emerged.[44] In the UK, Ben Goldacre recently argued that education is not evidence-based, citing a paucity of robust, "what works" evidence gathered through randomised controlled trials (RCTs).[45] Many scholars, however, see the dangers in pushing this kind of scientific approach to measuring outcomes as the solution to improving practice. Eric Bredo, for example, expressed concern about a narrowing of education research to an experimentation of "what works?" at the exclusion of broader questions, such as "what matters?".[46]

It is hard to avoid the conclusion that trying to turn teaching into a science cannot work, because it is not possible to contain what good teaching is within a scientifically controllable framework.

How should reform of education be approached?

I suggest there are five ways to approach education reform:

1   *Reinstate the high purpose of education for its own sake.* This will itself enable other worthwhile agendas to be pursued in the best possible manner. The rest of the chapter will be concerned with this.
2   *Puncture the exam culture.* The educational case against constant measurement, except where it is truly appropriate, is strong. Chapter 7 develops the argument that reliance on examinations is anti-educational.
3   *Personalise the curriculum for each student.* We need to acknowledge that the potential curriculum is as wide as life itself. Any one person, with their unique talents, needs and experience, can only access a tiny part of it. One-size-fits-all approaches to what is to be learnt do not work. See Chapter 8.
4   *Place trust in teachers.* Attempts to treat teachers as robots to do as they are told destroys the possibility of education happening. Moreover, it wastes teachers' time and energy on repetitive tasks instead of allowing a high vision of education to guide them. They must be given the freedom to behave professionally. It will both help to ensure that new teachers stay in the profession and draw on a wider calibre of teachers to come forward. See Chapter 9.
5   *Utilise to its full potential modern digital technology.* We no longer have to think of education in pre-digital terms. The key needs are for resilient and trustworthy people, not for memorised and probably out-of-date knowledge. Proper use of digital technology can enable deep-seated reform of the whole system to become a reality. Let technology free teachers to educate by giving them the time to do so. Chapter 10 explores these possibilities.

The purpose of education

The argument for points 2–5 above depends on a high view of the purpose of education. Caplan's book takes for granted the antithesis of the high view of education for which I argue. He takes issue with humanist objectors to his book: "The humanists deny that education is supposed to provide job training in the first place. Its primary function, rather, is to promote intellectual enlightenment, political wisdom, social cohesion, or spiritual fulfilment."[47] Caplan responds that while these are wonderful ideals, "humanist critics should have confronted my empirical evidence on education's (lack of) humanistic effects."[48] He asks:

> How often do academics *successfully* broaden students' horizons? Empirically the answer is bleak: while great teachers can turn students into Shakespeare fans, Civil War buffs, avant-garde artists and devoted violinists, such transformations are rare. Despite teachers' best efforts, most youths find high culture boring – and few change their minds in adulthood.[49]

Caplan provides no case against this ideal, only that his empirical evidence shows that the ideal does not work. The obvious response to this is to ask why. A high view of education is what we need to reach towards such ideals, and we seriously need to ask what is impeding reaching them. The very structure of the education system itself is part of the problem.

So what is the purpose of education? As Guy Claxton puts it in his book *What's the Point of School?*:

> Education is meant to supplement the upbringing provided by families and communities with a more systematic preparation for the future. That preparation involves cultivating the knowledge, skills, habits, attitudes, values and beliefs that we think young people are going to need if they are to thrive in the world that we foresee them living in.[50]

He uses the metaphor of "*epistemic apprenticeship*: the idea that school is protracted training in particular ways of thinking, learning and knowing."[51]

Part of what he says here is essential, namely that nurture in the home and local community does need supplementing. According to Dewey, a major purpose of school is

> to balance the various elements in the social environment, and to see that each individual gets an opportunity to escape from the limitations of the social group in which he was born, and to come into living contact with a broader environment.[52]

The successes of the Home Education movement are impressive, but they do depend on the advantages – intellectual, social and cultural – of the home-background. Schooling is important to ensure that all children have access to education. Claxton's focus on the future can be critiqued, however, according to Dewey, as noted above. It is not just the future that matters.

Regarding the purpose of education, strong emphasis has been placed on student learning. Thus, for example, Ken Robinson states: "the fundamental purpose of education is to help students learn."[53] Yet, is not education so much more? Learning can and does happen without teachers. Unwin and Yandell sum up so much of what a tiny, untutored child learns without being taught:

> We learn at least one language; we learn about other people and about ourselves; we learn a vast amount about the world around us – about how things work and how we can have an effect on what happens. We manage all of this without, in most cases, any formal program of instruction. In other words, we seem to be pretty good at learning (some things, at any rate) without being taught.[54]

Education, rather, should concern something much wider and deeper (see Figure 6.1).

Much depends on what is to be learnt, for learning is not just about students' activity. It includes "knowledge-building" for, as Michael Young states, learning is "epistemic."[55] What is taught is crucial. Tony Little suggests what has gone wrong:

> Throughout my years as a teacher I have never ceased to be amazed by the creativity and flexibility of the adolescent mind ... Unfortunately the conventional world of education stifles this. Our society's almost doctrinal emphasis upon deductive reasoning, convergent thinking and selective retention perversely excludes divergent thinking, approximation and, importantly, guessing.[56]

Little's comment parallels Iain McGilchrist's analysis discussed in the Introduction and Chapter 2 regarding the victory of the left hemisphere of the brain (LH) when, in fact, it is the right hemisphere (RH) which needs to be in control. The LH makes a good servant but a poor master. Lack of vision for what education really concerns emerges from the false thinking outlined in Part 1 (see Figure 6.2).

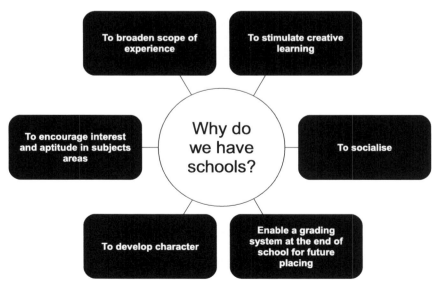

Figure 6.1 The purpose of schooling

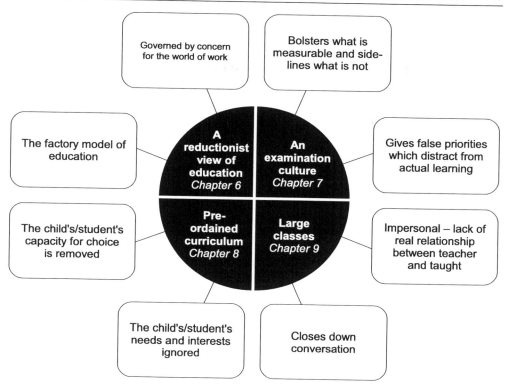

Figure 6.2 The education system creates the problems it cannot resolve

The hold of the fact/opinion divide, in particular, must be abandoned instead of reinforced. What is needed is the education of opinion through deeply and consistently helping people how to learn to make judgements for themselves about beliefs and values. The education of the emotion is also needed. And by that I mean education, not the therapeutic turn which Furedi rightly deplores.

This high purpose of education can only be achieved through activating its interest and sense of importance for each learner. This is where the insights of Dewey are supremely relevant. As he notes:

> The required beliefs cannot be hammered in; the needed attitudes cannot be plastered on. But the particular medium in which an individual exists leads him to see and feel one thing rather than another; it leads him to have certain plans in order that he may act successfully with others; it strengthens some beliefs and weakens others as a condition of winning the approval of others. Thus it gradually produces in him a certain system of behaviour, a certain disposition of action.[57]

He has an interesting passage on the importance of sheer interest: "The word *interest* suggests, etymologically, what is *between* – that which connects two things otherwise distant."[58] It is for schools to create the conditions in which the ideal can be realised.

How then can the purpose of education be summarised? I discussed this with a number of people who agreed on the following list of characteristics associated with being educated (see Box 6.2).

Box 6.2 What are the characteristics of an educated person?

A person who deserves to be called *educated* is someone who:

- ★   knows how to find information and to understand it by seeing it in its context
- ★   has wide interests; is not narrow-minded or unable to see connections between different aspects of life
- ★   is thoughtful; does not just take opinions and beliefs from other people without weighing their likely truth
- ★   has high ethical aspirations, and wishes to use knowledge and understanding for the common good
- ★   is self-assured, capable of self-criticism and not over-egoistic
- ★   is well aware of how little any of us know and accepts levels of uncertainty in all presumed knowledge
- ★   has strong convictions but holds them without dogmatism
- ★   knows how to listen carefully and to argue without personal invective
- ★   is wise and discerning in the use of knowledge and understanding

---

Is not the purpose of schooling to enable each child, each student, to progress as far as possible towards being such an educated person?

Utopia? Yes, indeed it is, but nevertheless an ideal worth investing in. Democracy can only flourish if there are large numbers of people working towards this utopian ideal, and formal education should play its part in promoting it. It is an ideal that encapsulates all that is best in the great stress on the autonomy of the individual, and the importance of science – the legacy of the Enlightenment – concern for community and the public good, and ethical responsibility towards all others. Such people *are* fit for democracy and able to take up their particular parts in responsibly running society, whether it involves just voting from time to time or holding positions of authority.

What I am arguing for is close to the traditional understanding of education as liberal and holistic. Tony Little associates it especially with values and character:

> As a nation we will only recapture a traditional strength, and give our young people the confidence to face change and uncertainty, if we loosen the grip of measurement-driven schooling and at the same time assert the demonstrable benefit of a school culture that celebrates academic excellence and the acquisition of skills, but which is firmly grounded in, and shaped by, personal relationships … I want young men to leave my school who are confident and independent-minded. I want them to feel that they are unique individuals. But the unfettered exercise of individualism is a curse. Edmund Burke knew it when he watched the unfolding of the French revolution in 1790 and wrote in words that seem remarkably relevant to us today: any society that destroys the fabric of its state must soon be "disconnected into the dust and powder of individuality" … How

relationships develop between young people and, just as importantly, between young people and adults should be right at the centre of our school programme, the starting point of all our discussions about syllabuses and systems.[59]

In quoting Little I am not supporting institutional class systems, but the opposite. He himself considers: "That there should be such a gulf of achievement between state and independent schools in the same country is a matter of national shame."[60] I want excellent education to be available for all, which is precisely the point of the radical reform of education I discuss in Chapter 10.

Notes

1 Joanna Dawson. 2018. Conversation and email exchange with author. March.
2 M. Donaldson. [1978.] 1986. *Children's Minds*. Fontana/Collins.
3 J. Dewey. [1938.] 2015. *Experience and Education*. First Free Press. p. 26f.
4 B. Caplan. 2018. *The Case Against Education: Why the Education System Is a Waste of Time and Money*. Princeton University Press. pp. 285 & 288.
5 J. Snyder. 2018. "We Don't Need No Education!" *Boston Review*. May 9. http://bostonreview.net/education-opportunity/jeffrey-aaron-snyder-we-dont-need-no-education. Cited in Caplan. *The Case Against Education*. p. 294.
6 J. Dewey. [1917.] 2015. *Democracy and Education*. Myers Education Press. p. 43.
7 A. Seldon. 2018. *The Fourth Education Revolution*. University of Buckingham Press. pp. 62 & 53.
8 Dewey. *Democracy and Education*. p. 124.
9 Ibid. p. 324.
10 Recent books are examples of this continuing approach, such as F. Green & D. Kynnston. 2019. *Engines of Privilege: Britain's Private School Problem'*. Bloomsbury; and R. Verkait. 2018. *Posh Boys: How English Public Schools Ruin Britain*. Oneworld.
11 P. F. Friere. 1972. *Pedagogy of the Oppressed*. Penguin. Quoted by A. Unwin & J. Yandell. 2016. *Rethinking Education*. New Internationalist. p. 129.
12 Dewey. *Democracy and Education*. p. 109.
13 I. Burbidge. 2017. "Outdated Public Services Must Empower People to Achieve Change." *RSA Journal*. July 5. https://medium.com/rsa-journal/outdated-public-services-must-empower-people-to-achieve-change-70d7c6a3f3f0
14 N. Johnstone. 2019. "Teachers at 'Outstanding' School Strike Over Violence." *The Times*. June 28.
15 Haim Ginott, an Israeli educational psychologist, notes that the quote was included in a letter that teachers received from their principals each year. M. Rozell. 2012. "So, I am Suspicious of Education." Teaching History Matters. April 12. https://teachinghistorymatters.com/2012/04/02/so-i-am-suspicious-of-education
16 Caplan. *The Case Against Education*. p. 291.
17 Dewey. *Democracy and Education*. p. 117.
18 Ibid. p. 60.
19 Ibid. p. 61.
20 Ibid. p. 118.
21 See J. Muller & M. Young. 2019. "Knowledge, Power and Powerful Knowledge Re-visited." *The Curriculum Journal* 30. pp. 196–214. The term "powerful knowledge" first appeared in M. Young. 2008. *Bringing Knowledge Back In: From Social Constructivism to Social Realism in the Sociology of Education*. Routledge.
22 M. Young. 2010. "Foreward." In L. Wheelahan. *Why Knowledge Matters in Curriculum: A Social Realist Argument*. Routledge. p. xii.
23 Dewey. *Democracy and Education*. p. 163.
24 See, e.g., P. Hirst. 1974. *Knowledge and the Curriculum*. Routledge.
25 See R. Barrow & P. White (Eds.). 1993. *Beyond Liberal Education: Essays in Honour of Paul H. Hirst*. Routledge.

26 I was told this by someone who knew her.

27 K. Robinson. 2016. *Creative Schools*. Penguin. p. 103.

28 J. Dewey. 1938. *Experience and Education*. Simon & Schuster. p. 17.

29 Ibid. p. 20.

30 Ibid. p. 28.

31 G. Claxton. 2008. *What's the Point of School?: Rediscovering the Heart of Education*. OneWorld. p. viiif. Quotes Dewey.

32 L. Wheelahan. *Why Knowledge Matters in Curriculum: A Social Realist Argument*. Routledge. p. 87. Wheelahan notes the impact of "three dominant approaches to the curriculum, which are constructivism, technical-instrumentalism and conservatism." Ibid. p. 1. Her choice of these three movements appears fair and sensible. At one pole is the traditional approach to the curriculum dominant in all schools till the 1960s. At the opposite pole is the most recent strongly challenging approach. The middle approach reflects the utilitarianism which has been a gnawing critique of the traditional academic approach throughout. For a review of Wheelahan's book, see M. Priestley. 2010. "Review: *Why Knowledge Matters in Curriculum: A Social Realist Argument*." *Scottish Educational Review* 42, no. 2. pp. 111–3.

33 B. Bernstein. 1990. *Class, Codes and Control: Volume 4 – The Structuring Of Pedagogic Discourse*. Routledge. p. 166.

34 M. Young & J. Muller. 2016. *Curriculum and the Specialization of Knowledge: Studies in the Sociology of Education*. Routledge. p. 141.

35 "Politics of Knowledge in Education: Elizabeth Rata." 2020. The Educationist. http://www. theeducationist.info/politics-knowledge-education-elizabeth-rata

36 A. Standish & A. S. Cuthbert. 2017. "Conclusion." In A. Standish & A.S. Cuthbert (Eds.). *What Should Schools Teach?: Disciplines, Subjects and the Pursuit of Truth*. pp. 135–44. UCL Institute of Education Press. p. 143.

37 Ibid.

38 E. Rata. 2020. "The Politics of Knowledge in Education: Elizabeth Rata." *The Educationist*. Originally delivered as lecture, May 2014, Bhopal, India). http://www.theeducationist.info/politics-knowledge-education-elizabeth-rata

39 Dewey. *Democracy and Education*. p. 73.

40 Ibid. p. 172.

41 See, for example, E. Rata. 2012. *The Politics of Knowledge in Education*. Routledge; B. Barrett & E. Rata (Eds.). 2014. *Knowledge and the Future of the Curriculum: International Studies in Social Realism*. Palgrave Macmillan.

42 D. Hayes & T. Marshall. (Eds.) 2017. *The Role of the Teacher Today*. SCETT. p. 137.

43 Dewey. *Democracy and Education*. p. 303.

44 See, e.g., the 2017 "Evidence-Informed Practice in Education: Meanings and Applications" special issue of *Educational Research* 59, no. 2.

45 B. Goldacre. 2013. *Building Evidence into Education*. http://media.education.gov.uk/assets/ files/pdf/b/ben%20goldacre%20paper.pdf. Partly in response, the UK has seen a development of "What Works Centres," which seek to apply robust evidence to improve public services. See, e.g., "Guidance: What Works Network." 2013. https://www.gov.uk/guidance/what-works-network. Similarly, the US has witnessed an increase in Federal Government-endorsed "what works" methodologies. See, e.g., R. E. Slavin. 2004. "Education Research Can and Must: Address 'What Works Questions." *Educational Researcher* 33, no. 1. pp. 27–8.

46 See, e.g., E. Bredo. 2006. *Conceptual Confusion And Educational Psychology*. Routledge

47 Caplan. *The Case Against Education*. p. 293.

48 Ibid. p. 296.

49 Ibid. p. 2.

50 Claxton, *What's the Point of School?* p. 27.

51 Ibid. p. vii.

52 Dewey. *Democracy and Education*. p. 24.

53 Robinson. *Creative Schools*. p. 71.

54 Unwin & Yandell. *Rethinking Education*. p. 28.

55 See, e.g., M. Young. 2015. "What is Learning, and Why Does It Matter?" *European Journal of Education* 50, no. 1. pp. 17–20, at 17.

56 T. Little. 2015. *An Intelligent Person's Guide to Education*. Bloomsbury. p. 71.
57 Dewey. *Democracy and Education*. p. 14.
58 Ibid. p. 136. Dewey notes: "One who recognises the importance of interest will not assume that all minds work the same way because they happen to have the same teacher and textbook." Ibid. p. 139.
59 Little. *An Intelligent Person's Guide to Education*. p. 31f.
60 Ibid. p. 30. Little adds, "[B]earing in mind that many UK independent schools are non-selective, the gap is even more striking."

Chapter 7

Exit examinations?

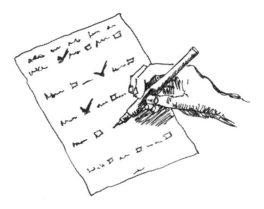

Dominance of an examination culture

For many people, perhaps most, education is mainly about passing examinations. The notion of the possibility of educating people without examinations would seem incoherent. Over one hundred years ago, when resigning after years in His Majesty's Inspectorate, the English educationalist Edmond Holmes asked:

> How did the belief that a formal examination is a worthy end for teacher and child to aim at, and an adequate test of success in teaching and learning, come to establish itself in this country? And not in this country only, but in the whole Western world? In every Western country that is progressive and up-to-date ... the examination system controls education and in doing so arrests the self-development of the child, and therefore strangles his inward growth.[1]

The development of testing into an examination structure may be seen as having a venerable history. As far back as 124 BCE, formal examinations were created in China to ensure the capability of those recruited to enter the Imperial civil service. The examinations were written under invigilated conditions for selection purposes.[2] In 1806 an exam system was first used in England by the East India Company to adjudicate between candidates for the civil service. It was specifically modelled on the Chinese imperial examinations. In 1847 Thomas

Taylor Meadows, the British Consul in Canton [Guangzhou], wrote a key paper in which he maintained that the exam system, which enabled appointment by merit only, was a major cause of efficiency in government. The Northcote-Trevelyan Report which followed in 1854 recommended that selection for the civil service be based on merit determined through standardised written examinations, which was doubtless preferable to what happened before, namely, preferment, patronage or purchase.[3] The civil service exam system adopted in England had huge international significance. It is unsurprising that the notion was soon applied to education and taken up by the universities, which had assessed students by oral examination since the Middle Ages.

The first public examinations for schools in Britain were introduced in 1858 in response to a demand from schools themselves as a way of marking their pupils' attainment. Schools approached universities – such as Cambridge and Oxford – and asked them to produce examinations that boys (note that girls were not included!) could take in local "centres" where they lived, such as schools or other suitable venues like churches or village halls. The University of Cambridge Local Examinations Syndicate – now known as *Cambridge Assessment* – was officially established on 11 February 1858. Its first exam took place on 14 December 1858.[4] Since then, the notion of written examinations has been adopted globally.

Disquiet at overemphasis on examinations

Nevertheless, in recent years there has been much concern about overemphasis on examinations, as shown by articles and correspondence in *The Times* over proposed changes in the UK. In 2017 Amanda Spielman, at the time chief inspector for schools in the UK, said she wanted quality education and complained that "pupils, parents and teachers are too hung up about examinations."[5] Alice Thompson, one of Spielman's interviewers, thought she was joking: "The whole system promotes examinations as *the* guarantor of education."[6] In a subsequent article, Nicola Woolcock, Education Correspondent for *The Times*, noted that Spielman said:

> It's deeply worrying to see secondary schools being encouraged to teach children narrowly to tests right from age 11. This is cutting down children's exposure to a full, rich curriculum and reinforces the idea that targets, predictions and data points are more important than the substance of education.[7]

Criticism in the press is supported by a wide range of academic disapproval. Thus Frank Coffield and Bill Williamson consider:

> Our schools, colleges and universities have been turned into exam factories, where teaching to the test and gaining qualifications and learning techniques to pass examinations are now what matters, rather than understanding, or being interested in, or loving, the subjects being studied. Stress levels are running high among educators and students, and all this pain is being endured in the cause of improving the international competitiveness of British business.[8]

The problem is certainly not confined to Britain. The United States offers striking examples of anxiety concerning the dominance of examinations, especially of what are termed *high-stakes examinations*. These are standardised tests used widely by governments throughout the world to hold teachers, schools and education providers to account. As Rachel Brooks notes:

> Since the 1980s they have become a key means for reforming educational systems – often supported by a wide range of stakeholders from across the political spectrum who see them as a neutral, fair and accurate means of assessing the performance of both individuals and schools.[9]

Examinations have generally been used as a crucial part of planned education, especially for purposes of accountability, where the proper use of resources needs to be safeguarded. However, the rise of high-stakes testing has exacerbated concern for accountability. Diane Ravich, Assistant Secretary of Education under George Bush in the 1990s, played a role in promoting examinations but subsequently became disillusioned. She came to see the strategies of national testing and accountability turn into a nightmare for American schools. Basic skills were effectively drilled into students, but they were often left ignorant about almost everything else. Indeed, this is the utilitarian danger. High-stakes testing and punitive regimes of accountability have, in her considered view, "transformed" education in American public schools, but very much for the worse.[10] Her powerful book, *Reign of Error*, received impressive reviews.[11] It found a timely follow-up in Anya Kamenetz's bestseller, *The Test: Why Our Schools Are Obsessed With Standardized Testing*.[12] The success of these books shows that much of the general public is tiring of the testing push of recent years, which has sucked the oxygen out of the room in a lot of schools.

Concern about overvaluing examinations is not new. It predates the high-stakes era. The term *diploma disease* was coined in 1976 by Ronald Dore in his book of that title.[13] Unwin and Yandell quote his sharply worded diagnosis: "More qualification earning is *mere* qualification-earning – ritualistic, tedious, suffused with anxiety and boredom, destructive of curiosity and imagination, in short anti-educational," and they comment that it is "as apt today as when [Dore] produced it."[14]

The case for examinations

How has the extraordinary emphasis on examinations come about? On the surface the case for examinations seems to appeal to common sense. Exams harness attention, develop memory skills, require disciplined pursuit of a definite attainable goal and promote motivation by enabling comparison with others – which appeals to the competitive spirit which almost all children have. In general, they encourage hard work and fight apathy and sheer laziness. Examinations also provide those responsible for educating with a seemingly reliable, fair and objective means of knowing how far they are succeeding. At quite a basic level testing can even be regarded as something children happily engage in naturally – almost as fun or a form of quiz.

In general, the value of testing appears to be supported by the public. A leader in *The Times* discussing Ofsted's new inspection formula commented:

> Teachers should be in no doubt that examinations still matter. Like the revision that has to precede them, they are an essential part of education. Without revision, knowledge may never be cemented in pupils' minds. Without examinations, pupils, their parents and employers may be left with no fair way of comparing their children's attainment with their peers or with national averages.

Ofsted was now offering "a new measure of the quality of a school's education that takes exam results into consideration but measures progress before outcomes. This measure will be called, not inappropriately, 'quality education.'" The writer considered that the measure would constitute "a rebalancing of a system that emphasised examinations but came to emphasise them a shade too much."[15]

Box 7.1 Advantages of examinations

Examinations appear to be definite, clear and objective, promoting at least five worthwhile goals. They:

1 encourage high standards in learning factual information
2 provide clear-cut criteria for assessing success and accountability, free from subjective bias
3 promote motivation in students to work hard and in teachers to teach effectively
4 aid social mobility through promotion of merit
5 ensure that society has a workforce sufficiently skilled for the modern world

---

Gordon Stobart, even though critical of the exam culture *per se*, considers that test-based accountability systems with consequences consciously linked to punishment and reward do have some positive effects. He gives the example of the expectation of year-on-year improvement, especially regarding traditionally low-performing groups of pupils. Examinations have challenged conceptions of intelligence and/or ability as being fixed or innate. He also notes that clear targets have encouraged some teachers to work harder and more effectively. Examinations offer a common language with which to communicate.[16] (See Box 7.1).

It is mostly the case that even those who criticise how the exam culture works in practice, with its many unfortunate consequences, still do not question the inherent value of assessment. Ken Robinson, for example, states: "Neither I nor many other critics of high-stakes testing are questioning the need for assessment, which is a vital part of education, but the form it now takes, and the harm it is causing."[17] Later he notes that "Assessment is an integral part of teaching and learning. Properly conceived, both formal and informal assessments should support students' learning and achievement in at least three ways." He sees these as providing motivation, achievement and standards.[18] Discussing the PISA league tables of the OECD, he writes: "The aim is to offer a regular, objective guide to international standards in education. No one could object to that."[19]

I do however object! I fear the dangers of playing the exam game. It unleashes forces damaging to education as a whole. I question whether the benefits outweigh the harm and disadvantages. Little, former Head of Eton, recounts a fascinating conversation with heads of top-performing schools in PISA assessment in Shanghai, who were, themselves, worried:

> As one of the most distinguished heads in Shanghai put it to me: "We know we are on a juggernaut heading for the cliff edge and we want to change direction but we don't know how ... high-performing Chinese schools are fascinated by the philosophy and methodology of the best British schools.[20]

It is time to consider in more detail the case against examinations.

The case against examinations

Unwin and Yandell offer trenchant criticism of an education system "in which the tail of assessment wagged the dog of learning." Extensively quoting Holmes's critique, referred to above, they note that "the echoes in the world of the early twenty-first century are chilling."[21]

Unwin and Yandell discuss five myths concerning learning The third, which they see as the "most deeply implicated in the history of schooling," is the myth that "Learning is individual." In powerful language they state that

> it assumes that learning is the property of an individual and that learning happens within a single learner's head. Plagiarism is the cardinal sin within the religion of schooling precisely because it entails a transgression of this article of faith.[22]

Scathingly, they continue:

> With glorious circularity we know that learning is individual because the assessment regimes constantly demonstrate that this is the case ... Assessment separates sheep from goats, high-fliers from also-rans, leaders from hewers of wood. It underpins the notion of meritocracy and sustains the illusion that social justice can be achieved through social mobility.[23]
>
> It ignores the fact that "learners are irreducibly social beings, situated in history and in culture."[24]

Each of the five presumed advantages of examinations listed in Box 7.1 has downsides.

1 Encourage high standards in learning factual information

Whilst it may be the case that examinations encourage high standards in learning factual information, this gives a high priority to facticity per se. It can promote a narrow approach to learning that expects to find straightforward information. Many educationalists associate this approach with Dickens's character Mr. Gradgrind, who insisted that children were "little pitchers" to be "filled so full of facts."[25] For example, Anthony Seldon comments that the depiction of Gradgrind

> may always have been something of a caricature. But the reality of fact-based learning remained the norm up to the present day, bolstered during the last two decades by a new band of enthusiasts for exam success as the sole validator of school success.[26]

Reliance on constant testing can subtly indoctrinate people into a simplistic understanding of knowledge which excludes discernment. Robinson notes: "All sense of nuance and complexity is usually lost in the process."[27] Instead, education should be encouraging a real, first-hand search for knowledge with all its uncertainty.

It is not that factual information is unimportant, but only that constant attention to it can easily smother other, and arguably more important, aspects of learning. Moreover, it fails to address a whole range of questions concerning information, including:

i   We live in an age of information overload; increasingly, is it not selection of what is important, relevant and appropriate that matters?

ii In an age that has been dubbed *post-truth*, do not pupils need to learn how to tell whether given information is reliable, whether it is fake or whether it embodies false generalisations?

iii Such capacity depends on trusting the source of the information, which is especially relevant regarding what the media broadcast but also applicable in the case of examinations and those who set and mark them. How far can we trust them? Do they have an agenda?

iv What is the point of the information-gathering? The use of information raises a whole set of important questions to be addressed, which is closely associated with the next point:

v Do not issues of privacy, surveillance and potential criminal exploitation need to be addressed?

By focusing attention so much on learning and remembering specific information, these other important questions can easily be ignored. Yet, they are crucial regarding how information is deployed. What do we use the information *for*? Such ignoring is the more likely to happen in conjunction with the second presumed advantage of examinations, because the claim to objectivity can appear to resolve these other problems.

2 Provide clear-cut criteria for assessing success and accountability, free from subjective bias

The capacity for examinations to monitor performance and progress rests on their presumed objectivity. In the struggle for fairness, guarding against the intrusion of subjective notions and bias, the claim is that examinations enable the best means possible for accurate assessment of basic knowledge and skills. Unwin and Yandell note what assessment is presumed to offer:

> a studied impartiality, an objectivity that transcends the messiness of individual identities, interests and interactions, the contingencies of lived experience ... This kind of assessment is the cornerstone of the new technical-rationalist education system since it is what enables inputs and outputs to be measured and compared, judgements to be made and action to be taken.[28]

What seems to be missing from much criticism of the exam culture is awareness of the powerful effect of implanting in young minds the notion that there are straightforward right or wrong answers, regarded as objective. This reinforces the fact/opinion divide discussed in Chapter 2, which disables intelligent debate about reasons for opinions and subtly conveys scientism because only such evidence looks to be objective and, therefore, worth considering.

Moreover, the well-intentioned search for ways of assessing that are fairer to the breadth and depth of education founders on automatic disrespect for anything subjective. Yet, it is the opposite of what democracy needs from its citizens, namely, the capacity to think seriously about and discuss what is *not* straightforward and objective. People need the capacity for discernment regarding what is highly complex, multilayered or emotionally-held. As Unwin and Yandell note in their first myth, which considers that "Learning is linear": "Learning is a much messier, more complicated business, than a linear scale of levels or grades would suggest."[29] Tests have been reified "as if test scores or grades had the same solidity and materiality as say, shoe sizes."[30] One might add that even shoe sizes vary between one manufacturer and another!

The presumed objectivity is challengeable in any case. Rachel Brooks, who examined the examination process as a sociologist, denies that it is objective:

> While educational assessment can be perceived as an entirely objective process … sociological analyses have demonstrated convincingly that it is instead a value-laden social activity which, rather than measuring what is already in existence, creates and shapes what is measured.[31]

Joe Bower discusses a possible reason for this:

> When we try to reduce something that is as magnificently messy as real learning, we always conceal far more than we ever reveal. Ultimately, grading gets assessment wrong because assessment is not a spreadsheet – it is a conversation.[32]

A particular example which can be cited is the discrepancy between what is taught in schools and what is taught in universities. A former colleague told me that on occasions BA undergraduates at Durham University mentioned how they had been advised to forget what they had learnt at A level as they would now be "studying the subject properly." This was strikingly confirmed in an experiment set up by Sam Wineburg involving eight professional historians and eight high-school students. They were given documents relating to the battle of Lexington and asked to rank the documents in order of trustworthiness. The conclusions of the two groups were diametrically opposed![33]

Assessment can get it wrong not only because its claim to be scrupulously fair is false. It fails to prioritise what is most significant because of the passion for measuring everything. Elliott Eisner expressed the problem clearly:

> Not all – perhaps not even most – outcomes of curriculum and instruction are amenable to measurement … Some fields of activity, especially those which are qualitative in character, have no comparable rules and hence are less amenable to quantitative assessment. It is here that evaluation must be made, not primarily by applying a socially defined standard, but by making a human qualitative judgement … it is only in a metaphorical sense that one can measure the extent to which a student has been able to produce an aesthetic object or an expressive narrative. Here standards are inapplicable; here judgement is required.[34]

Once again the search at all costs for objectivity, discussed especially in Chapter 2, uproots what education should really be about. The need is for learning the capacity for judgement.

Unwin and Yandell pick this up as the fourth of their myths concerning learning, namely that "The assessment of Learning is objective and reliable":

> Only in the most trivial cases is assessment merely a matter of measuring. And reliability comes at a cost: the more reliable a test, the less information it can provide about the breadth of a child's learning and development. There is, in other words, an inverse relation between reliability and validity.[35]

This is a massive indictment of over-reliance on examinations. It is interesting that John Katzman, despite being the founder of a business based on the preparation of students for a wide range of standardized tests, has become an outspoken critic: "These tests measure nothing of value. It's just an utter disrespect for educators and kids married to an utter incompetence."[36]

It is true that the marking of an essay will always reflect subjective views unless specific, itemised points must be included, in which case it is back to the presumption of objective assessment. Yet, after all, how can creativity be measured? It cannot be in such a way that disregards anyone's subjective experience. As Nikhil Goyal comments: "We need to stop giving so much emphasis to test scores whether they plummet or escalate. They're artificial, manufactured, and narrow indicators of intelligence."[37]

3 Promote motivation in students to work hard and in teachers to teach effectively

The view of examinations as motivators comes with a big downside. It encourages teachers to teach to the test and students to value only what is examined. As Robinson says, "Only some areas of education lend themselves to being standardised. Many of the most important developments that schools should be encouraging do not."[38]

He notes that "standardized testing has become an obsession in itself ... the pressure is everywhere to teach to the tests and give scant attention to what is not tested." As schools become exam factories, learning becomes limited and people lose sight of the purpose of education.[39] Robinson gives an important quotation from FairTests's *National Resolution on High-Stakes Testing*, which, while it relates to experience in the United States, is applicable everywhere that examinations are overvalued:

> [T]he overreliance on high-stakes standardized testing in state and federal accountability systems is undermining educational quality and equity in US public schools by hampering educators' efforts to focus on the broad range of learning experiences that promote the innovation, creativity, problem solving, collaboration, communication, critical thinking, and deep subject-matter knowledge that will allow students to thrive in a democracy and an increasingly global society and economy.[40]

The dominating examination culture has had the effect of making teachers and their students regard non-measurable subjects as unimportant. Yet, an educated person is someone with wide interests and a spirit of enquiry and thoughtfulness. Whatever the official rulings on the curriculum, the vast majority of children in state schools are *not* receiving a balanced and broadly based education, a subject that will be discussed further in Chapter 8.

4 Aid social mobility through promotion of merit

The role of examinations in social mobility also needs questioning. Stobart's acknowledgement that examinations break down fixed notions of potential has already been mentioned.[41] Yet, once again, damage is done when such positive outcomes fail to consider other matters of importance, especially regarding how acquired skills and knowledge are used.

This question brings into play, above all, character – the values and beliefs by which a person lives. The substance of these are important, as discussed in Chapter 4. Brilliance can be wayward and corrosive; clever people can go most astray. Ability to do a job successfully, of course, matters. When undergoing an operation, a patient's life is dependent on the extreme skill and knowledge of the surgeon. Equally crucial, however, is the surgeon's commitment to humane values and care. These are not to be thought of as some kind of either/or, but as both/and. Over-concentration on merit tends to ignore the latter.

It is worth asking: what is the goal of social mobility? Is it not to enable people to utilise their gifts, expertise and experience for the good of society as well as for themselves? People should not be chained to the expectations of their birth and economic/cultural/social situations. Social mobility is concerned to help people find the best way for them to reach towards their potential as caring and socially-minded citizens. All this requires much more than concentration on merit of a particular nature.

A factor constantly forgotten in official planning of education is, as Robinson puts it, "[p]eople don't come in standard versions."[42] People are unique, so their education cannot be laid down in advance. Education must concern each student's particular talents and capacities, particular background in home and environment of nurture, specific gifts and weaknesses of character. Generalised schemes examining some skills apart from others are likely to misfire regarding actual individuals.

5 Ensure that society has a workforce sufficiently skilled for the modern world

The achievement of workforce goals depends on appreciating what skills and know-how are in fact needed. It is inadequate to presume that the real world, including the business world, needs only the cleverness and skills which formal qualifications recognize. Many are the complaints about graduates' ill-preparedness for the world of work as it actually is today, let alone for what it will be in the future. The impact of Artificial Intelligence will very probably highlight what examinations cannot measure, namely, character, commitment to civilised values, psychological maturity and the capacity to listen and learn and change appropriately according to changing circumstances. Even qualities such as a sense of humour are likely to be needed.

The current system pays attention to what is no longer important. It is failing to prepare pupils for the real world. Andreas Schleicher, Special Adviser on Education Policy at OECD, expressed himself candidly when talking to Robinson:

> The world economy no longer pays you for what you know; Google knows everything ... We see a rapid decline in the demand for routine cognitive skills in our world and the kind of things that are easy to test and easy to teach, the kind of things that are easy to digitise, automate and outsource.[43]

Why prepare children to do what computers can do better? It is a sentiment expressed by a number of writers. But the question mark it puts beside all presumed fair and objective assessment is rarely raised.

Two additional potential outcomes are highly significant.

I Temptation to cheat

The aim to get top results at all costs can actually encourage dishonesty and lack of integrity. On cheating, Unwin and Yandell cite the example of Atlanta, Georgia, which claimed to be a shining example of the *No Child Left Behind* policy's transformation of education in one of the poorest districts in the United States. According to Unwin and Yandell,

> there was a flaw in the success story ... If the increases in the test scores, particularly in schools in the poorest areas, seemed to be too good to be true, that's because they were. The spectacular gains were the product not of better teaching but of something much simpler: cheating.

Teachers resorted to telling pupils the answers or altering what students had written after the papers were collected. "They cheated because of the intolerable pressure on them to meet targets that they knew they could not achieve in any other way."[44]

Rachel Sylvester exposes similar dishonesty operating in the UK in a 2018 article in *The Times*:

> Figures from the Department for Education show that an average of 41 children are permanently excluded from schools in England every day, an increase of 15 percent since last year, but many more are being informally "managed" out of the system. The schools inspectorate, Ofsted, found that 19,000 pupils were removed from the school roll in 2017 just before taking their GCSEs. A quarter of these children appeared on a different school's register and a quarter went into alternative provision, but half simply disappeared. Amanda Spielman, the chief inspector, is convinced that schools are edging out "the most disruptive, hardest to teach children" to bring up their overall results. They are "gaming the system, they've lost sight of what they are here for."[45]

Sylvester concluded the article with: "An education should be judged on the society it fosters not just the results of examinations."[46]

2 Promotion of stress, health and identity problems

Sitting for examinations can cause high levels of stress and contribute to mental and physical health problems. There is growing concern today about the increase in mental health problems, especially amongst teenagers but also younger children. The examination culture is promoting, in response, the therapeutic turn in education, which was discussed in Chapter 6.

Moreover, assessment practices can have a profound effect on pupils' identities. John Couch described the impact the typical education he received had on him and other students:

> It was understood that the seemingly never-ending series of standardised tests we were given would show how "smart" we were, in the process judging us, labelling us, sorting us, and attempting to forecast our future ... We were warned that these tests meant everything and would define us in the eyes of our teachers, families, friends, and future employers. Even then, watching many of my fellow students struggling with those tests, I knew there was something inherently wrong with the way things were.[47]

Examination results can encase a personality within an identity – one denoting failure or success as a person – regarded as factually objective. Character wise, the latter can be as damaging as the former. Lack of self-esteem is serious, but perhaps even more so is the bloated ego. Business is now beginning to recognise that the charismatic whizz-kid may not be as valuable as the team leader.

People need to learn to believe in their own inalienable worth as persons. At the same time, however, they need to develop the capacity for critical as well as affirming self-knowledge. Similarly, they need to work towards extending to others a spirit of generosity towards the identity of the other person, yet retaining the capacity for critical discernment. These are difficult goals, and giving people a measure for comparing themselves with others according to external criteria is profoundly unhelpful. See my discussion of critical affirmation in Chapter 3.

When discussing their second myth, "Learning is context-independent," Unwin and Yandell give a relevant cartoon alongside Einstein's quote: "Everybody is a genius. But if you judge a fish by its ability to climb a tree, it will live its whole life believing that it is stupid."[48] Such lack of trust in people and institutions is a major factor in causing distress because people tend to internalise the lack of trust. It also increases fear, which can push people into becoming automata who just do as they are told, like a machine, failing to use their own sensitivity and experience. This is profoundly discouraging for the flourishing of democracy which seeks to involve every citizen in producing wise government.

Alice Thompson ends her article in *The Times*: "We have failed those waiting for their results because they have been told a lie: that examinations are all that matter."[49] Box 7.2 sums up the anti-educational case against examinations.

Box 7.2 Why examinations are anti-educational

1   Examinations embody and effectively communicate, both explicitly and implicitly, the fact/opinion divide discussed in Chapter 2 – a major fault in the thinking of the West. The exam system is dangerous, therefore, conditioning the teacher and taught, as well as the general public, into a warped understanding of knowledge.

2   Examinations are powerfully distracting. They swallow up huge resources – time, expertise and finance – mostly to the detriment of what schools should be pursuing. They seriously reduce the purpose of education. Through the operation of the null curriculum, they help to disable a balanced education for all.[50]

3   They permit other undesirable features. These include encouragement of dishonesty, promotion of tension resulting in physical and mental ill-health, and failure to give all pupils a positive experience of the foundational values essential for civilised life, let alone a democracy.

4   The exam culture is failing to develop what will be needed in the future. The arrival of the digital age requires not treating students as robots to be stuffed with information but as human beings capable of reflection.

5   A schooling system set on promoting competition and rivalry and power-seeking individuals is actively discouraging democracy. Instead, schools should be prioritising what Queen Elizabeth II called for in her Christmas 2018 television broadcast: "respecting different points of view, coming together ... never losing sight of the bigger picture."[51] Nothing less is worthy of the name of education.

Many people basically agree and sense that radical reform in education is needed, especially regarding the use of examinations. Yet, little in practice seems to be able to change the overall mindset of the times. The problem lies in the unexamined assumptions, such as the four discussed in Part I of this book, which are rarely questioned and therefore are difficult to dislodge – what Tyack and Cuban noted as "the basic grammar of schooling."[52] Their continuing impact keeps the exam culture alive (see Figure 7.1).

A responsible attitude towards examinations

Informal and formal assessment

Formal assessment concerns grading, comparison with other people, publicly-published results and the like. Informal assessment, on the other hand, goes on all the time – that is what learning is about. It is a natural part of doing or writing or saying anything. In conversation we assess what someone has said and agree, disagree or question it. When doing any task, we naturally note whether we are succeeding with it, whether we are coming up against a problem, whether we need to think how to get around a problem, whether we have addressed the problem or not and to what degree we have.

Good teachers are, as Joe Bower told Robinson, assessing both themselves and their pupils all the time:

> I am a very active teacher who assesses students every day, but I threw out my grade book years ago. If we are to find our way and make learning, not grading, the primary focus of school, then we need to abandon our mania for reducing learning and people to numbers.[53]

He abandoned grades, noting that instead of grades being tools for teachers, teachers are now tools used by grades.[54]

If teachers are constantly assessing whether they are communicating or not and what progress their students seem to be making or not, why make such a fuss about compartmentalising themselves and other pupils? It constitutes a waste of time and effort, which is itself very serious, for both are precious resources.

Reasons for some formal assessment

If knowledge itself cannot be dealt with in a unified, measurable manner, should we abandon all forms of formal assessment? There are two reasons why some form of formal assessment is needed:

(i) The importance of developing rigour in thinking beyond dependence on scientific/empirical evidence

To give the impression that there is no distinction between knowledge and lack of knowledge, between discernment and lack of discernment, would be to fall into the relativist trap whereby the question of truth – relating what we think with what is actually the case, whatever we may happen to think – is ignored. The lure of postmodernism needs resisting. In subjects like the sciences and maths, logic and scientific/empirical evidence denote clearly that there are right and wrong answers to many questions, although very far from all. The ubiquity of latent scientism will always preserve a sense of truth in these areas. Awareness of

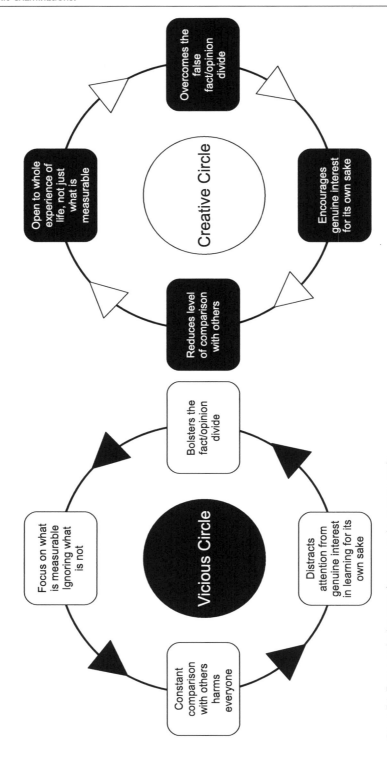

Figure 7.1 Exams and education: A vicious and a creative circle

levels of understanding in other subjects cannot be thus neatly listed, yet the difference between them is still hugely important. It is the purpose of education to try to communicate these subjects to students and develop the skills necessary for perceiving them. Some form of formal assessment requiring such discernment can correct wrong impressions here.

(ii) The need to provide information to potential future employers

There is the obvious need that the running of any society has to consider – the appropriate employment of people in work for which they have the aptitude, knowledge and skills necessary for efficiency. A high view of education can still, and must, find a place for what Caplan, whose ideas were discussed in Chapter 6, describes as the *signalling* role of educa-tion, which is just a special case of what economists call "statistical discrimination": using true-on-average stereotypes to save time and money.[55] A final examination at the end of schooling makes public a certain level of intellect and expertise, which can serve as a rough guide for employers to consider. In a perceptive passage he notes that, however desirable it might be to take each individual applying for a job seriously, the sheer scale of the problem of finding the right employees for jobs prohibits that level of individual attention. Instead, society trusts a signalling scheme in which individuals are matched up against a presumed norm. This works, so Caplan advocates that the education that legitimises such signalling needs to continue.

Overemphasis on externally-judged qualifications should be avoided, but to rely on interviews alone is unrealistic when very large numbers of candidates for jobs are potentially possible. Sheer time constraints demand a weeding-out process. Interviews supported by qualifications suggests a practical way forward. There is no need for formal testing to accompany the whole of a pupil's career in school. Finland manages very well educationally with a policy of holding just one final examination.[56]

Suggestions for educationally valuable assessment

Given that some form of formal assessment is required, what should it look like? As already pointed out, future society is unlikely to want human robots. Rather, there will be a need for human beings who can think for themselves, who value others in a spirit of generosity and goodwill, and who show the resilience and adaptability required to cope with an ever-chan-ging and complex world. In terms of subject-knowledge, future-focused education means not emphasising so-called facts, which can be easily ascertained and kept up-to-date via a computer, but rather understanding and discernment.

Take history as an example. It is hugely important that people develop a sense of history, an awareness that the present has emerged out of the past, and an understanding that there is a huge amount to be learnt from the mistakes of the past as well as from its outstanding achievements. All this depends on the capacity to search for and work towards a proper understanding of the past and not rest content with a figment of imagination about it. The search for truth is essential. That truth, because it is complex and necessarily non-demon-strable beyond changeability, will never be able to be captured in lists of actual informa-tion, such as how history used to be taught, thereby boring generations of students.

When I taught history in a secondary school, I experimented with a different approach for examinations. I set a paper, for example, around a topic quite unknown to the students. I provided them with three or four source materials and asked them to evaluate the sources for obvious bias and likely truth content. The students could come up with a summary of how they thought the topic should be understood. Students found this both interesting and refreshing. It revealed very clearly those who had already begun to think like historians. It did not rely on memory work but on close reading of a text and on relating clues to each other in trying to resolve a mystery; it drew on detective skills. In the process it showed up levels of individual bias that students may have had. This approach can work just as well with much younger children. Elizabeth Ashton, for example, used to do similar work with ten- and eleven-year-olds exploring the problem of poverty in Victorian England.[57]

Another form of examination that I found worked very well was inviting pupils to be the examiner. They were presented with three or four different views on a topic they had studied and asked to adjudicate the views for knowledge, understanding and a practical way forward. It was quite illuminating. The structure did require some memory skills, but not of the type needed for a context-free quiz, but what is actually necessary in day-to-day living. It required the capacity to discern regarding persons and situations.

The point about these types of examination question is that they are educative in themselves. They constitute one of the ways of enabling students to learn. For Couch, quoted above, an examination question was life changing. At the University of California, Riverside, one of his physics classes had a final examination with only one question – and one not directly addressed before in any lecture or textbook.[58] It was a shock for all those sitting the examination. It caused Couch to question the complete basis of the education he had received.

In situations where official grading cannot be avoided, sharing the examining with pupils offers an educational way forward. Thus Bower used this technique by asking students to grade themselves and found that his own assessment and theirs usually were quite close. In any case, it resulted in students taking seriously their own progress. Timothy Walker, discussing how the Finnish education system operates, notes how students share in grade giving – *perustella*; they are asked to justify what they have said or written. Walker comments that, in this way, success in examinations has become so closely aligned with education as to be almost its equivalent.[59]

The concept of *continuous assessment* offers for many an alternative to written examinations. As Goyal argues, assessment and portfolios are different from testing:

> A test is used to tell whether a student memorised and regurgitated enough material. An assessment, on the other hand, is a process of evaluating, documenting, and reflecting. Many schools are using digital portfolios to showcase students' work – essays, videos, and presentations.[60]

Portfolios of work are, indeed, excellent for the final end-of-schooling assessment.

To put too much emphasis on continuous assessment can, however, chain both students and teachers to the examination system once again. It takes a lot of time and effort which can be better spent on actual learning. So when practised, continuous assessment needs to be kept low-key and fluid. Moreover. forms of dishonesty can enter in if it is taken too seriously. Searching the internet for essays, for example, is a practice difficult to eradicate.

The word *continuous* itself is ominous, as though everything is being watched and noted for purposes of grading. Even what is said or how a student contributes to discussion can be monitored. Instead, we need to let assessment just happen almost unconsciously; it is a natural and unavoidable part of learning and teaching. To focus on it makes it a form of surveillance, which is unhelpful for the true purpose of education as understood in Chapter 6.

Concluding thoughts

Formal assessment should be kept in its properly lowly place, because in itself it is neither forwarding knowledge and wisdom, which is the purpose of education, nor is it helping the true self-esteem and well-being of children and students. The exam culture is a major cause of failure of the education system actually to educate.

The temptations posed by an exam culture are, indeed, great. The pull of the *zeitgeist* is so strong that we should be careful of conceding too much to the over-desire to measure, compare and standardise achievement.

One of the most damning indictments of the examination system is a comment by Ian Small, late Head of the highly successful Bootham School. Regarding its place near the top of the League Tables, he told the *Times Educational Supplement* that he was ambivalent: "The figures are accurate, but I don't believe in them because I don't know what they mean."[61] The interviewer noted that Small endeavoured to give his students indices other than examination scores to measure their self-worth. He directed plays and pumped resources into the Music department. According to Small, "It's about recognising the light in every child."[62]

Notes

1 E. Holmes. 1911. *What Is and What Might Be*. Constable. Quoted by A. Unwin & J. Yandell. 2016. *Rethinking Education*. New Internationalist. p. 102.
2 J.-A. Baird, T. Isaacs, D. Opposs & L. Gray (Eds.). 2018. *Examination Standards: How Measures and Meanings Differ Around the World*. UCL Institute of Education Press.
3 Northcote-Trevelyan Report [*Report on the Organisation of the Permanent Civil Service*]. 1854. https://www.civilservant.org.uk/library/1854_Northcote_Trevelyan_Report.pdf
4 See "Our Heritage." 2020. Cambridge Assessment. https://www.cambridgeassessment.org.uk/about-us/who-we-are/our-heritage
5 R. Sylvester & A. Thomson. 2017. "Amanda Spielman Interview: 'There Are Children in this Country for Whom British Values are Meaningless.'" *The Times*. December 16.
6 A. Thompson. 2018. "It's a Bit Late Now to Say Examinations Aren't Everything." *The Times*. August 15.
7 N. Woolcock. 2018. "Children Drilled for Examinations from Age of 11." *The Times*. August 22.
8 F. Coffield & B. Williamson. 2012. *From Exam Factories to Communities of Discovery: The Democratic Route*. UCL Institute of Education Press. p. 46.
9 R. Brooks. 2019. *Education and Society: Places, Policies, Processes*. Macmillan International & Red Globe Press. p. 159. She notes: "The origins of high-stakes testing can be traced back to the early 1980s in the USA. A key moment was the publication of a report entitled 'Nation At Risk: The Imperative for Education Reform.'" p. 160.
10 D. Ravitch. 2010. "Why I Changed My Mind about School Reform" *Wall Street Journal*. March 9. p. 2. Quoted by Unwin & Yandell. *Rethinking Education*. p. 48.
11 D. Ravitch. 2013. *Reign of Error: The Hoax of the Privatization Movement and the Danger to America's Public Schools*. Alfred A. Knopf.
12 A. Kamenetz. 2015. *The Test: Why Our Schools Are Obsessed With Standardized Testing — But You Don't Have to Be*. Public Affairs.
13 R. Dore. 1976. *The Diploma Disease: Education Qualification and Development*. Allen & Unwin.
14 Unwin & Yandell. *Rethinking Education*. p. 19.
15 "New School Grades: Ofsted has a New Inspection Formula, but Examinations Still Matter." 2018. *The Times*. October 12.
16 G. Stobart. 2008. *Testing Times: The Uses and Abuses of Assessment*. Routledge.
17 K. Robinson. 2015. *Creative Schools*. Penguin Books. p. 170.
18 Ibid. p. 180f.
19 Ibid. p. 167. The Organisation for Economic Co-operation and Development is hugely influential.
20 T. Little. 2015. *An Intelligent Person's Guide to Education*. Bloomsbury. p. 29f.

21 Unwin & Yandell. *Rethinking Education.* p. 103.
22 Ibid. p. 107.
23 Ibid. p. 108.
24 Ibid.
25 C. Dickens. 1854. *Hard Times.* Dickens Journals Online. http://www.djo.org.uk/household-words/volume-ix/page-141.html
26 A. Seldon. 2018. *The Fourth Education Revolution.* University of Buckingham Press. p. 22.
27 Robinson. *Creative Schools.* p. 161.
28 Unwin & Yandell. *Rethinking Education.* p. 104.
29 Ibid. p. 105.
30 Ibid. p.106.
31 Brooks. *Education and Society.* p. 155.
32 Quoted in Robinson. *Creative Schools.* p. 172.
33 S. Wineburg. 1991. "On the Reading of Historical Texts. Notes on the Breach between School and Academy." *American Educational Research Journal* 28, no. 3. pp. 495–519. Quoted in Unwin & Yandell. *Rethinking Education.* p. 75.
34 E. W. Eisner. [1967] 2004. "Educational Objectives – Help or Hindrance?" In D. J. Flanders & S. J. Thornton (Eds.). *The Curriculum Studies Reader.* 2nd ed. pp. 85–92. Routledge.
35 Unwin & Yandell. *Rethinking Education.* p. 108f.
36 John Katzman, co-founder of *The Princeton Review,* quoted in Robinson. *Creative Schools.* p. 164. Robinson also quotes Monty Neill, executive director of FairTest: The National Center for Fair and Open Testing: "The tests don't measure very much of what's important, and they measure in a very narrow way." Ibid. p. 161.
37 N. Goyal. 2016. *Schools on Trial.* Doubleday. p. 65.
38 Robinson. *Creative Schools.* p. 160.
39 Ibid. p. 161.
40 "National Resolution on High-Stakes Testing." 2015. FairTest: The National Center for Fair and Open Testing. http://fairtest.org/national-resolution-highstakes-testing. Quoted in Ibid. p. 162f.
41 Stobart. *Testing Times.*
42 Robinson. *Creative Schools.* p. 160.
43 Robinson interview of A. Schleicher, Director for Education and Skills and Special Adviser on Education Policy to the Secretary-General at the OECD (Organisation for Economic Cooperation and Development). Quoted in Ibid. p. 168.
44 Unwin & Yandell. *Rethinking Education.* p. 111f.
45 R. Sylvester. 2018. "Schools are Cheating with Their GCSE Results." *The Times.* August 21.
46 Ibid. Another article in *The Times* notes that "TeachFirst found that 10.3 percent of pupils on free school meals passed the English baccalaureate [in 2017], while 10.7 percent had faced a permanent or temporary exclusion." B. King. 2018. "Poor Teenagers More Likely to be Excluded than Get Five Good Passes." *The Times.* August 22.
47 J. Couch with J. Towne. 2018. *Rewiring Education: How Technology Can Unlock Every Student's Potential.* BenBella Books. p. 1f.
48 Unwin & Yandell. *Rethinking Education.* p. 107.
49 A. Thompson. "It's a Bit Late Now…"
50 The null curriculum is discussed in Chapter 8.
51 Queen Elizabeth II. 2018. "The Queen's Christmas Broadcast 2018." The Royal Family. https://www.royal.uk/queens-christmas-broadcast-2018
52 D. Tyack & L. Cuban. 1995. *Tinkering Toward Utopia: A Century of Public School Reform.* Harvard University Press.
53 Bower quoted in Robinson *Creative Schools.* p. 172.
54 J. Bower & P. L. Thomas. 2013. *De-testing and De-grading Schools: Authentic Alternatives in Accountability and Standardization.* Peter Lang.
55 B. Caplan. 2018. *The Case Against Education: Why the Education System is a Waste of Time and Money.* Princeton University Press. p. 15.
56 See P. Butler. 2016. "No Grammar Schools, Lots of Play: The Secrets of Europe's Top Education System." *Guardian.* September 20. https://www.the guardian.com/education/2016/sep/20/grammar-schools-play-europe-top-education-system-finland-daycare

57 Conversation with Dr. Elizabeth Ashton, who showed author examples of what the children produced.
58 Couch. *Rewiring Education*. p. 4.
59 T. D. Walker. 2017. *Teach Like Finland: 33 Simple Strategies for Joyful Classrooms*. W. W. Norton.
60 Goyal. *Schools on Trial*. p. 65f.
61 "Ian Small: Gentle and Unaffected Headmaster of Bootham School in York, Whose Love of Acting Highlighted an Inner Flamboyance." 2018. *The Times*. December 12.
62 Ibid.

Chapter 8

Resolving the curriculum nightmare?

Once liberated from the constricting notion that learners have to be tested regularly to show what they have learnt or make sure they are being taught properly, we can turn to what they should be learning. The word *curriculum* is broadly used to denote this aspect of education. It is derived from a Latin word meaning "a race" or "the course of a race," which in turn derives from the verb *currere*: "to run/to proceed."[1] As Brighouse and Woods note, there are two ways of looking at the curriculum: "the first from the perspective of the subject, the second in the round – that is to say everything school does."[2] On the whole, the content of learning is usually what people mean by the curriculum, so this chapter will focus on Brighouse and Woods's first perspective.

The curriculum as a contested area

The content of learning has become a contested area, as discussed in Chapter 6. Furedi neatly summarised how he sees the problems and solutions:

> Firstly, education needs to become depoliticised: politicians need to be discouraged from regarding the curriculum as their platform for making statements. Secondly, society needs to challenge the tendency to downsize the status of knowledge and of standards … Thirdly, we need to take children more seriously, uphold their capacity

to engage with knowledge and provide them with a challenging educational environment.

Developing these points I would like to add:

1 The politization of education is profoundly mistaken

The role of politicians cannot be entirely divorced from what happens in education because of the administrative and financial role of government. The government has to retain responsibility for the overall structure nationally, for which appropriate legislation is needed to hold it in place. Political input into education is therefore unavoidable and is not necessarily to be distanced; it depends on whether the involvement supports genuinely educational goals or not. What is imperative is that education does not become a political football and educational reasons are foremost in deciding what to do. For education can only yield its true treasures if it can be itself. It must retain its integrity and not be at the whim of extra-educational causes, however worthy they may be.

From a political point of view centred on the concept of anti-elitism, subject-based teaching is under attack. Furedi strongly confronts this emphasis:

> A ... destructive trend haunting education is the enthronement of philistinism in pedagogy. The striving for standards of excellence is frequently condemned as elitist by apparently enlightened educators. Forms of education that really challenge children and which some find difficult are denounced for not being inclusive. There have always been philistine influences in education but it is only in recent times that anti-intellectual ideals are self-consciously promoted by educators. The corrosive effect of anti-elitist sentiments is evident in all the subjects discussed by authors in [*The Corruption of the Curriculum*].[3]

The book has chapters on the teaching of English, geography, history, foreign languages, maths and science, which all represent a serious indictment of what has been happening in schools. Furedi considers that: "Over the past two decades the school curriculum has become estranged from the challenge of educating children ... issues that are integral to education have become subordinate to the imperative of social engineering and political expediency."[4]

The removal of politicisation will meet considerable resistance, even though the need for reform in education is acknowledged. Alex Moore argues, "The rate and scale of change in the wider socio-economic world has brought us to a place from which we can – and perhaps must – contemplate some radical curriculum possibilities and changes."[5] Many educationalists, however, regard opponents as politically motivated. Moore draws attention to "the fundamental political and ideological debates that underpin curriculum theory, policy and design." He sees everywhere a political choice at work. Thus, he regards traditional curricula as "despite much rhetoric to the contrary, locked into a time and mood when education was primarily aimed at a small elite."[6] He notes: "The way in which ubiquitous neoliberal discourses of self, alongside just-about-compatible conservative discourses of tradition, have dominated – and continue to dominate – curriculum development and design in England, the USA and some Western European countries in particular."[7] Many advocates of the knowledge-based curriculum note, however, an opposite danger – this time from the impact of anti-elitism. Barrett and Rata express it like this: "We recognise that any challenge to the sociology of education's widely accepted positioning of knowledge and curriculum as instruments that simply reproduce educational and social inequality is likely to be read by many as reactionary, conservative or elitist."[8] Yet, educationalists, of whatever political persuasion, should seek reform of education on genuinely educational grounds.

2 The debasing of the concept of knowledge is serious

To leave the transmission and discovery of knowledge out of what constitutes education, as discussed in Chapter 6, makes a travesty of it. To quote Michael Young, there is "knowledge that is 'worth knowing,' in every field and subject, and it is the right of all children, regardless of what may be their initial resistance, to have access to it."[9] Similarly, Standish and Cuthbert represent a countervailing view to the low esteem in which knowledge is held by noting that the priorities of schools need to be concerned with broadening access to valued knowledge.

What is important in the reinstatement of the importance of knowledge is bringing to the fore the concept of sharing in a search for knowledge. The notion that knowledge is like a definite, objective bloc of material to be handed on needs to be resisted. As Unwin and Yandell note, "A curriculum cannot simply be delivered like a sack of rice."[10] This is very different from the traditionalist notion, encapsulated by a statement by Michael Gove when he was Education Secretary in the UK, that we should concentrate on providing "a world-class curriculum that will help teachers, parents and children know what children should learn at what age."[11] This assumes that adults *can* know what children should learn. Gove thus undermines a genuine understanding of knowledge, and this is a direct effect of the fact/opinion divide, discussed in Chapter 2, which puts facts on a pedestal by comparison with "mere" opinion. In reality, the search for knowledge is unending with enormous difficulties to be surmounted in becoming certain of it. All this needs to be shared with pupils and is remote from so much typical teaching, especially teaching to the test, which is declamatory and claims to be based on fact.

The emphasis on the seeking of knowledge carries with it an important corollary. It is essential to understand that children should want to study for study's own sake, for learning's sake, not for the sake of attaining extraneous ends, however laudable in themselves – a further reason for distancing political agendas.

3 A low opinion of the capacities of many children lies behind much failure in education

Furedi's critique of what he terms the "therapeutic turn in education" was discussed in Chapter 3. He may have reacted over-sharply regarding attempts to make students feel good and on the positive effects of praise. Yet, in a society that frequently treats people as automata, may it not be good to acknowledge that education is dealing with persons who have feelings? Indisputably, praise can achieve results. One of the greatest motivators within a classroom situation is the creation of a culture of success. As a headteacher, Stuart Freed, told me:

> Nothing succeeds like success! Find something to praise and use it as a springboard to improve something less well done. When I was teaching electronics, my students had to learn how to solder. It's a medium level skill that many youngsters find challenging. Once demonstrated, it has to be developed through practice. If several joints are done poorly and a couple well, focus on those, explain how the judgement is made, ascertain why they are better and watch how additional joints are improved.[12]

He found that this approach really worked. Of course, indiscriminate praise should be avoided; praise should always be deserved. It then can give a feeling of confidence to the learner, who is thus taken seriously as a person. It achieves what Furedi wants, namely, respect for the child.

A major reason for low expectations of students has been overemphasis on cognitive skills which can be measured. Many children do not do very well, hence the importance of not only challenging traditional notions of IQ in favour of appreciating different aspects of intelligence and understanding – see below for details of such alternatives – but also of down-positioning the examination culture. Measurement revolves around comparing children with each other; it glorifies competition and takes attention away from what matters, namely, the knowledge itself. Concern about measured success or failure can so easily take centre-stage. The presumption of the importance of measurement itself makes a travesty of education.

I want to add an additional point to Furedi's three specific points,

4 The curriculum needs to nurture the foundational values of truth, fairness, compassion and beauty

As discussed in Chapter 4, the pursuit of truth must be especially to the fore; the way in which the curriculum is presented needs to share with students concern for truth. As Bernard Williams puts it "Truth is the basis for the authority of scholarship, at all levels of education." Yet, dogmatic stances should be avoided. He goes on to note: "Nevertheless, scholars must also live with an understanding of the fallibility of our accounts of truth."[13] Education, therefore, must also acknowledge the role of uncertainty and controversy, yet within a spirit of reliance on *partial and provisional* certainty, which I argued in Chapter 2 is needed in order to act.

Education must also be concerned with how to think ethically. *Social justice*, which has such political associations, can be better reached via concentrating on nurturing students in the foundational values of fairness and compassion. They should internalise these values and learn to apply them in all the varied circumstances of their lives and their world. Working towards social justice requires not just concern with legislative approaches but with educating feelings. Fairness and compassion are at the heart of striving to create a more just world. Concern for beauty also has its part to play. Drab, ugly surroundings tend to stifle the spirit, whilst beauty enhances it, bringing together cognitive and affective capacities.

Is the notion of a core curriculum for everyone educationally tenable?

A core curriculum can be thought of as a universal, structured, pre-ordained approach to the teaching of content; it lays down what children should learn and at what age. In most countries the core curriculum of subjects is legally-required for all schools. The main reason for this has probably always been a practical one: how to cope with mass education and the need for knowledgeable teachers. The overall, explicit rationale, however, is to provide a broad and balanced education for all. It appears to be a sound notion – working towards inclusivity, learning what is needed for society and using time and resources efficiently. One might ask: what can be the matter with that? Yet, the chapter will argue that we should question this for at least three reasons.

1 Is it educationally effective?

To require learners to learn what is presented to them, as it were from on high, is to court disaster. It naturally freezes up the spirits of curiosity, interest and excitement in the pursuit of a self-chosen goal. Enlightenment, and therefore understanding, is a more deeply personal experience. Similarly, the top-down approach ignores the natural detective capacities, by which we learn most effectively, and the sense of achievement in the search for knowledge. Learning happens when the learner can see the significance of the learning – motivation, choice, freedom to pursue and, if necessary, change tack.

The very notion of a core curriculum to be taught to all is, thus, at loggerheads with Dewey's key point about learning. Anything truly and deeply learnt involves the choice and willpower of the learner. Pushing a given curriculum on all children makes impossible an education system that honours Dewey, whose theory is discussed in Chapter 6.

2 Does the imposition of a curriculum undermine responsible educational development?

It can be argued that insistence on a core curriculum is a major factor in *disabling* education for democracy. It has a levelling effect which deprives pupils from developing as the unique individuals they are. They are taught to relate to what is presented to them, not to think and make decisions for themselves. Unwin and Yandell quote Edmond Holmes, who identified the effects of a centralised curriculum focusing on skills and factual knowledge enforced through testing and inspection: "Within such a system, there is no space for creativity, no space for dialogue, no space to explore and exploit the interests and experiences that the learners bring with them. Schooling is a transmission process driven by fear."[14] Perhaps *fear* is too strong a word, yet fear of failure to reach standards set by society can be powerful. This is especially so when an examination culture is operating and examination results carry important consequences (see Figure 8.1).

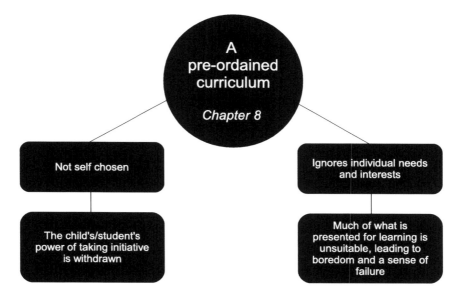

Figure 8.1 What's problematic about a pre-ordained curriculum?

3 Should the hornet's nest of difficult questions concerning competition between subjects be tolerated?

There are many difficult questions. Which subjects should be on the curriculum? How much time should each be given? What resources – both human and material – should be dedicated to each subject? The answers to these questions reflect the general status of each subject. We create and perpetuate the conditions of the competitive marketplace. Time spent on one subject is time not spent on something else. The endlessly stated high intentions of providing pupils with a rounded education may be rendered hopeless by our insisting on prioritising certain aspects of education which operate against such a rounded education.

What is actually delivered in schools comes close to how Robinson summarises the current most common priorities:

> At the top are maths, languages, and sciences. Next are the humanities, history, geography, and sometimes social studies and religion. At the bottom are the arts and physical education. "The arts" usually mean music and the visual arts. Drama, when it is taught at all, is usually deemed the lowliest art, except for dance, which is a rarity in most systems.[15]

The introduction in the UK of the ill-named English Baccalaureate is making this situation worse. Its emphasis on the core subjects – English, science, mathematics, a foreign language and either history or geography – is the most recent expression of the explicit curriculum. Coffield and Williamson argue that it represents a reactionary view of the curriculum which "will sideline (and so devalue) subjects like Art, Music, Physical Education, Vocational Education and Technology, which should be integral to everyone's initial education."[16]

In order to help sort out this hornet's nest concerning content, I shall discuss three particular difficulties.

1 The need to guard against a disjointed curriculum

The curriculum has traditionally been subject-based, and for good reason. As Unwin and Yandell argue, "The divisions between disciplines are not simply arbitrary."[17] They represent huge investment of intellectual enquiry. They also constitute one of the great achievements of the West. Children may be considered deprived who are not encouraged to have access to the knowledge and understanding embodied in these disciplines.

A curriculum organised around subjects, however, can easily teach the false notion of the separation of subjects, as though they have nothing to do with each other. Unwin and Yandell note how "the subjects appear on a secondary student's timetable: Tuesday morning, Biology; Wednesday afternoon, Geography. One effect of this is to discourage students from making connections between their learning in different areas of the curriculum."[18] A compartmentalised understanding of knowledge (or rather misunderstanding) is the result for so many who fail to think holistically. Dewey's comment is highly relevant. Looking back on the effects of this required subject-division, he wrote:

> One trouble is that the subject-matter in question was learned in isolation; it was put, as it were, in a water-tight compartment. When the question is asked, then, what has

become of it, where has it gone to, the right answer is that it is still there in the special compartment in which it was originally stowed away ... it is not available under the actual conditions of life.[19]

From a specifically educational point of view, however, Ken Robinson considers that the conventional idea of an academic subject is too limiting because *subjects* suggest discrete areas of knowledge, edged by clear, permanent boundaries. The world is not divided up into compartments, so neither must education be. Robinson continues:

In practice, knowledge in all its forms continues to evolve outside schools, the boundaries between different subjects constantly overlap ... in a sense, there is really no such thing as an academic subject. There are only academic ways of looking at things. Academic work is a mode of analysis and it can be applied to anything: foreign languages or particle physics, poetry or geology.[20]

Some educationalists have provided alternatives to subjects as a way of organising the curriculum. Charles Fadel, founder of the Centre for Curriculum Redesign in Boston, MA, considers that education curricula need to be deeply redesigned around four dimensions: Knowledge, Skills, Character and Meta-Learning.[21] His reasons echo those of many of the educationalists discussed above, namely, as a response to the sudden growth in societal and human capital needs, because the world of the twenty-first century bears little resemblance to that of the nineteenth, adapting to twenty-first century needs means revisiting each dimension and the interplay between them.[22]

Howard Gardner developed the notion of the different aptitudes which schools should develop.[23] He defined seven different types of intelligences: musical-rhythmic, visual-spatial, verbal-linguistic, logical-mathematical, bodily-kinaesthetic, intrapersonal and interpersonal. The list is not a hard-and-fast one. Gardner has since given consideration to adding "naturalistic – the ability to recognise flora and fauna and to make productive use of nature" and perhaps "existential intelligence or spirituality."[24] Gardner's theory has not received universal support, but it has helpfully extended the range of abilities with which many schools are concerned. Anthony Seldon, when Head of Wellington College in the UK, took up the notion in a different way: "We prefer the four couplet model of the 'eight aptitudes' ... namely, 'logical' and 'linguistic,' 'personal' and 'social,' 'cultural/creative' and 'physical,' and 'spiritual' and 'moral.'"[25]

It is interesting to compare this with an important initiative for reform set up by the RSA entitled *Opening Minds*. It organises learning around five main competencies: learning, citizenship, relating to people, managing situations and managing information. These competences are broad areas of capability, developed in classrooms through a mixture of instruction and practical experience.[26] Each of the five key competences contain a number of individual competences, which are expressed in terms of what a school student could achieve having progressed through the curriculum.

A more recent approach is built around what is termed the *Five Pillars of the Mind*.[27] Tokuhama-Espinosa proposes replacing antiquated curriculum models with neurologically anchored "pillars." Starting from research into pre-literacy and pre-numeracy skills, she found that 16 neuronal networks are needed. Subsequently she discovered that these 16 fell into just five distinct types of studies.[28] "Everything humans learn is either a symbol and/or a pattern and/or an expression of order and/or a category and/or a relationship."[29]

A curriculum designed around these pillars would correspond precisely to the way in which our brains work and how they come to terms with material given and organise it, networking to form ever more connections. Patricia Wolfe, author of *Brain Matters*, describes Tokuhama-Espinosa's book as "cutting-edge ... Teaching relationships using the five broad pillars makes infinitely more sense in this day when most content can be found by 'Googling.'"[30] Ideally, Tokuhama-Espinosa wants the pillars approach to replace the traditional curriculum: "In this completely revamped curricular model, students would have five classes a day, with each class devoted to one pillar across all areas of study."[31]

> The imagined benefits are vast: natural trans-discipline instruction; reduced content load; flexible learning for all students working towards their strengths; better diagnosis of learning problems; higher probability of differentiation; elimination of age as a criterion for grade work; and greatly reduced scheduling problems – no more infighting about which subject teacher gets the early morning slot! But the required changes to reap those benefits would also be far-reaching ... This makes its immediate use unlikely.[32]

What the competency approach may not offer is the depth of understanding developed within subjects. Standish and Cuthbert discuss this question, and they quote Leesa Wheelahan who "observes that while competency-based education provides students with access to content it does not offer access to 'systems of meaning in disciplinary knowledge.'"[33] She suggests that where students are denied access to disciplinary knowledge, class divisions are likely to be reinforced because "unless students have access to the generative principles of disciplinary knowledge, they are not able to transcend the particular context."[34] The political point Wheelahan incorporates may or may not be valid, but an understanding of methodology, its strengths and its weaknesses undoubtedly broadens horizons for students and enables them not to be so limited by their inherited culture.

What is crucial, of course, is the way that subjects are taught. At their best they share with students questions concerning truth and evidence and integrity in the use of knowledge. Often subject teaching has been closely associated with the transmission of factual material in which questions concerning the presumed facts are not presented at all. This deficiency is serious. The important question is not so much whether we teach the Tudors or WWI or the exploits of Genghis Khan, but how can we avoid indoctrination in the way we present material? For example, how do we avoid giving an imperialist or an anti-imperialist understanding? Neutrality is not possible. See the section below on indoctrination.

Instead, we need to help students think about issues, for example, by allowing them access to seemingly contradictory materials. I well remember how history came alive for a class when I was teaching on the English Civil War. One week I rigorously put across a Royalist perspective. I followed it the next week with an equally rigorous Roundhead viewpoint. They learnt that history can be manipulated, that it is not easy to come by the truth or decide which side should be taken in disputes, that consequences can be of enormous significance, that compromise – so far from being something to be scorned – is essential for civilised life together because people do have different ideals and needs and interests. What is needed is the capacity for educated judgement. These are lessons which are extraordinarily important for the flourishing of democracy.

Moreover, it should be noted that the false separation of subjects into different compartments can to some extent be surmounted. Just because knowledge is organised under

Indian parable of the elephant and the six blind men who feel what it is in different ways. All are right to a certain extent, but limited and they fail to get a picture of the elephant as a whole.

Side
"This is a wall"

Ear
"This is a fan"

Tail
"This is a rope"

Tusk
"This is a spear"

Leg
"This is a pillar"

Trunk
"This is a snake"

Figure 8.2 Truth seen from different perspectives

subject headings does not mean that knowledge is disconnected. Constant reference to other subjects can help. Geoff Scargill, a headmaster, makes the sensible suggestion of a specifically linking lesson every week in secondary schools.[35] It is possible, indeed necessary, to do what Coleridge asked for, namely, to "distinguish without separating."[36] The hand can be distinguished from the body without being separated from it. History is not the same as geography, but it does not have to be artificially disconnected. It is important to note that different perspectives on a theme do not necessarily denote incongruity (see Figure 8.2).

There have also been attempts to get round this problem by emphasis on multi-disciplinary work and projects. W. H. Kilpatrick, a colleague of Dewey at Columbia University, wrote *The Project Method* in 1918. As Pring notes, "[Kilpatrick] translated Dewey's educational ideas into a curriculum in which the practical and interdisciplinary *project* provided the relevant interest to motivate the learner, while initiating the learner into the different kinds of knowledge relevant to the project's solution."[37]

It needs also to be borne in mind that there is no need for rigidity regarding how subjects are presented. Jerome Bruner advocated the spiral curriculum. Quoting Bruner, Gary Thomas writes: "One starts somewhere – where the learner *is* – then the teacher should revisit these basic ideas repeatedly, building on them."[38] Ted Wragg has put forward the idea of the "cubic curriculum" – i.e., three-dimensional with subjects, cross-curricular themes and different teaching styles, such as discovery, observation, teamwork, demonstration or practice. Thomas comments:

> The important point about Wragg's cubic model and Bruner's serial one before it is that there is no either/or about the way the curriculum is conceived. It is not either subject knowledge or the development of imagination through project work. Rather, it is a question of integrating forms of information and styles of learning in such a way that the learner learns usefully and meaningfully, with understanding.[39]

2 The need to enquire in depth as to the priorities adopted in the curriculum

What is more difficult to resolve than the disjointed curriculum is the question of priorities in content. In practice certain subjects are simply assumed to be truly core subjects at the centre of the constellation. Others are admitted from time to time on the basis of the popularity of certain ideas or at the behest of forceful people. I know of a primary school which favoured boxing as a helpful way of teaching self-discipline. Another made drama a top priority because the Head happened to be a former actress. Most people would probably agree that such subjects are not essential for all. But which are?

The prioritising of certain subjects over others reflects value judgements which are questionable. Instead of assuming that every child needs to do certain subjects, we should be asking: do they? In order to make this section as incisive as possible, I want to consider the role of three subjects: (i) one commonly of high status (mathematics), (ii) one in the middle (history) and (iii) one of low status (music).

(i) Mathematics

Does the high status of mathematics in schools need challenging? Huge disquiet is expressed about shortages of maths teachers because it is assumed that every child must persevere with the subject, if possible, throughout their school careers. The question why is rarely raised.[40]

Sir Martin Taylor, chairman of the Royal Society's Vision Committee, said: "Science and mathematics are at the absolute heart of modern life … [They] also provide the foundations for the UK's future economic prosperity."[41] Of course, maths and science are crucially important both for modern life and for the economy, but are they the most important priorities? The Royal Society clearly thinks they are in that no mention is made of anything else as being at the absolute heart of modern life. This is a good example of how, without explicitly claiming priority, it is implied. This is how the status of subjects in schools becomes established, not by proper overview of all subjects and wrestling with all potential priorities, but by pressure groups articulating their specific concerns in a way that claims their importance without mentioning the possibility of other voices and concerns.

The question remains: does the importance of maths warrant every student studying maths throughout their school careers, especially when it is at the expense of other subjects? When thinking about priorities, consideration must be given to the consequences regarding what is left out.[42] By insisting on so many hours a week on, say, maths, we are effectively depriving pupils of similar time being devoted to so many other subjects, including the one to which I will turn now.

(ii) History

It is possible to argue that an understanding of history is crucial for responsible citizenship to avoid unnecessarily negative judgments concerning the past and the role of tradition. If it is crucial, then why should history be starved of time and resources? The importance of teaching disciplinary knowledge regarding history for education into democracy has been clearly and persuasively discussed by Christine Counsell, a leading curriculum expert who is, at the time of writing, a member of Ofsted's curriculum advisory panel. I will quote at some length from her chapter "History" in *What Should Schools Teach?*[43]

Counsell begins by noting:

> Without knowledge of a collective past, we can neither think nor act socially or politi-
> cally. This is why knowledge of history is emancipatory. Only when young people can
> generalise appropriately, draw on enough precedent to give explanatory power to their
> arguments, and share enough common terms of reference to challenge the grounds of
> *others'* generalisations and arguments, can they hope to engage with educated discourse
> and especially serious political discourse.

She then explains just why teaching history should not be conveying a series of presumed
historical facts to be memorised:

> While many facts are known incontrovertibly (we really do know that the Battle of
> Hastings occurred in 1066 and that the Muslims first ruling Cordoba were exiles from
> Syria), collections of facts come together in generalisations and stories. Thus, the inter-
> pretative process is brought to bear in the very generalisations we make, in the facts
> selected, rejected or ignored in each story. To leave children ignorant of the way that
> the interpretative process works, both the legitimate and important reasons why
> respectable accounts will differ, and the pernicious reasons why some might inherit
> partial, deliberately deceptive, stories, would be dangerously irresponsible.

She considers it is irresponsible because, if properly taught about the nature of history,
people are in a much better position to make educated judgements:

> A pupil in possession of adequate disciplinary knowledge will realise that whatever cur-
> riculum they are taught, it is not the same as the whole domain ... Any curricular diet of
> substantive knowledge will always be the result of selection and will be subject to con-
> scious and unconscious biases of those who select the content – from politicians to
> policy-makers, to lobbyists to teachers.

Such teaching can help to guard students against the worst dangers of the three curricula discussed below: the *explicit curriculum*, the *implicit curriculum* and the *null curriculum*. This
makes for genuine education which will stand the recipient in good stead because it involves
learning to think independently and with sufficient empathy and understanding to hope to
make sound judgements. Respect for sound scholarship will enable students consciously to
adopt such principles and appreciate the ongoing nature of the search for knowledge.

(iii) Music

The third subject I want to discuss is a low status one – music. I want to stimulate some
discussion on the all-important question of priorities by arguing provocatively for the inclusion of music as being essential for all children throughout their school careers.

What music can do for education is huge:

I Music can improve educational performance in general for all children

There is increasing scientific evidence of the power and usefulness of music in the development of the brain.[44] It can greatly aid efficient learning of basic skills in literacy and
numeracy, enabling especially those children who may not be cognitively minded to master

the subjects more easily. It can help towards advanced skills in language, maths and science for those with higher cognitive capacities; it can enhance their performance, thereby helping to produce the linguists, mathematicians and scientists needed by society.

2 Music is universal and has social bonding capacities

Music comes long before language. Even a foetus in the womb responds to rhythm. Babies and tiny children pick up other facets of music, such as loudness, pitch, tone, colour, tempo and phrasing, long before they learn language. Mother-infant interaction universally entails both singing and rhythmic movement, such as rocking.[45] Every civilization the world has known has valued the part that music can play in celebration and bringing communities together. Music retains its special ways of communicating and understanding throughout life. Stammerers can sing. Impressive work in trauma-management and in the treatment of dementia confirms just how powerful music can be.

3 Music can teach cooperation and relationship skills

Harmony is a crucial aspect of making music. Music comes into its own fully when it is shared, so that people effortlessly learn to give-and-take, listen to others, share with others, and relate to others in a way which can bring pleasure to all. Even more, music-making can work in some of the most difficult areas of relationships. The extraordinary success of the Venezuelan *El Systema* movement, now copied in many countries, shows just what can be done to help children growing up in highly deprived areas to reach towards a qualitatively different way of life.[46]

4 Music can play a crucial role in emotional education and in enabling emotional maturity

Music is perhaps the most powerful of all the ways in which emotion can be expressed. It offers a hugely important outlet for all children, disturbed or otherwise – a way of coping with tensions and preventing the build-up of negative emotions. For music presents an emotional encounter through the medium of sound. Music evokes emotion and emotion affects physiological change. Consequently, music has the power to change us not only mentally but also physically. The core of individuality is based on one's unique set of emotions. Music can enhance emotional intelligence and deliver enormous psychological benefits throughout life. When emotional management is so crucial a feature of civilized society, why do we ignore a powerful means of educating it?[47]

5 Music is valuable in itself

Music is not just valuable for other purposes but in itself. The science writer Philip Ball powerfully argues that

> the case for musical education should not rest on its "improving" qualities even if these are real. The fact is that music, no less than literacy, gives access to endless wonders. To cultivate those avenues is to facilitate life-enhancing experience.[48]

Perhaps the chief reason for serious music education is to share the sheer joy of music. Music is indeed a universal language which can be understood and enjoyed right across barriers of class, culture, race, language, etc. It can speak to all children. Our society is too cerebral, too rushed, too technologically stressed; serious music education can help to correct this, acting as a valuable counter-balance. As Ball notes, "Music is not simply a kind of mathematics. It is the most remarkable blend of art and science, logic and emotion, physics and psychology, known to us."[49] Moreover, the whole canon of Western classical music is a magnificent achievement. It is increasingly appreciated worldwide, yet neglected by a majority of people in its homeland.

So why is music not taught with sufficient time and resources to enable all children/students to benefit from it throughout their school careers?[50]

Before leaving this section on priorities, I want to inject a note on the distinction between education and indoctrination.

Avoiding indoctrination

Whatever the subject taught, and by whatever method, we need to be focused on education and avoid any form of indoctrination. We need to be aware of how easily the latter can happen. Education, unlike nurture in the home and local community, is deliberate management of what the child/student should know, value and believe. It cannot be neutral in any of these matters, because what is on offer in schools inevitably reflects the views of society and its educational authorities.

The issue of indoctrination does not matter if all that is put across is beyond dispute as true. Indoctrination happens when what is, in fact, controversial is assumed to be true and children and students are not presented with alternative views. Their minds are filled up with what they are told. They can then become incapable in later years of thinking outside the box into which they were either nurtured or educated. The essence of an indoctrinated person is an inability to conceive of other possibilities than those currently presented. As such, the person cannot think about alternatives or meaningfully choose between them because they are blind to them.

Indoctrination can happen largely unintentionally, but nevertheless actually, through the three curricula which effectively operate in schools:

i   *explicit curriculum* – what is presented, namely, the content of teaching, what is actually said
ii *implicit curriculum* – how it is presented; innumerable factors which are rarely, if ever, focused on because they are the way in which the content of teaching is conveyed through the organization of the school, its ethos, relationships between staff and pupils, etc.
iii *null curriculum* – what is not presented, what is never discussed and, therefore, what pupils are not encouraged to think about. Or, if mentioned, it is done with a sneer, negative tone or critical note to discourage anyone taking it seriously

Teaching presumed factual information that students learn for exams offers a prime way towards indoctrination, because it largely bypasses their capacities for thinking and reflecting on the material presented to them. Sharing what the subject concerns, its insights, its limitations and the difficulties of arriving at the truth, on the other hand, educates. An example was already given above in Christine Counsell's approach to teaching history.

What then should be taught in schools?

A broad and balanced curriculum is an obvious answer. Very few educationalists would disagree with the notion of a broad and balanced curriculum, even though they may understand *broad and balanced* in different ways. Robinson, for example, considers that a

> balanced curriculum should give equal status and resources to the following: the arts, humanities, language, art, mathematics, physical education and science. Each address major areas of intelligence, cultural knowledge, and personal development. As well as providing a framework for what all students should learn in common, the right balance of these disciplines allows schools to cater to the personal strengths and interests of students as individuals.[51]

The question is: does it?! Religion and philosophy and moral education receive no mention in the list, although they figure under humanities, as he notes on the following page.[52] This draws attention to the great vagueness and seriously divergent views operating regarding what we mean by terms such as the *humanities*. A colleague told me, for example, how she noticed that Heads frequently confused *humanities* with *environmental studies*. See my discussion in Chapter 4 on the importance of the humanities and arts for emotional development.

The possible range of subject matter for the curriculum is huge, however. I suggest that the following two principles above all need to be borne in mind.

1 The need to try to share an interest in and openness towards the vastness of human experience and its insights

Interest and openness includes the sciences, maths, technology, languages, humanities, arts, religion, philosophy, politics, practical subjects, sport and health studies. Those leaving school who fail to appreciate how important and worthwhile all these areas are have been deprived in their education. This is so, even though they may not pursue the subjects much for themselves. We can, all of us, only develop a fraction of understanding in any of these subjects, but the holistic viewpoint remains essential.

Regarding the sciences, I would like to underline the importance of teaching not just understanding of scientific method with respect to skills and facts, but also awareness of its limitations as discussed in Chapter 2. It will help to prevent the damaging tendency towards scientism, which is false. It will enable science to deliver its hugely important contribution to civilisation without harming respect for other areas of the curriculum.

Regarding the arts, I have given some detail on the importance of music education for all children, right from the beginning. Respect for music should include respect for all the arts, literature, drama, poetry, the visual arts and crafts and dance.

In short, inclusivity in the subjects noted above for all children, regardless of their strengths, is essential. It is a means of providing an adequate, broadly based approach to education.

I consider that there should be a new category of subject, namely *Education in Beliefs and Values*. It is largely absent in schools today but, actually, crucial for the sustenance of education and, in particular, democracy. As Unwin and Yandell note, "Questions of knowledge are not neatly separable from values and beliefs."[53] Brighouse and Woods agree that "any curriculum is based on beliefs about values and purposes – about what is worth knowing, about which skills are worth acquiring, about what education is for."[54]

Education in Beliefs and Values should comprise: philosophy, moral education, religious education, citizenship and consideration of spiritual development (see Box 8.1).

Such *Education in Beliefs and Values* should not teach particular beliefs and ideas as true but invite students to think for themselves about their possible truth and relevance on the basis of some knowledge about them. It would not be indoctrinatory, rather the opposite. In the modern world help is urgently needed to safeguard students against being taken in by the easy lies thrown up by social media and the capacity of digital technology to deliver fake news.

Box 8.1 Education in beliefs and values

* *Philosophy* should be taught in a wide, holistic sense, as discussed in Chapter 2, avoiding the narrow understanding of reason based only on logic and empirical/scientific evidence.
* *Moral education* needs to concern itself with nurturing the foundational values (see Chapter 4).[55]
* *Religion* should be separated from the cultural, sociological matrix in which it has generally been put because, as Chapter 5 discussed, it is a *sui generic* subject in its own right. The view that it is just part of sociology constitutes a form of secularist indoctrination.
* *Education into politics* should be part of the school curriculum, namely, fairly presenting to children differing political views and helping them to learn to judge them for themselves. Partisanship should be exposed for what it is – failure to control emotional attachment to certain issues, tending to see things in terms of black or white and ignoring the wider view. It is often associated with the single-issue syndrome. Politics is an enormously difficult field. Nuanced thinking is required for making decisions in a highly complex and ever-changing world. Preparation for citizenship should focus especially, therefore, on how to make decisions within a situation where people disagree, as discussed in Chapter 3.
* *Development of spiritual understanding*. The difficulty of defining the word *spiritual* should not deter teaching the subject, because it deals with what clearly lies beyond literal, straightforward language. The notion of *spiritual* is close to practices such as mindfulness and meditation as aids to wellbeing.

The lack of ease with which many people regard the word "spiritual" calls for some elucidation. The development of spiritual understanding concerns reflection on the inner life which, as persons, we all have. It involves a sense of wonder and of interconnectedness – a holistic view of life. *Spiritual* is closely associated with what Ken Robinson says:

As human beings we all live in two worlds. There is the world that exists whether or not you exist. It was there before you came into it, and it will be there when you have gone. This is the world of objects, events and other people; it is the world around you. There is another world that exists only because you exist: the private world of your own thoughts, feelings and perceptions, the world within you ... Our lives are formed by the constant interaction between these two worlds, each affecting how we see and act in the other. The conventional academic curriculum is focused almost entirely on the world around us and pays little attention to the inner world. We see the results of that every day in boredom, disengagement, stress, bullying, anxiety, depression, and dropping out.[56]

Seldon is unafraid to use the word *spiritual* regarding the lack of it in education. He notes:

> Atheist thinkers dominated the late third revolution era with their dismissal of those who did not accept their materialistic, mind-dominated interpretation of truth. These thinkers tend to conflate religion and spirituality, and highlight the excesses of religious fanatics while denigrating the human and artistic achievements of those inspired by faith. Their appalling black and white approach to truth is typical third education revolution thinking. Its leading atheistic thinkers, may never have encountered the spiritual in their own life, but were single-minded in their determination to use the power of their intellects and academic and literary authority to disparage the quest for the spiritual in others.[57]

In another passage he links consciousness with the spiritual:

> When we are fully conscious, and fully present, we know life at a much deeper level, including the spiritual, but we can only experience this ourselves wholly, not by thinking alone. Only by living in the present moment, being fully aware of passing thoughts and feelings, do we become entirely awake and fully human, a state AI will never replicate.[58]

It is important that even young children should be encouraged to think for themselves about beliefs and values. It is never too young to begin the journey toward independent thought. This is in contradiction to much cognitive development theory – itself a clear example of positivism at work – which has now been radically reassessed.[59] Educated judgement is achieved not by telling people what to think but by cultivating their own genuine capacity to think and reflect.

2 The importance of relating to the needs and interests of the learner

The second principle for curriculum construction avoids the key problem with the concept of a core curriculum of subjects, namely, the disruption to the way in which learners learn. Often a core curriculum defies how learning happens and helps to create the problems which education then proceeds vainly to resolve. Therefore, concern for the person, for the student, should dominate discourse about the curriculum. It is acutely important, for example, to steer clear of identity politics. What matters is respect for each child as a person, not as belonging to a particular category of race, colour, gender or creed.

The prime concern must be at the personal level, moral and spiritual as well, so that students are helped to be in touch with an holistic vision of life. We need to return to the basic question of what education is for and about: why it is important to enable people to become educated, as discussed in Chapters 1 and 6. As Standish and Cuthbert say, "Following the insights of Michael Oakeshott among others, we argue that education is about cultivating our humanity."[60]

To fail to treat students as persons is anti-educational. As the old adage put it, "Education is not filling a bucket but lighting a flame." Probably few educationalists would openly disagree. Yet, the constant priority of management issues behind the scenes easily comes to treat those to be educated like pawns to be moved around or like robots. It is hugely important to resist this tendency. The insight so persuasively expounded by Dewey concerning the need for learning to be pupil-directed holds. Ways must be found to permit, in the current language, *ownership* of the curriculum by students. Personalised curricula offer the way forward.

Objections to not having a core curriculum for all may be alleviated by the following considerations:

(I) ACCEPTING THE PARTIALITY OF ANYONE'S KNOWLEDGE

The responsible goal of equality does not require everyone to do the same thing, but to move as far as possible towards realising his/her own potential. The volume of knowledge there to be known and mastered is infinite. All that even the most gifted can do is understand a very little. Today the danger is, indeed, information overload. We have to acknowledge that any one person can only reach an infinitely minuscule understanding of the world. Talent and interest need to be the drivers in learning what a person sees as important and helpful.

Nor is it helpful for educationalists to set limits on a student's progress. Dividing people into academically minded and practically minded groups, for example, fails to show respect for people in their diversity. Opportunity of access should be for all, even though only some will be attracted to it or able to take it on. Why do we not celebrate the fact of difference between people instead of trying to treat everyone as the same? Society needs its poets, but it does not need everyone to be a poet.

(II) THE CRUCIALITY OF DEVELOPING DISCERNMENT

What is crucial is not how much people know but how sound their capacity for making judgements is when faced with a breadth of themes and challenges. Potentially, the most important consideration of all is helping students to avoid being dogmatic. The ongoing nature of knowledge needs to be taught. Levels of uncertainty need to be accepted, indeed celebrated. Students need to be helped to think "by using the shrewd guess, the fertile hypothesis, the courageous leap," as Thomas argues.[61] Teaching such thinking skills should be at the centre of the curriculum. In the conclusion to their book, Cuthbert and Standish argue for

> an understanding of what disciplinary knowledge entails, and a commitment approaching an ethical value in making it the central organising principle of educational policy and practice ... Education is centrally about knowledge, but it also has a concomitant ethical dimension that needs to be considered not as an issue separate from knowledge, but in their relationship ... There are two ethical values at play in the selection of content, its mode of teaching *and* the pedagogic relationships required – truth and freedom."[62]

A curriculum in which the learner has genuine choice, and so to which 100 percent commitment can be given, is in a far better position to achieve such sound judgement. Being ill-at-ease with an imposed curriculum will waste everyone's time, cultivate boredom or rebellion, and, in fact, de-educate the student. I believe that the crisis facing democracy in the West today has roots in such misuse of years spent in school.

How can a personalised curriculum work in schools? After considering the role of the teacher in Chapter 9, Chapter 10 considers the logistics of sufficient reform of the education system and proper use of digital technologies to enable all children to have access to the broad and balanced curriculum which is right and possible for them. But personal interest and choice must be preserved, for the most part, in the proper meaning of a personalised curriculum made possible by digital technology. The way forward for a properly educational approach to curriculum is to weld together Dewey's insights on learning with a carefully thought-out range of subjects to be presented to pupils.

Notes

1 See, e.g., Online Etymology Dictionary. 2020. www.etymonline.com
2 T. Brighouse & D. Woods. 2013. *The AZ of School Improvement*. Bloomsbury. p. 30.
3 F. Furedi. 2007. "Introduction: Politics, Politics, Politics!" In R. Whelan (Ed.). *The Corruption of the Curriculum*. pp. 1–10. Civitas. p. 8.
4 Ibid. p. 1.
5 A. Moore. 2015. *Understanding The School Curriculum: Theory, Politics and Principles*. Routledge. p. 9.
6 Ibid. p. 3.
7 Ibid.
8 B. Barrett & E. Rata (Eds.). 2014. *Knowledge and the Future of the Curriculum*. p. 1. Cf. E. Rata. 2012. *The Politics of Knowledge in Education*. Routledge.
9 M. Young. 2017. "Foreword." In A. Standish & A. S. Cuthbert. *What Should Schools Teach?: Disciplines, Subjects and the Pursuit of Truth*. UCL Institute of Education Press. p. xiii.
10 A. Unwin & J. Yandell. 2016. *Rethinking Education*. p. 72.
11 M. Gove. 2011. "Press Release: National Curriculum Review Announced." January 2011. https://www.gov.uk/government/news/national-curriculum-review-launched. Quoted in F. Coffield & B. Williamson. 2012. *From Exam Factories to Communities of Discovery: The Democratic Route*. UCL Institute of Education Press. p. 8.
12 S. Freed. 2019. E-mail correspondence with author. October.
13 B. Williams. 2010. *Truth and Truthfulness: An Essay in Genealogy*. Princeton University Press. Quoted in Standish & Cuthbert. *What Should Schools Teach?* p. xxi.
14 Unwin & Yandell. *Rethinking Education*. p. 102.
15 K. Robinson. 2016. *Creative Schools*. Penguin. p. 134.
16 Coffield & Williamson. *From Exam Factories to Communities of Discovery*. p. 35f. They argue it is reactionary to emphasise the core subjects: English, science, mathematics, a foreign language and either history or geography. A long-running campaign against traditional core subjects because of the impact on the creative arts is still running at the time of writing. See, "BACC for the Future." 2020. ISM: Incorporated Society of Musicians. https://www.baccforthefuture.com
17 Unwin & Yandell. *Rethinking Education*. p. 74.
18 Ibid. p. 75.
19 J. Dewey. 1938. *Experience and Education*. Simon & Schuster. p. 48.
20 Robinson. *Creative Schools*. p. 141.
21 Fadel argues that there are three kinds of education needed, culminating in a fourth: (i) Knowledge, i.e., "what we know and understand," which involves themes, such as interdisciplinarity, traditional (e.g., maths), modern (e.g., entrepreneurship) or global learning; (ii) Skills, i.e., "how we use what we know," including creativity, critical thinking, communication and collaboration; (iii) Character, which is "how we behave and engage in the world," including mindfulness, curiosity, courage, resilience. ethics and leadership. Taken together these produce (iv) "Meta-Learning" or "how we reflect and adapt," including metacognition, growth and mindset.
22 The CRR openly propagates its recommendations and frameworks on a worldwide basis. It brings together non-governmental organizations, jurisdictions, academic institutions, corporations, and non-profit organizations including foundations.
23 H. Gardner. 1983. *Frames of Mind: The Theory of Multiple Intelligences*. Basic Books.

24 Gardner, H. "Multiple Intelligences: Prelude, Theory and Aftermath" in Sternberg R.J., Fisker S. T. & Foss D.J. eds. 2016 *Scientists Making a Difference* Cambridge University Press.
25 A. Seldon. 2018. *The Fourth Education Revolution*. University of Buckingham Press. p. 101.
26 "RSA Opening Mind Competence Framework." 2020. RSA: Opening Minds. www.rsaopeningm inds.org.uk/about-rsa-openingminds/competences
27 T. Tokuhama-Espinosa. 2019. *Five Pillars of the Mind: Redesigning Education to Suit the Brain.* W. W. Norton.
28 Tokuhama-Espinosa. *Five Pillars of the Mind.* p. 13. "I propose that if students were allowed to advance through different levels of mastery … If we were to teach children to identify the symbols, patterns, order, categories, and relationships around them in a routine fashion throughout their early years and education, they would then naturally call upon this way of thinking as they approached anything new throughout their lifetimes … if students were allowed to advance through different levels of *mastery* based on a pillar hierarchy, rather than being grouped by age, there would be less school failure."
29 Ibid. p. 3.
30 P. Wolfe. Quoted on the cover of *Five Pillars of the Mind*. Wolfe is the author of 2010. *Brain Matters: Translating Research to Classroom Practice*. 2nd ed. ASCD.
31 Tokuhama-Espinosa. *Five Pillars of the Mind.* p. 130.
32 Ibid. pp. 129f & 32. Tokuhama-Espinosa calls this Option C. She sees options other than this as possible. "Option A uses the pillars as method; Option B uses the pillars hierarchy to reach *mastery*." Ibid. p. 119. The term *mastery* refers to an incremental style of teaching which is today much in favour.
33 Standish & Cuthbert. *What Should Schools Teach?* p. 142
34 L. Wheelahan. 2010. *Why Knowledge Matters in Curriculum: A Social Realist Argument*. Routledge. p. 106f.
35 Geoffrey Scargill. 2019. Conversation with author. June.
36 This is my convenient summary of what Coleridge argues for in many of his works – his response to Wordsworth's "The Tables Turned": "Our meddling intellect/Mis-shapes the beauteous form of things:–/We murder to dissect." Coleridge saw a middle path – distinguishing not to divide or separate but in order to understand and better see things whole.
37 R. Pring. 2007. "Introduction: Genesis and Nature of the Book." In R. Pring (Ed.). *John Dewey*. Bloomsbury. p. 2.
38 J. Bruner. 1977. *The Process of Education*. Harvard University Press. p. ix.
39 G. Thomas. 2013. *Education: A Very Short Introduction*. Oxford University Press. p. 99.
40 In a letter in *The Times*, Nicola Woolcock reports on a report written by experts at the Royal Society including Charles Clarke, former education secretary. The report "sets out a roadmap for changing science and maths teaching in schools over the next 20 years." It says the government should create new baccalaureate-style qualifications so that all young people study science and maths until the age of 18. N. Woolcock. 2014. "Pupils 'Should Study Maths and Science to 18.'" *The Times*. June 26. p. 17.
41 "Current Education Systems Will Not be Fit for Purpose in 20 Years." 2014. The Royal Society. June 26. https://royalsociety.org/news/2014/vision-for-science-maths-education
42 Many are conditioned to believe maths is of vital importance to modern life. Yet, apart from personal finance, many have never needed much of it!
43 C. Counsell. 2017. "History." In Standish & Cuthbert. *What Should Schools Teach?* pp. 73–87, at pp. 73 & 74f.
44 See, e.g., S. Hallam. 2015. *The Power of Music: A Research Synthesis of the Impact of Actively Making Music on the Intellectual, Social and Personal Development of Children and Young People*. UCL Institute of Education Press. Hallam's research draws on more than six hundred pieces of scientific research.
45 See, e.g., D. Levitin. 2006. *This Is Your Brain on Music*. Atlantic Books. p. 262.
46 See, e.g., "Building a Better Future." 2020. The Hilti Foundation. www.hiltifoundation.org; Sistema Global. 2020. "About Sistema Global" and "Quick Facts: El Sistema in Venezuela." Sistema Global: Friends of El Sistema Worldwide. https://sistemaglobal.org
47 See, e.g., R. Scruton. 2018. *Music as an Art*. Bloomsbury Continuum. pp. 65–8, 84 & 103.

48 P. Ball. 2011. *The Music Instinct: How Music Works and Why We Can't Do Without It.* Vintage Books. p. 8.
49 Ibid. p. 2.
50 See B. Watson. 2018. "Enabling Education for All: Change the Mindset, Change the System." RSA. March. https://www.thersa.org/discover/publications…articles/rsa…/enabling-education-for-all. See also "What Can Music Do for Education?" (May 2019) and "Towards an Additional Paper for Politicians" (October 2019) available from bgwatson@waitrose.com.
51 Robinson. *Creative Schools.* p. 142.
52 On p. 143 Robinson put languages under humanities, but in the earlier list he gave them a separate slot.
53 Unwin & Yandell. *Rethinking Education.* p. 80.
54 Brighouse & Woods. *The AZ of School Improvement.* p. 72.
55 See my 2017. "Religious Education and Moral Education." In L. P. Barnes (Ed.). *Learning to Teach Religious Education in the Secondary School: A Companion to School Experience.* 3rd ed. pp. 164–81. Routledge.
56 Robinson. *Creative Schools.* p. 52.
57 Seldon. *The Fourth Education Revolution.* p. 318f.
58 Ibid. p. 320.
59 The powerful influence of Piaget has been much discredited. See, e.g., O. Petrovich. 1988. *An Examination of Piaget's Theory of Childhood Artificialism.* Oxford University Press; O. Petrovich. 2018. *Natural-Theological Understanding from Childhood to Adulthood.* Routledge.
60 Standish & Cuthbert. *What Should Schools Teach?* p. xxi.
61 Thomas. *Education.* p. 98.
62 Standish & Cuthbert. *What Should Schools Teach?* p. 135f.

Chapter 9

What is the role of the teacher?

The high calling of the teacher

One of the finest chapters in Ken Robinson's book *Creative Schools*, it seems to me, is that on "The Art of Teaching." It is brimful of enthusiasm for the vocation of teaching and its crucial importance for those who are taught. He quotes the effect on Thomas Friedman, the world-renowned *New York Times* columnist, of his teacher, Hattie Steinberg:

> Those of us on the paper and the yearbook that she also supervised, lived in Hattie's classroom. We hung out there before and after school ... None of us would have articulated it then, but it was because we enjoyed being harangued by her, disciplined by her and taught by her.[1]

This reminds me of one of the most outstanding teachers I have ever met – the cellist William Pleeth. His enormously positive, though critical, approach, his capacity for 100 percent attentiveness, and his respect for the personality of the student and concern for them to develop in their own best way were remarkable.[2] No wonder Jacqueline Du Pré called him her "cello daddy." She described him as an extraordinary teacher who knew exactly how to guide someone or to correct an error with kindness and understanding.[3]

Robinson begins his chapter on *The Art of Teaching* with reference to another utterly outstanding classroom teacher, Rafe Esquith, who taught for more than 30 years in the same elementary school classroom in Los Angeles. Esquith taught Shakespeare to nine- and ten-year-olds. Robinson spoke of an amazingly sophisticated performance of *The Tempest* in that classroom with live music including three-to-four-part singing. Moreover, the children all knew the play from memory. The performance reflected Rafe's single-mindedness and high commitment to teaching. It is a wonderful example of what can be done in a low-income area with a large percentage of immigrants.[4]

Robinson goes on to mention by name at least another ten outstanding teachers. The cover of *Maverick Teachers – How Innovative Educators are Saving Public Schools* by David E. Baugh and A. J. Juliani notes: "Despite dwindling resources and high-stakes testing, public school teachers all over the country [USA] are managing to breathe life, passion and excitement into their classrooms." Angela Duckworth comments on the book:

> Did a teacher change your life? Can you teachers learn how to do the same? The stories of these extraordinary teachers will remind you how you got into education in the first place and will inspire you to change your own teaching game.[5]

Returning to Robinson, he makes many crucial points about teaching, of which I will note three.

(i) Metaphors

Robinson discusses the all-important question of the metaphors with which we think about teaching. The factory model has never been satisfactory. Gardening is so much truer:

> Education is a living process that can best be compared to agriculture. Gardeners know that they don't make plants grow. They don't attach the roots, glue the leaves, and paint the petals. Plants grow themselves. The job of the gardener is to create the best conditions for that to happen. Good gardeners create those conditions, and poor ones don't. It's the same with teaching.[6]

As Iain McGilchrist notes, metaphors are hugely important; they define our attitude towards the world:

> Metaphoric thinking is fundamental to our understanding of the world, because it is the *only* way in which understanding can reach outside the system of signs to life itself. It is what links language to life.[7]

(ii) Developing students' creativity

The importance of developing students' creativity is widely acknowledged today. Robinson speaks wisely about the nature of creative work. He insists that being knowledgeable and appreciative of tradition and of the work of other people is not inhibiting but, on the contrary, goes hand-in-hand with authentically creating work oneself. "Appraising" and "making" belong together:

> Creative work in any domain involves increasing control of the knowledge, concepts, and practices that have shaped the domain and a deepening understanding of the traditions and achievements in which it is based … Appraising involves a deepening *contextual knowledge* of other people's work – of how, when, and why they were made – and growing powers of *critical judgment* – both artistic and aesthetic – in responding to them.[8]

Placing contemporary versus the traditional is a damaging and unnecessary dichotomy; it is both/and rather than either/or.

(iii) Relationship

Relationship is central for effective teaching. There needs to be genuine respect and deep concern for the welfare of each student. It involves finding points of contact in interest, experience and understanding. Without such bonding, little can be achieved. Teaching is a matter of person-to-person relationship. The reality of this is perceived intuitively by the young, for children are very perceptive. As Rob Carpenter puts in the preface to his book:

> At ten years old … I knew which staff were more compassionate and those who had a tendency to abuse their privilege. I knew that Mrs. Lewis, the dinner lady, genuinely loved children and did not resent turning the skipping rope in all weathers, because she liked to make kids feel good about themselves.[9]

It is worrying that the relationship aspect of teaching is something which educators often have not highlighted enough. Robinson quotes Rita Pearson, a distinguished professional educator in America for more than 40 years, as saying: "One of the things that we rarely discuss is the value and importance of human connection, relationships."[10] As Robinson put it, "Rita gave them something to build from and an incentive to keep trying. Most important, she made it clear that she was rooting for them."[11]

The reality today

How does a high concept of the vocation of the teacher compare with the day-to-day reality of teaching in so many schools in the West today? This understanding of teaching is a long way from how many working teachers see it. A joyful commitment to the importance of teaching does not seem to be reflected in the huge numbers of UK teachers who are leaving the profession early in their careers. The Association of Teachers and Lecturers Union surveyed newly qualified teachers (NQTs) in 2015, asking what their motives were for becoming teachers:

> Of the 858 respondents, over 80 percent responded that they enjoyed working with young people and 75 percent said that they wanted to make a difference. Nearly 80 percent of respondents described the excitement of celebrating pupils' "lightbulb moments" as a significant reason to enjoy teaching … Of those teachers who took part in the 2015 survey, a frightening proportion will have left the profession already. Government figures for dropout rates for teachers in their first five years of work are over 30 percent.[12]

In the intervening years the situation has become even worse. A 2019 *Guardian* article on a survey conducted by the National Education Union, the UK's biggest teaching union, noted that a "fifth of teachers plan to leave the profession within two years" and "two-fifths of teachers want to quit in five years blaming 'out of control' workload pressures and 'excessive' accountability."[13] As Anthony Seldon says: "Teachers should be able to devote their best energy to teaching students." It does not appear that many of them can. Seldon quotes a 2016 survey of 4,450 respondents in which "82 percent stated that their workload was unmanageable ... and 73 percent of respondents said their workload was affecting their physical health and 76 percent their mental health."[14] He develops the point about workload:

> Lesson planning has become inordinately burdensome for teachers under the scrutiny of the inspection body in England, Ofsted, and the demands of ever-expanding numbers of senior managers in schools, whose job is to monitor the performance of teachers ... A teacher will often have to write down a detailed lesson plan, outlining learning objectives, evaluation and content for the entire lesson.[15]

He quotes a report from the Independent Teacher Workload Review Group in England in 2016, "These burdensome and unhelpful practices have arisen due to the real and perceived demands made by government and Ofsted, and how school leaders and teachers have reacted to them."[16]

Allen and Sims note, "Teachers *have* been given greater non-contact time, which takes them out of the classroom and lowers the burden of covering absent colleagues, but it has been overwhelmed by the rate of bureaucratic activities."[17] They summarise: "Schools have fallen victim to an audit culture in which teachers feel obliged to create a paper trail that proves to people not present at the time that unwritten activities really happened."[18]

Seldon also considered the question of class size and referred to Dewey's suggestion of eight to twelve as being ideal. This is far removed from the situation today, which increases workload for teachers. Large classes of 30 or more do make matters worse despite the apparent findings of some research that smaller classes are not a significant factor.[19] They certainly are regarding, for example, the problem of marking in the secondary school, especially for teachers of subjects like English and history.

Large classes also contribute considerably to the problem of discipline, which is for many teachers – and often for the more sensitive and gifted teachers – a nightmare. If this does not feature particularly in the reasons teachers give for leaving the profession, I suspect it is because of a certain embarrassment at failure. After all, very strong-minded people with definite views can control almost any class. Inability to keep discipline can easily appear to reflect the inadequacy of the teacher.

When asked what needs to be done, one respondent to the 2019 survey was clear: "Trust being given back to teachers, less paper pushing and more focus on the children. Less emphasis on SAT's results."[20] Easier said than done! Behind the disturbing figures regarding teacher discontent lie more substantial reasons than work overload: the ubiquity of examinations and the difficulty of maintaining discipline in classes.

The impact of deeper forces at work

Firstly, the most important and sustained cause of the trouble is the top-down authoritarianism of governments chained to a bureaucratic, high-stakes approach to teaching (see

Chapter 6). Constant surveillance of instruction and the emphasis on testing are disasters for teachers. Gary Thomas expresses why they disable teachers:

> These efforts divert teachers from their experience and instincts, deliberately forcing them to bypass the teaching intelligence they have learned and nurtured. Those top-down efforts tell teachers: "Do it this way" … These initiatives fail because they disable teachers; they prevent teachers acting and reacting as they see fit as reasoning professionals. They immobilise teachers, disconnecting them from their experience and their intelligence as professionals – substituting a set of routines and procedures for professional understanding and acumen.[21]

Secondly, the proliferation of neoliberalism has done much damage to the status of teachers. Market forces threaten either to bypass the teacher altogether or reduce the teacher's role still further by treating them as a mere go-between. In their discussion of Bridge International Academies (BIA) and the role of Pearsons, Unwin and Yandell quote Carolina Junemann and Stephen J. Ball:

> The strategic feature of BIA's business model … involves a radical standardisation of processes and methods, including curriculum and pedagogy … A scripted curriculum, providing instructions for and explanations of what teachers should do and say during any given moment of a class, is delivered through tablets synchronised with BIA headquarters for lesson-plan pacing, monitoring and assessment teaching.[22]

Unwin and Yandell ask pointedly: "Who needs a qualified teacher when you can have a tablet?"

Thirdly, insisting on educational research as the preferred means of improving practice has a braking effect on change. The assumption that evidence-based research constitutes the way forward weakens trust in the inspirational aspect of teaching. It is notable, for example, that Allen and Sims's *The Teacher Gap* constantly refers to what research now shows us, as though without research we could not have intuited such insight. They disapprove, for example, of studies that

> advocate change without the scientific approach necessary to provide strong insights that can help school leaders and policymakers improve teaching and learning. In the absence of good evidence, we have been flying blind or, at best, feeling our way forward. Fortunately, the last decade has seen an explosion of rigorous research on teachers … This has attracted a new generation of researchers committed to a more scientific approach.[23]

See Chapter 6 for important discussion of this.

Fourthly, a more subtle problem facing teachers has been the impact of much current educational orthodoxy, which insists that today's world is novel and requires a significant amount of re-thinking. The presumed need for fresh initiatives creates a rather frenzied atmosphere of accommodating constant change. Time and effort must be spent on keeping up with the latest professional development courses, requirements and fashionable ideas. The pressure can seriously limit day-to-day satisfaction in doing one's job.

An example of the over-focus on the novelty of today comes across in Roofe and Bezzi-na's book, *Intercultural Studies of Curriculum*. They have high hopes for what education can achieve:

> As borders continue to narrow and societies grapple with catering to diverse needs that arise as a result, the role of teachers has become more critical. Teachers are needed to aid in nurturing the habits and consciousness necessary to create a society where every-one feels valued and respected regardless of cultural context. For this to happen, how-ever, teachers need to be properly prepared.[24]

They speak of an "emerging curriculum agenda" which "involves connecting with stu-dents and showing them how to use knowledge in real-life situations," as though this is something new. Moreover, they use a social justice lens to spotlight teacher prepara-tion.[25] Discussion in Chapter 8 noted some anxiety about the potential politicisation of the concept of social justice as a driver in education. Schools cannot be expected to carry the whole burden of society. More relevantly, the high view of education has always tried to help "everyone feel valued and respected regardless of cultural context." It should not be presented as a radically new concept that changes the very notion of education. Fail-ure in practice does not mean that social justice was deliberately not intended. To say that it was is simply viewing education as a political tool when it has always been more than that.

In light of these formidable forces at work in our society, it is unsurprising that teachers in the West are, and feel, undervalued. An immediate response to the Birmingham Starbank School incident, which was discussed in Chapter 6, is that it is just one more example of how teachers have been sidelined through an absence of trust. As Unwin and Yandell put it, "It has become common to marginalise the role of the teacher and to silence teachers' voices, particularly when the voices attempt to speak as one, through organised trade unions."[26] Roofe and Bezzina are correct to contend:

> Ongoing professional development should provide the space teachers need to reflect, debate and challenge notions about how they teach and how they help students to navigate the constant changes given their realities ... teachers need to be given the autonomy to make curricular decisions but they will not be confident to do so if the successes of their endeavours are delivered only by test scores.[27]

Such marginalising and lack of respect for teachers' professionalism is not new. Unwin and Yandell refer to a 2008 controversy over the teaching of creationism in schools, which resulted in the resignation of Professor Michael Reiss, Director of Education at the Royal Society. Reiss was not advocating Creationism, but he was grappling with the problem facing teachers as to how to relate to students whose views appeared to be opposed to evolutionary theory.[28] This controversy is close to the heart of serious issues concerning what and how teachers teach, to which I will return below.

Unwin and Yandell's comment is amply justified. Reiss's most vociferous critics were eminent scientists, for whom no such classroom problems had ever arisen. Reiss was acknowledging the plain fact that students arrive in a science laboratory with widely diver-gent worldviews, and some of their ideas do not sit easily with evolutionary theory – a pro-blem that is both deeply ethical and intensely practical. However expert in other fields they were, most of Reiss's critics had no teaching experience and, thus, were pontificating wildly outside their areas of competence. Unwin and Yandell summarise it thus:

> For the Fellows of the Royal Society, as for an increasing number of national govern-ments ... decisions about curriculum content should be made by experts – by academics or by government ministers and their advisors. The role of teachers is to deliver curri-cula, and the role of pupils is to learn what they are taught.[29]

These forces are getting in the way of teachers being truly educators. As Allen and Sims point out, the "first sense in which we face a teacher gap is the disparity between what we know about the importance of teachers, and how we treat them."[30]

What is the proper role of the teacher?

Below I give various perspectives on the proper role of the teacher.

Unwin and Yandell discuss the traditional notion of education as transmission. The teacher is

> the one who is knowledgeable, whose role is to transmit knowledge to the pupil, the one who is not-yet-knowledgeable. The teacher, or the teacher's teacher, determines in advance what is worth knowing; the pupil is the (sometimes) grateful beneficiary of this knowledge. In this process of knowledge transmission, the teacher is assisted by artefacts that have usually been specifically designed for educational purposes including text-books, worksheets, displays and so on. For much of the history of formal education, this model of education has been massively influential, informing the day-to-day practice of teachers and their pupils.[31]

Few today would agree with this notion, if challenged, even though in practice it still flourishes. Instead, Robinson neatly sums up good teaching: "Expert teachers fulfil four main roles: they *engage, enable, expect and empower*."[32] The teacher must first gain the attention of the student, then give opportunity for students to choose to learn. The teacher should believe in the student's ability to move forward and should help the student take ownership of the learning so that it is truly something the student does, not something that is done for them.

A more technical approach is offered in the following list of "six components of great teaching" by Coe, Aloisi, Higgins and Major:

1   *Pedagogical content knowledge*. This term refers to a teacher's understanding of how to adapt teaching approaches to fit the specific needs of the subject content.
2   *Quality of instruction*. This relates to how teaching method promotes the student's progress.
3   *Classroom climate* (including motivation). The term *climate* is increasingly used to indicate the general atmosphere of the classroom and how it helps or hinders students' learning. Are its vibes encouraging a positive and receptive attitude to learning?[33]
4   *Classroom management* (including behaviour management). This has as its primary concern the importance of discipline. A disruptive class can teach nothing.

5   *Teacher beliefs* (own theories about what does and does not work in teaching). This refers to the practical sensibility of the teacher, regarding what may be effective or not. It is a pragmatic awareness.
6   *Professional behaviour* (including self-evaluation and reflection). This relates to the capacity to be self-aware and self-critical as well as self-affirming. It is associated with who the teacher is as a person – with character and motivation.[34]

See also Richard Gerver's list of some of the most important knowledge and skills possessed by great teachers (Box 9.1).[35]

Box 9.1 What makes a great teacher?

1   Great teachers know how to create a strong culture. "They have the ability to create dynamic and vibrant environments where students feel safe, respected and stimulated."
2   Great teachers know how to set high expectations. "They raise their students' sense of aspiration and value ... The safe and respectful climate they produce is crucial in accomplishing that."
3   Great teachers prioritise what really matters. "Teachers know how to personalise and prioritise the needs of each and every child. They possess levels of emotional intelligence, and through deep knowledge and understanding of their students and of their job, they are able to sift through the thousands of variables in order to respond to need in highly targeted ways."
4   Great teachers plan. "They know how to deliver complex programmes and processes in logical and coherent ways, flexible enough to adapt yet clear enough to succeed."
5   Great teachers execute. "Every day, teachers execute their plans irrespective of the variables thrown in their direction."
6   Great teachers learn constantly. "The truly great teachers are confident enough to collaborate and share strengths and weaknesses and they are as committed to learning as they are to teaching."
7   Great teachers persevere. "Under often intense pressure and scrutiny, teachers always bounce back."
8   Great teachers are resourceful. "They may not know it but teachers are incredibly entrepreneurial."
9   Great teachers empathise. "Most important of all, teachers know and understand their students on a deeply personal level."

Unwin and Yandell summarize how they see the skills of the teacher:

> The teacher's role is far from straightforward. Teachers need to become adept at interpreting situations, organising learning and managing events. They need to be proactive, to know their subjects and their students, to motivate, facilitate, communicate, organise and plan. They develop the ability to know what is going on in all areas of the classroom (as if they had eyes in the back of their head). They become multi-taskers. They need to create structures, clarity and momentum.[36]

More than this, teachers inspire. I would argue that what is missing from Coe, Aloisi, Higgins and Major's list of components of great teaching is a vision of what education really is about. Inspiration needs vision. Gerver, researching the traits of people who have left an indelible mark on humanity, noted a number of characteristics they have in common: "They all possessed a profound sense of a higher purpose, something that drove them on and helped them to change the world."[37]

In Chapter 6 I suggested nine characteristics of an educated person (see Box 6.2). These characteristics are the ideal to which we need to work as teachers – enabling every student to progress as far as possible for them to realise this goal.

Five ways in which the teacher can help to educate students

The teacher is the one who puts flesh onto the ideas concerning what education really is about. As such, the role of the teacher is critical.

1 Being a role model

The teacher especially needs to embody the foundational values outlined in Chapter 4. To be absolutely committed to these values is the most important aspect of being a teacher, for it is what one is in oneself that counts most. Being a role model involves a four-fold attitude of concern:

Concern for truth is especially important because education is particularly closely concerned with knowledge. This makes particular demands on teachers, which I will return to in (4) below.

Concern for fairness involves, for example, taking care to avoid favouritism of any kind; trying to treat all students equally and fairly – to accord importance to every one. It involves commitment to social justice, but it is much more. It actually means taking each person seriously whatever their outward identity.

Concern for compassion is perhaps the most important of all as a basis for powerful education. This is the one that takes relationship most seriously and can have the most enabling effect upon the student. It involves trying to be alongside the student. See (5) below for further comment on this.

Concern for beauty tends to be neglected, as though it is just being vaguely artistic, and as such subjective. Yet in fact the climate of teaching is hugely affected by the beauty or ugliness of surroundings.

An attitude of four-fold concern is much more likely to be caught than taught. Yes, the teacher must be able to explain why these principles are so basic, but it is in day-to-day living that they come alive. They are conveyed through enthusiasm, attentiveness, discipline, persistence and confidence in working towards the progress of students which the teacher displays. Students are well able to discern teacher authenticity. Tharby quotes research which concluded that "Authentic teaching is perceived when teachers are viewed as approachable, passionate, attentive, capable and knowledgeable."[38] Tharby's advice to teachers is: "Recognise your students as individual people and be yourself," with which I agree provided the commitment to foundational values is first in place.[39]

A living example of what is to be taught is always the quickest and most responsible way forward. As Claxton and Lucas put into the mouth of Ruby in *Educating Ruby*: "Your teachers showed us how to discuss and disagree respectfully, so we naturally treated each other like that."[40] Gerver notes, "For example, if you want the students to take risks, to learn from mistakes, to respect and support each other, the staff has to work that way first."[41]

Commitment shows itself by what people are, how they treat others and how they approach knowledge. Thus, an ex-student of Kenneth Wilson spoke of his

> enthusiasm, honesty and passion which was unlike anything we had experienced before. Kenneth Wilson joyfully opened my mind to all the glorious possibilities of what we can achieve when we blend the arts, the various disciplines, literature, music and science … But it is not only what he did; it was the way he did it … He was a gentle teacher but intellectual honesty and integrity were always the underpinnings of everything he did. There were no easy answers; as a partner in dialogue he would stretch you, challenge you, make you commit to considering all sorts of options and possibilities. And in return he was always appreciative when you did the same.[42]

This is how the foundational values can be nurtured.

2 Being alive to the present and not hemmed in by pre-constructed planning

This involves being open towards fresh possibilities and delighting in improvisation when appropriate. Roofe and Bezzina note "the critical and central role that teachers play in creating aha moments."[43] Such moments do not happen to order. They usually emerge from something special or unusual that happens to take place. The teacher's role, therefore, has to have an important aspect of improvisation about it. It must have sufficient space to accommodate such moments.

Teachers need to live in the present, learn flexibility and relate to what is happening now. Carpenter sums it up like this:

> Expertise comes from the confidence to experiment, apply learning in new contexts and play creatively with learning elements – it is the organic model of improvement … teachers become artists; they have the confidence to discover new possibilities and shape them into brilliance.[44]

Some kind of a notion of what we are going to teach and how the lesson time ideally will be used is, of course, essential. The notion, however, of a very detailed and exact plan is not only a waste of effort but also likely to interfere with the direct engagement of the teacher with those before them. The lesson is likely to be ordinary and probably dull, instead of taking off and, hopefully, perhaps even permitting one of the precious aha moments.

In view of officialdom's fondness for detailed lesson plans, this point should be pursued further. The sheer intricacy and changeability of the mode of teaching as the teacher relates to students they are actually teaching, moment by moment, cannot possibly be centrally decided beforehand. Robinson quoted one of his outstanding teachers: "Good teachers know that however much they have learned in the past, today is a different day and you cannot ride yesterday's horse."[45] I recall meeting a very distinguished missionary who worked in the slums of Calcutta and taught at the university there. When I asked him the secret of his success, he replied: "Never answer a question until it is asked." In the short time I was with him, several Hindu children looked in where he kept open house, and they were not short of questions![46] Robinson says the same: "In place of offering answers to questions they haven't asked, expert teachers provoke questions in students so that they are inspired to explore them."[47]

Teaching is about having such genuine understanding of what it is one is teaching that one can improvise, listen to where students actually are and lead them forward in probing their own interests and questions. The precious spark of live interest, open-mindedness and authentic thinking for oneself must be allowed to take over when it happens. It must not be constrained by list making, note taking or the like, which currently take up so much of teachers' time and effort.

3 Resisting the mania for producing immediate results in teaching

Claxton and Lucas note, "One of the absurdities of the current education system is the single-minded obsession with results at any price."[48] This panders to the urge to be able to say that such-and-such has been taught and that the recipients successfully learned it. In point of fact, the really important results of teaching may not be known until years afterwards. Gerver writes, "I often say to teachers and school leaders that they may never see the full effect of their decisions but they must trust that their impact will be felt."[49]

The quality of teaching and discussion in the classroom cannot be neatly measured. In any attempt to communicate, we naturally note how far we are succeeding and, if not, we try some other tack. To make a great fuss of this is fundamentally mistaken. As Thomas says,

> Good teachers develop "with-it-ness"[50] ... and they are able to shift from one teaching style to another as necessary. Good teachers learn to multitask, attending to students' individual activities as well as managing the larger group. They respond to the class as well as leading it; they reflect on their successes and failures and they adapt.[51]

Even emphasis on so-called formative assessment can be unhelpful. The product of real education cannot be measured. The teacher's role is immensely important, but it has been misconstrued. The role is not to deliver a preconceived, preordained package to students treated as automata on the analogy of a factory designed to turn out manufactured products. Rather, it is for teachers to ensure that wide opportunities are given to pupils to explore for themselves. Teachers must encourage, guide and critique students' learning, act as role models and open up avenues so that each individual's interest and enthusiasm for learning is aroused for what it is that is important for them to learn at any particular moment.

May I just share my own experience. One of the most important things I tried to do as a teacher was to encourage students really to think for themselves. I never knew whether I was succeeding at all. In a sense, it did not matter, because that was not my responsibility, it was theirs. My job was to try to stimulate thought by as many interesting ways as I could think of. It took all my time, energy, enthusiasm and concern to relate to the students. There was no time for formative assessment and its procedures, just off-the-cuff, common-sense reactions to whether students were interested and understanding or whether I needed to adopt a different tack. I just hoped that I was opening vistas for them and that some of the things I said or suggested would ignite a genuine response in the students. You can imagine how gratified I felt when, as long as 50 years later, I met up with a group of former pupils who volunteered: "You taught us how to think for ourselves!"

Fundamentally, the role of the teacher is to give opportunities, not to enforce understanding upon the mind of the student. In the end, measuring success is impossible and irrelevant.

4 Counteracting the impact of the exam culture with its inculcation of false notions of knowledge

The teacher must be on guard especially against the intrusion of the exam culture with its simple reliance on recital and memorisation of facts. It tends to convey dangerous mistruths, namely:

i   That facts can be reliably known. Anxieties concerning post-truth and fake news are not going to be laid to rest without helping students learn how we can be sure that proclaimed facts are actually facts and may not be mistaken.

ii That the most important thing is remembering facts instead of understanding and using them wisely. Especially in an era of information overload, questions of relevance and purpose are not peripheral. Moreover, paying attention to these can help to close the often very wide gap between school and real life.

iii That these particular facts that we choose to examine are all that are needed or are the most important. This is not an easy point to get across. By voicing what Paul thinks, we are not voicing what Mary thinks. By choosing to talk about examination results, we are failing to talk about their impact on teachers. To the retort "Well, we can't say everything all the time – this is just absurd," we may reply that it is true, but we need to remember that this IS what is happening. By saying one thing we ARE concealing something else that could be said. Our views on matters are likely to be very partial and dependent on what we have heard, whilst there may be a host of things we should have heard.

The issue of selectivity and omission is an enormous problem besetting what to teach in the curriculum. Thus, if study of the medieval period in history focuses on superstition or dungeons in castles while it fails to encourage understanding of the vision and skills that built cathedrals, little real understanding of the medieval mind and heart will be conveyed. Again, if all we say about Cecil Rhodes is how much he believed in the British Empire and we do not mention, for example, his scholarships enabling "colonials" to share in British education at the highest levels, then a skewed judgment of him will result, as has happened in student protests against him.

To counter the power of the exam culture, the teacher should share with students, including the very young, something of the complexity of knowledge and the levels of uncertainty which are unavoidable. They should explain that we can have partial and provisional certainty but only on the basis of understanding how easy it is to be misled.

It is important that the teacher shares the questioning needed to avoid dogmatic attitudes and damaging prejudices. This involves not just giving information but stating what a subject discipline concerns (see Figure 9.1). It can help students to see that understanding history is a complex and controversial matter, just as is understanding our world today. We can rely on a commitment to the foundational values, which can enable us to be constantly open to questioning without collapsing into indecision. If the teacher can help students to see this, democracy will be hugely strengthened.

A particular difficulty is seeing history in the round instead of focussing just on one issue. I call this the single-issue syndrome which can be really damaging, disregarding the foundational values of truth and fairness and compassion.

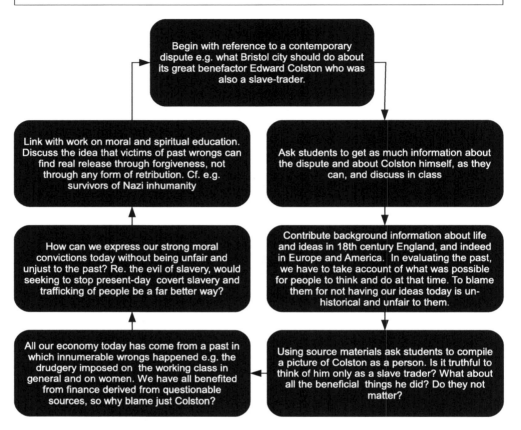

Figure 9.1 A disciplinary approach to teaching history

Awareness of such complexity can be taken on board early on. Indeed, simplistic reliance on what we have been taught as fact is the product of damaging education which has failed to share with young children the actual problems of knowledge and of communication of knowledge. By enabling students of all ages, including the very young, to begin to wrestle with criteria for discernment, such as those listed in Chapter 2, the teacher can help students move towards wisdom and not just knowledge.

5 Critically affirming teaching

The notion of critical affirmation, discussed in Chapter 3, is helpful for the teacher in two ways.

Firstly, it helps to build sound relationships with people. It affects how we treat people, especially regarding initial reactions. It is a welcoming attitude, yet it is also discerning at the same time. Critical affirmation can enable us to be honest and still be kind. This is important for the teacher correcting mistakes. We all need to be challenged. However, unless it is accompanied by warmth of relationship, by affirmation of the student as a person, a spirit of criticism can be destructive. Constantly pointing out what is wrong will deflate and frustrate students.

In learning to play a musical instrument, for example, criticism is essential, because there is a difference between a right note and a wrong one, between a note that is in tune and one that is not, between a note that is rhythmically right and one that holds up the rhythm, between a note that is expressive and part of a phrase and one that is isolated and conveys nothing except a sound, between combined notes which constitute real and meaningful music-making and just a collection of sounds which might just as well be termed noise. Criticism is essential for the student to progress. Yet, how it is given is all-important. Critical affirmation seeks to bring the student alongside and help her/him to see what needs work. Instead of feeling deflated or distanced from the teacher, the student absorbs something of the teacher's high intentions for performance and can delight in making progress.

Secondly, critical affirmation has a powerful cognitive aspect. We need to teach people how to engage in critically affirming thinking and discussion. The term *critical thinking* is constantly invoked, yet it is seriously deficient, as was pointed out in Chapter 2. Criticism puts down rather than builds up. Critically affirming thinking, however, is concerned with building up and utilising criticism in order to achieve a task. It encourages a search for what can be held in common – a real desire to understand the position of another or an opponent and together move towards truth. Instead of the adversarial approach, which has done such harm, critically affirming thinking assumes that opponents do have insights. A lot of the difficulties experienced in apparently contradictory views are often due to oversight, to what is not understood in another's position and to an unwillingness to accept that one's own position could be inadequate in any way.

As such, critically affirming thinking could offer a real way forward regarding democracy. Schools could teach it and help students experience its advantages. The teacher can draw on immense opportunities for teaching this. Anything controversial can be utilised according to its relevance to and the interests of the group. How far is what is said helpful in taking thinking further forward, or how far is it merely critical, negative or damaging to other people's self-esteem and the like? Discussion should be subjected to critically affirming thinking in the learning of any subject.

Critically affirming thinking can make the search for knowledge into a satisfying endeavour for all who take part. It is not there to condemn or slight what is possibly mistaken, but to build up and to work together towards more adequate statements. Moreover, it can be taught in the classroom (see Box 9.2).

Box 9.2 Teaching critically affirming thinking

* Ask students to note all emotionally charged words used in what people say, newspaper cuttings, tweets, etc. Such words could be used equally by both sides in a dispute. They do not take the argument forward at all because they do not refer to any evidence. The offensiveness of much conversation and public debate depends a great deal on the use of words which are emotionally charged.
* Ask students to write or talk about a controversial issue in such a way that another student cannot tell which side they are on. This is far from easy, but it is an exercise that

does help concentration on both the strong and the weak points on both sides. Any conclusion is thereby likely to be more intelligent and sensitively reached.

⋆   Ask students to note what a statement hides as well as what it says. Ask them to list various things which could have been said but were not, or people who could have been listened to but were not.

⋆   Use the device of prompts to give a vocabulary to students. Carpenter, for example, effectively used prompts in his school, such as:

"That is an interesting opinion. However ... "
"In my opinion ... What do you think?"
"I would also add that ... "
"I like ... idea but would like to add/include ... "
"I agree with ... because ... /I disagree with ... because ... "
"I particularly agree with the viewpoint because ... However, I would add that ... "[52]

The prompts referred to in the Box 9.2 are a very useful way of forwarding the search for common understanding and reaching towards truth because they offer a way of expressing disagreement without rancour. They also focus on HOW a conversation is being conducted. They can present other, non-threatening ways of challenging in a debate, which can reduce the emotional temperature of the debate and enable movement forward by all sides towards a wiser understanding of the issue.

Gerver speaks about the importance of lack of cynicism. Reflecting on attitudes in South Korea, China, Singapore, Finland, New Zealand and other countries, he comments: "Their first reflex is not to undermine or disprove but to engage. The default setting is not 'I don't agree so I will undermine you', but 'That's interesting. What can I learn from that?'"[53] This is critically affirming thinking in practice.

Trusting teacher integrity

I have suggested a formidable list of perceptions and skills that are part of the role of the teacher. Teaching attracts people who are gifted in communicating a love of knowledge. To do this requires great sensitivity, care and concern for those with whom we are trying to communicate, an awareness of the complexity and ever-changing nature of the task as well as a deep level of knowledge of the subject matter and how it is to be approached. These are qualities which require thoughtful consideration of a very wide set of issues. The best teachers are inspirational and truly present in the classroom. They do not throw their weight around. They are not submissive or compliant to instructions. They take responsibility themselves and are unafraid to use common sense, if necessary, to defy regulations. They are people of character who want their students to become people of character, not pale imitations of their teachers. They want people who think for themselves on the basis of a controlled emotional response to situations and a real concern for the welfare of others.

At the heart of it all, however, is a simplicity: a desire to communicate knowledge, understanding and wisdom through real concern for the personality and progress of the student. It concerns the twin attitudes of respect for truth and respect for people, and it brings them together.

It is essential, however, that teachers be trusted to pursue such a goal. Over-regulation of teachers must stop. It creates an atmosphere of servility and even fear, whereas education concerns liberation and delight. What has happened to the sheer joy that teaching can bring? What has happened to the confidence and excitement that are needed for joyful teaching and for which people are prepared to work hard?

A particular problem is the traumatisation of so many teachers as a consequence of how they were treated throughout their own education. Many have been taught to follow the rules, not to think for themselves and use common sense where the rules are clearly misplaced. An example from the perspective of healthcare illustrates this point. A district nurse arrived to give an injection to a patient who regularly received injections. Because written permission with a doctor's signature was forgotten one week, the nurse was put to immense trouble to search out a doctor to sign a new form. The nurse was a charming, caring person who could easily have used common sense to wink at the bureaucratic mistake, but she dared not because she could have been reported for endangering the patient. In fact, the danger was the other way round. The patient did not receive necessary medication until hours after she should have had it. Moreover, the doctor whose signature was regarded as all-important did not know the patient at all. He was, therefore, trusting the nurse! The bureaucratic mindset itself inhibited the provision of health-giving care.

I have given these details because they parallel so closely the problems facing teachers. Truly inspirational teachers, for example, do not need to make detailed lesson notes and then meticulously tick boxes after lessons to show that objectives were achieved. As mentioned above, bureaucratic labour increases teachers' workload considerably. Yet, it would require a very brave person to refuse to waste time on drawing up such detailed plans or commenting on them because the authorities could take a dim view and the teacher would be jeopardising their career. In fact, the teacher's energies are best spent on looking forward to the lesson and being truly present in the classroom, attentive to the students and adaptive to particular circumstances. Occasionally, this may require the complete jettisoning of what was planned. Recent excitement over something, a tragedy in the school, something very important affecting a member of the class, etc., may necessitate improvising important engagement with a topic of concern to all. The point needs always to be remembered that it is education that matters, not attempts to measure it.

A fine example of trusting teachers comes from Finland. Teachers in Finland have a very high status and a great deal of respect within society:

> In Finland, teachers are highly valued. The teaching career is prestigious, demanding, and reserved for the most talented and hard-working. Only one fifth of all applicants to primary teacher education programs in Finnish universities are admitted. Admission depends not only on high academic achievements, but on interest and passion to become a teacher. Once Finnish teachers are hired and in classrooms, they are given a lot of responsibility. With such a high quality human capital, school management can be performed differently. The country does not have classroom inspectors or supervisors. In its place, principals act as pedagogical leaders and provide teachers with trust and steering, instead of control. Teachers are encouraged to work in close collaboration with their peers, constantly mentoring and tutoring each other.[54]

Thus, teachers and trust are regarded as cornerstones in the Finnish education system.

How then can we encourage trust in and the trustworthiness of teachers? According to Allen and Sims, the third and most important sense of the "teacher gap" is "the difference between the quality of teachers we currently have, and the quality of teachers we want."[55] They go on to make the important point:

> Of course, not all teachers can and will thrive in a trust culture. Those that cannot must therefore be managed out in order to maintain the vitality of the profession for the benefit of teachers and pupils. Audit systems should be restricted for use on this tiny minority of teachers who are unsuited to the job … As headteacher Stephen Tierney describes it: "You deal with the exceptions; what you don't do is build a universal system around it that affects all teachers and school leaders."[56]

Otherwise untrustworthiness becomes more likely because submission and compliance are expected of people instead of sensible thinking and responsible involvement. This goes against the very nature of the job of a teacher. If the purpose of schooling is to produce educated people and citizens who enable democracy to work well, then teachers must model intelligent, sensitive and compassionate thinking for themselves. The attempt to control teachers, therefore, perverts the purpose of having them at all. So-called accountability is a fraud and must be abandoned because what it accounts for is not what schools exist to achieve.

Those in control of education need to realise that trusting teachers is not some impossible ideal but the necessary ground for any education worthy of the name to happen. The argument for giving teachers space and allowing them to develop their own professional expertise is extraordinarily strong. Confident and inspired teachers inspire students to progress to the best of their abilities. Caretaker teachers obeying instructions produce switched-off students. It is far better to trust teachers nurtured in the foundational values to act like a beacon in navigating the ever-changing circumstances of the classroom.

The future

Are teachers going to be redundant? This constitutes a real anxiety for many. An education revolving round fact-memorisation will not in the foreseeable future need teachers. All will be able to access the information they want or need via the internet. Similarly, straightforward, basic literacy, numeracy and IT skills can be taught via online programmes. Language labs can teach languages. Excellent-quality commercial materials, using the latest pedagogical devices, can bring what used to be good teaching into every home or workplace. So what role remains for a teacher?

Gerver, whose wide experience of education in many countries, deep commitment to education and optimism for its future gives his thinking some authority, writes:

> I often get asked if I think that technology will replace the teacher and whether I think that is a good thing. If teaching is no more than the acquisition of facts, then I would argue teachers are already obsolete, not just because of technology but because anyone can share facts. To inspire a thirst for knowledge and a desire to learn, however, is a human experience and one that technology cannot replicate – not yet at least. Technology is a wonderful catalyst and also a brilliant vehicle of communication and of democratising information, but it is not able to model the wonderful human traits that

define us. TED talks[57] are not brilliant, provocative and inspirational because of the technology used to broadcast them. The technology makes them accessible but the way we feel about them is entirely down to the people presenting them. So it is there that I want to focus: on the presenter, the teacher. Great teachers are great leaders; they inspire others to strive, to develop and to achieve. They take information, often complex, and facts, often sterile, and they make them live; they make them matter so that they become tools in the box of a student as they develop their knowledge and understanding of the world.[58]

Use of digital technology can free teachers to educate. So, far from implying a threat of any kind, technology can bring salvation. I share the optimism of Seldon, who writes: "The problem of teacher workload is utterly integral to the third education model and has become steadily worse over the years rather than better. AI promises total transformation."[59] I would strongly argue that, far from making teachers redundant, digital technology will liberate them. Chapter 10 discusses how this can happen.

Notes

1 T. L. Freidman. 2001. "Foreign Affairs: My Favorite Teacher." *New York Times*. January 8.
2 See, e.g., "5 Views on Teaching and Performance from William Pleeth." 2019. The Strad. September 10. https://www.thestrad.com › playing-and-teaching › 129.article
3 See, e.g., A. Blyth. 2017. "Jacqueline de Pré Interview: 'You Must Have Spontaneity and Too Much Study Destroys That.'" Gramophone. September 6. https://www.gramophone.co.uk › feature › jacqueline-du-pré-interview
4 K. Robinson. 2015. *Creative Schools*. Penguin Books. p. 97. Rafe Esquith taught in Room 56 at Hobart Elementary School in Los Angeles, CA.
5 D. E. Baugh & A. J. Juliani. 2019. *Maverick Teachers – How Innovative Educators are Saving Public Schools*. Routledge.
6 Robinson. *Creative Schools*. p. 102.
7 I. McGilchrist. 2009. *The Master and His Emissary: The Divided Brain and the Making of the Western World*. Yale University Press. p. 115. See the discussion of metaphor in Chapter 6.
8 Robinson. *Creative Schools*. p. 103f. Robinson put this into practice in *Learning Through Drama*, published in 1977, one of the outcomes of the Drama 10–16 project for the Schools Council.
9 R. Carpenter. 2018. *A Manifesto for Excellence in Schools*. Bloomsbury. p. ix.
10 Robinson. *Creative Schools*. p. 108f. He quotes Rita Pierson, a distinguished American professional for more than 40 years. See "Rita Pierson: 'Build Relationships with Your Students.'" 2013. PBS: TED Talks Education. https://www.pbs.org › wnet › ted-talks-education › speaker › rita-pierson
11 Robinson. *Creative Schools*. p. 108.
12 Carpenter. *A Manifesto for Excellence in Schools*. p. 8f.
13 S. Weale. 2019. "Fifth of Teachers Plan to Leave Profession within Two Years." *The Guardian*. April 16. https://www.theguardian.com/education/2019/apr/16/fifth-of-teachers
14 A. Seldon. 2018. *The Fourth Education Revolution: Will Artificial Intelligence Liberate or Infantilise Humanity?* University of Buckingham Press. p. 68.
15 Ibid. p. 38.
16 Seldon. *The Fourth Education Revolution*. p. 69f.
17 R. Allen & S. Sims. 2018. *The Teacher Gap*. Routledge. p. 89. According to Gibson, Oliver and Denniston, "Teachers overwhelmingly report that the love of detail, duplication or bureaucracy in their job is unnecessary of unproductive. They most frequently complain about how they are asked to record, input, monitor and analyse data (56%) and about excessive marking expectations (53%)." S. Gibson, L. Oliver & M. Denniston. 2015. "Workload Challenge: Analysis of Teacher Consultation Responses" Department of Education Research Report (DfE-RR445). Department for Education.

18 Allen & Sims. *The Teacher Gap*. p. 89.
19 M. M. Chingos & G. J. Whitchurst. 2011. "Class Size: What Research Says and What It Means for State Policy." Brookings Institute. Quoted in Seldon. *The Fourth Education Revolution*. p. 73.
20 Weale. "Fifth of Teachers Plan to Leave Profession within Two Years."
21 G. Thomas. 2013. *Education: A Very Short Introduction*. Oxford University Press. pp. 42–4.
22 C. Junemann & S. J. Ball. 2015. *Pearson and PALF: The Mutating Giant*. Education International. p. 19f.
23 Allen & Sims. *The Teacher Gap*. p. 6.
24 C. Roofe & C. Bezzina (Eds.). 2017. *Intercultural Studies of Curriculum: Theory, Policy and Practice*. Palgrave Macmillan. p. 9. They speak of "the emerging curriculum agenda."
25 Ibid. p. 231f.
26 A. Unwin & J. Yandell. 2016. *Rethinking Education: Whose Knowledge Is It Anyway?* New Internationalist. p. 126.
27 Roofe & Bezzina. *Intercultural Studies of Curriculum*. p. 234.
28 Unwin & Yandell. *Rethinking Education*. pp. 81–3.
29 Ibid. p. 83 on Professor Michael Reiss at the 2008 Liverpool Festival of Science.
30 Allen & Sims. *The Teacher Gap*. p. 4.
31 Unwin & Yandell. *Rethinking Education*. p. 26f.
32 Robinson. *Creative Schools*. p. 104.
33 See, e.g., R. Kamb. 2012. "Key Factors in Creating a Positive Classroom Climate." Committee for Children. August 12. https://www.cfchildren.org. See also K. Gulbrandson. 2017. "Three Ways to Foster a Positive Classroom Climate" Committee for Children. https://www.cfchildren.org
34 R. Coe, C. Aloisi, S. Higgins & L. E. Major. 2014. "What Makes Great Teaching? Review of the Underpinning Research." Sutton Trust. October. www.suttontrust.com/researcharchive/great-teaching. Quoted in D. Hindmarch, F. Hall, L. Machin, & S. Murray. 2017. *A Concise Guide to Education Studies*. Critical Publishing Ltd. p. 38.
35 R. Gerver. 2019. *Education: A Manifesto for Change*. Bloomsbury. p. 28f.
36 Unwin & Yandell. *Rethinking Education*. p. 136f.
37 Gerver. *Education: A Manifesto for Change*. p. 14.
38 Z. D. Johnson & S. LaBelle. 2017. "An Examination of Teacher Authenticity in the College Classroom." *Communication Education* 66, no. 4. pp. 423–39. US college students were asked to describe the behaviour of authentic and unauthentic teachers. Quoted in A. Tharby. 2018. *How to Explain Absolutely Anything to Absolutely Anyone*. Crown House Publishing. p. 37.
39 Tharby. *How to Explain Absolutely Anything to Absolutely Anyone*. p. 38.
40 G. Claxton & B. Lucas. 2015. *Educating Ruby*. Crown House Publishing Ltd. p. 57.
41 Gerver. *Education: A Manifesto for Change*. p. 69.
42 R. Fisher. 2017. *Methodist Recorder*. May 26. In an obituary of Kenneth Wilson, Fisher recalled his experience as a student in 1984 being taught by Wilson, who had been the Principal of Westminster College, Oxford and the first Director of Research at the Queen's Foundation, Birmingham. Wilson was awarded the OBE for services to education.
43 Roofe & Bezzina. *Intercultural Studies of Curriculum*. p. 232.
44 Carpenter. *A Manifesto for Excellence in Schools*. p. 157.
45 Robinson. *Creative Schools*. p. 107. He quoted Eric Thomas, an outstanding teacher of horsemanship, who noted that riding "changes every second, and you've got to change with it."
46 Fr. Pierre Fallon (1912–85) was a Belgian Jesuit priest, missionary in India and Professor of French literature at the University of Calcutta.
47 Robinson. *Creative Schools*. p. 107.
48 Claxton & Lucas. *Educating Ruby*. p. 61.
49 Gerver. *Education: A Manifesto for Change*. p. 101.
50 A phrase of Walter Doyle, the American classroom researcher.
51 Thomas. *Education: A Very Short Introduction*. pp. 42–4.
52 Carpenter. *A Manifesto for Excellence in Schools*. p. 44.
53 Gerver. *Education: A Manifesto for Change*. p. 16.
54 J. Saavedra, H. Alasuutari & M. Gutierrez. 2018. "Teachers and Trust: Cornerstones of the Finnish Education System." World Bank Blogs. December 28. https://worldbank.org/education/teachers-and-trust-cornerstone

55 Allen & Sims. *The Teacher Gap*. p. 6.
56 S. Tierney. 2017. "Teacher Monitoring: Lessons from Pig Wrestling" @LeadingLearner. November 19. https://leadinglearner.me/2017/11/19teacher-monitoring-lessons-from-pig-wrestling. Quoted in Allen & Sims. *The Teacher Gap*. p. 121.
57 TED is a nonpartisan non-profit organisation devoted to spreading ideas, usually in the form of short, powerful talks. TED began in 1984 as a conference where technology, entertainment and design converged. Today it covers almost all topics
58 Gerver. *Education: A Manifesto for Change*. p. 48.
59 Seldon. *The Fourth Education Revolution*. p. 72.

Chapter 10

Fast forward in the digital age?

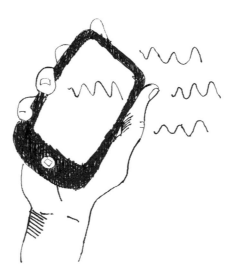

Much excellent education is happening now. There are those lucky enough to live near an exceptionally good school with outstanding staff and rich cultural resources in the neighbourhood. Many independent schools achieve a very high quality schooling for an elite financially able to afford it. Others benefit from exemplary homeschooling because of the strong educational capacities of parents. At the moment, however, such a quality education is not available for all.

The need for radical reform

There are strong moral grounds for trying to create a just society in which this kind of inequality of educational opportunity is addressed. Moreover, democracy needs educated citizens. The traumas of recent years in the running of democracy call pragmatically for urgent action. Democracy deserves better support from education, which has failed to be true to itself. The digital world opens up new possibilities for the reform needed.

Earlier chapters in this book have indicated how, to some extent, education itself may be seen as the culprit because of the way it is organised. The insightful work of Dewey on how learning best happens has not had a chance to become a reality for most because of the rigidity of the educational system. In fact, the current system creates many of the problems it cannot then resolve.

What is needed for quality education?

This chapter concerns how the high view of education given in Chapter 6 might be delivered in practice. I want to start with some common sense considerations.

(i) We are all individuals, with diverse backgrounds, abilities, temperaments, interests, needs, opportunities and experiences

In a democracy we are encouraged to value diversity, yet we try to pre-package education and make individuals fit into it. In particular, why put children/students in classes that are arranged chronologically? This model is rarely questioned because it is based on the assumption that age is important for learning. However, are there not a range of other factors that matter more, such as experience or non-experience, motivation, innate talent or lack of it?

(ii) We all know that we learn effectively when we are really and genuinely interested

Without explicit teaching babies learn so many skills, including language, through sheer interest in what is happening around them. When adults and, increasingly, governments decide what they should learn, the spontaneous curiosity which ensures learning may easily be absent. Learning can turn into drudgery, setting up a vicious circle of inability and failure instead of a creative circle of delight and achievement. Are we surprised that children thus oppressed do not learn well or that the situation can lead, moreover, to discipline problems?

(iii) We all know how easily concern for exam results replaces the proper purpose of education

To impose a regime of testing is a distraction which affects both those who teach and those who are supposed to be learning. It also risks creating cocky self-assurance among those who successfully pass exams and a lack of self-esteem among those who fail them. Notably, examinations are a breeding-ground for the social injustice we elsewhere bemoan. Moreover, this risk is without any necessary connection with education in knowledge, skills and understanding.

(iv) We all know that what really matters in life is the kind of people we are, the values we hold and try to live up to

Integrity and trustworthiness are the cement that bind civilised society together. Yet, we impose on people in their most formative years a regime in which there can be a grave mismatch between who they are as persons and what they are obliged to do or pretend to do. It can engender not only boredom and failure to achieve the potential of which they are capable, but also a split personality between what students have to do outwardly and what they really think inwardly. This split provides ample soil for the development of deception and non-integrity. While it includes the propensity for cheating and dishonesty, it can go far deeper than that.

Bearing these factors in mind we may look afresh at what is needed for learning. Is it not along the following lines?

Elements for learning

1 Access to interesting and stimulating material, together with freedom to explore it at one's own pace and following one's own interest

A broad and balanced curriculum remains the ideal, but in delivering it the emphasis must be not on *demanding* attention, but on *inspiring* it. Learning needs to be voluntary unless immediately essential, otherwise there can be waste, boredom, dissatisfaction and anger. The curriculum does need to be personalised.

2 The inspiration of being with others who want to learn together, with many opportunities to interact with people

Education is a social activity. Dewey was insistent that real learning is an interactive process that requires active participation not passive observation. As the old adage puts it, understanding is most easily "caught not taught." A strong personal and social dimension is important, both through having sufficiently small classes and having time for communal activities.

3 Sufficient structure to encourage the hard work and attentiveness needed to learn, yet without over-tension

Emphasis should be on the acquisition of self-discipline, reducing dependence on any stick-or-carrot approach. The informal kind of assessment which is a necessary and normal part of learning and teaching should be trusted without reliance on formal testing for motivating children/students. The signalling use of exams right at the end of a student's school career is all that is needed.

To sum up, a positive, enquiring and open atmosphere encouraged through conversation with others who share curiosity and freedom from dogmatism provides one of the best encouragements to education. If this is so, what kind of education system do we need?

A blueprint for organising education fit for a democracy

Even under present schooling arrangements, there could be much improvement. The following are needed:

1   A clear emphasis that persons are at the centre of education, not the content taught, measurable comparisons, administrative efficiency, etc.
2   Smaller classes so that teachers have the time to get to know children/students properly and are able to adopt something like a tutorial style of teaching, which is as appropriate for five-year-olds as it is for university undergraduates
3   A great reduction in whole-class work through the constructive use of technology, thus freeing teachers to devote quality time to conversation and informal discussion

4   Schools that resemble well-run modern libraries and provide much more of a sense of freedom for individual responsible choice and opportunities for greater interaction

5   Strong emphasis on character development and self-discipline instead of reliance on rules and regulations

6   The aim of a truly balanced curriculum, which should be genuinely broad in being fair to the arts, humanities, philosophy, religion as well as practical studies, sports, etc.

7   The involvement of helper-adults for different activities and children/students taking part in community work of various kinds, which can help prevent the isolation of schooling from real life

The educational focus should be on teaching skills of discernment, using both minds and hearts, and nurturing those values foundational for any civilised society: concern for truth, fairness, compassion and beauty, as discussed in Chapter 4. This should happen through the way the whole school experience is delivered. It involves, for example, the visual aspect of buildings and grounds as well as the expectation that staff treat everyone connected with the school with courtesy and respect.

Ideally, however, far bigger change is needed in how schooling is approached. Educationally inappropriate aspects need to go. A reformed system of education needs to be much more visionary.

The need for more far-reaching reform of education

A real breakthrough on how education is organised needs to enable each child/student to have their own personalised curriculum. It needs to liberate teachers from endless distractions that disable their focus on being educators. Time and space should be available for all the truly communal and creative activities which, in today's typically rushed climate, are mostly left out.

I would like to see pilot schemes set up and the notion of a "learning village" explored. Key aspects of this new education system should include the following.

(i) A personalised curriculum for all

Classes should include no more than eight to twelve children/students – as Dewey suggested. Teachers should see themselves as mentors – tutors guiding those committed to their care into as full an education as students' potential allows. Children/students progress at different speeds, and to try to teach concepts before they are ready is to spell disaster. Equally, damage is done when children/students are held back or hindered through boredom. Self-directed learning of information and basic skills should be encouraged by teachers for real educational progress.

A special feature of the timetable would be time together in which conversation and discussion takes place on a regular basis. Not only is this a crucial skill necessary for the flourishing of democracy, it is also an integral part of education. It is by sharing that inspiration is given. Much of the rest of the time the children/students will engage with digital programmes, where the teacher monitors what they are learning and how they are getting on, and makes suggestions. For young children this will involve teaching reading and numeracy skills.

The tutorial teachers would be supported by specialist staff who visit the school on a regular basis, for example, language specialists, drama specialists and music specialists. In addition, there should be weekly trips away from the school campus for the children to visit sports facilities, such as swimming pools, or do some kind of community work. As the children get older, visits from specialist historians, geographers, scientists, artists and mathematicians could be included. The classes should also join up for various communal activities, such as assemblies (see Figure 10.1).

The role of the teacher in these schools would be primarily tutoring and mentoring, responsible for encouraging the overall education of each student. I envisage teachers as having characteristics such as the following:

* Are committed to the foundational values
* See each child/student as a unique person whose development really matters
* Have the capacity to relate to children/students, especially the ability to listen to and talk with them in a way that holds their attention
* Have wide interests and a holistic view of life – *not* gifted at everything but open to seeing that everything can be interesting and important
* Are prepared to be flexible, change course when necessary and work with other classes
* Are capable of multi-tasking
* Have considerable expertise or skill in computers, digital management and technology, e.g., information literacy (IL), which can be broadly described as "knowing when and why you need information, where to find it and how to evaluate, use and communicate it in an ethical manner"
* Are realistic when setting aims – not perfectionists

(ii) A broad and balanced choice of subject matter available for all voluntarily to access

So that more resources are available than just those in each school, I envisage that each town will have several dedicated spaces to which all schools have access: e.g. a science bloc, a

	Monday	Tuesday	Wednesday	Thursday	Friday
20 minutes	Assembly	Assembly	Assembly	Assembly	Assembly
3 hours	Individual learning + tutorial time	Individual learning + tutorial time	Individual learning + tutorial time	Individual learning + tutorial time	Individual learning + tutorial time
	Lunch Break				
2 hours	Sciences	Music	Arts/Crafts Drama	Humanities	Sport
20 minutes	Discussion Time	Discussion Time	Discussion Time	Discussion Time	Discussion Time

Figure 10.1 Possible timetable for a primary school

languages centre, a humanities centre, an arts centre and a sports centre. Subject-specialist teachers could work in these centres, and teaching could be organised according to students' individualised interests and abilities.

There would be, therefore, basically two kinds of teachers. In addition to the tutorial teachers discussed above, there would be subject specialists who are very knowledgable about their particular subjects. Some would operate in special buildings or areas devoted to that specialism. Such teachers would only be expected to deal with students who want to learn their specialism. The enormous frustration encountered by subject teachers in mixed-ability classes could thus become a thing of the past. I suspect that this one measure alone could reverse the problem of teacher recruitment and sustainability in the profession. It would ensure that all that has been good about the traditional system will continue without the disadvantages for so many, both teachers and students. Other specialist-subject teachers would visit schools on a peripatetic basis to fire enthusiasm for their subject and inspire teaching in the schools (see Figure 10.2).

(iii) Focus on character development

The priorities for all teachers should concern character development as much as acquisition of knowledge and skills. Thus, for example, if any child/student does not fit in properly with their class, there needs to be flexibility to put them in a different class. Those with severe problems or special needs, such as learning, socialisation or mental health difficulties, should automatically be able to have one-to-one attention and support from sympathetic staff to help them re-focus and, thereby, reduce the need for specialist intervention. Almost all disciplinary problems should be nipped in the bud, therefore, by teachers using sensible ways of directing attention elsewhere and through conversation to enable anti-social attitudes to be overcome early on. Safety regulations could be reduced and normalised to better reflect how

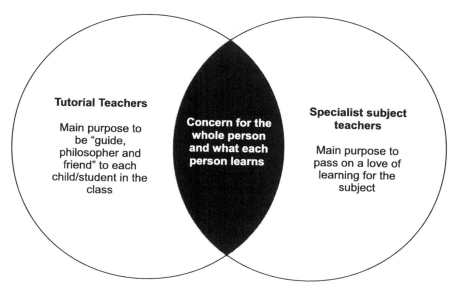

Figure 10.2 The role of the teacher

out-of-school life operates. The emphasis throughout would be on helping children/students to become trustworthy *on their own*.

As part of character development, the isolation of official education from the real world needs to be discouraged. At the specialist centres, adults could be welcome to study specialisms which interest them. A mix of some older people with the younger students might represent a more natural environment. There should be considerable opportunities for work in the community of which the school is part. For example, students could visit people in care homes, help to keep public spaces and gardens tidy and attractive or similar initiatives.

Enter digital technology

In all previous ages, what I have suggested as to how education should be organised would look like pie in the sky, completely unrealistic. However, we have entered a new age in which technology can help enormously. As Louise Starkey notes: "The innovations that have emerged at the start of the digital age include home computing, the World Wide Web, online social networks, mobile or wireless capability and communication technologies."[1] The ripples caused by common use of these tools can take us far beyond what was before possible. The proper use of digital technology could enable the system of education to treat people as persons and not as units in an administrative scheme.

The difference digital technology could make

Artificial Intelligence (AI) can support teachers and enable them to educate:

1   By enabling children/students to learn online much of the repetitive rote learning needed to acquire skills, a task for which digital technology is ideally suited.
2   By supplying excellent quality material on a wide range of subjects to enable teachers to inspire interest and, indeed, to inspire teachers themselves. Impressive resources are already available and should be used.[2]
3   By coping with the timetabling logistics to ensure every child/student has a curriculum suited to them. Enlightened headteachers have always been prepared to juggle the timetable so that individuals are able to study what they need. When everyone has individualised timetable requirements, algorithms will prove essential.
4   By managing the problems associated with transport to specialist areas, because much teaching will take place in specialised locations or outside of school grounds.
5   By providing administrative help with repetitive or bureaucratic tasks, such as taking registers, marking straightforward skills work, etc., for which digital technology and algorithms are ideally suited.

In *The Fourth Educational Revolution*, Anthony Seldon draws attention to the extraordinary impact that AI will have on schools. He envisions schools of the future in which AI, if properly used, will highlight the human over the mechanical:

> Schools of the future won't have conventional classrooms, and each student will begin their day with their personal work-plan. If we use AI well, we will retain the best of the third education revolution benefits, e.g., the social experience, the positive interactions

with staff, the stimulating careers for teachers, and the academic ambition and seriousness.[3]

His description of how *smart* schools might look perhaps sounds rather fanciful, but is an ideal worth working towards:

> Built of natural materials which are local to the area in which the school is located … they will have green areas and plants inside and out. They will be powered and watered by local sustainable supplies, and some of their food will be grown by the students. They will have animals which students will help look after. Inside, there will be a series of large open plan spaces, with flexible seating, which students will use to work in alone or participate in discussions, projects and group work in designated zones. The school day will allow for some 30 percent of time in front of each child's AI software, which will give them learning plans. Human values will permeate every pore of the school's curriculum, values and structure. Dedicated space will be given to the arts and physical activity, both of which will figure prominently in the smart school. Areas will be set aside for quiet reflection.[4]

Matt Bower considers that "Technology is changing everything in our world, including education." He notes it is not "a panacea that will solve all educational ills … in fact, using technology poorly can render a learning experience confusing and meaningless."[5] He nevertheless sees enormous possibilities for those working on the design of technology and ends his book on the need to work "scientifically and artistically" regarding the design knowledge we acquire and develop. This "can have a colossal positive effect on people's lives and indeed society."

It is not hard to find other extravagant claims made about what digital technology can achieve. In *Rewiring Education*, John Couch, Apple's first Vice President of Education, quotes Steve Jobs: "All books, learning materials and assessments should be digital and interactive, tailored to each student and providing feedback in real time."[6] Couch gives information about seven examples of transformative technologies which have the most power to rewire education: artificial intelligence, adaptive learning, intelligent assistants, the internet of things, mobile technology, 3D printing and interactive books. He notes that the sheer speed of the Internet as well as the advent of social media is allowing information to pass between people at lightning speed. People are finding out about things that solve their problems faster; when things actually do solve problems, they tend to spread faster. Couch considers that the technology currently being developed which has the most transformative potential is augmented reality (AR): "if we can get it quickly enough to the millions of students that can benefit from it, it could change the future of education as we know it."

It is worth putting such optimism beside an important statement for the need for reform in education from Diana Laurillard of the London Institute of Education:

> The processes of teaching and learning have to engage pupils' attention so that they enjoy study; the knowledge and skills they need must link to their interests so they are motivated to study; they need constant personalized support and encouragement at the pace and level to keep them engaged; the content and process of learning must be compatible with their social culture; they need to be able to see the long-term value in the hard work of study – every teacher with a vocation to teach wants to provide all this,

but in a non-elitist system this level of personalization cannot be offered for every student. The promise of new technology is that it can, for every one of those learner needs. It is an engaging and highly responsive medium; it can gather content according to interest; it can respond to individual needs of pace and level; it fits with the style and forms of youth culture; it can link the classroom to the workplace and in doing so enable teachers to provide much more of what only they can do for students.[7]

Current reluctance to reform

The wherewithal to reform education through digital technology is here already, but the ingenuity and sensitivity to apply it properly is still in its infancy. The need for reform does not appear to have made much impact on how education is managed. Kieron Sheehy and Andrew Holliman's book on education and new technologies begins with a thought experiment that imagines Mary, a time traveller from 1927 Europe, visiting our world today:

> It would be obvious to our time traveller that "modern lives" have been technologically transformed … and that activities are very different from those in her own time. However, if Mary visited a school she would probably feel very much at home, recognising many familiar structures and practices. The buildings would serve largely the same function, and she would find classroom spaces which have the form of desks, chairs and classroom boards. The reading, handwriting and arithmetic activities the children carry out would be entirely comprehensible to her. The dizzying array of online and technologically mediated experiences which she would have encountered elsewhere would seem less obvious modern settings explicitly designated for educational activities.[8]

The educational world appears to be unable to relate to this in more than a superficial way. Thomas notes: "The world of knowledge has been turned on its head in a period of only two decades or so by the Internet, and in our thinking about the curriculum we haven't yet worked through the consequences."[9]

   Back in 2001, Cuban noted that teachers in his study adapted computer use to fit with their traditional practices rather than adapting the way they teach to take account of the opportunities offered by computers.[10] Laurillard makes the same point:

> We focus the majority of technological provision on what we already understand – information systems, data gathering, communication processes, presentation – rather than using it to tackle the really difficult problems presented by our ambitions for universal and effective education. Imaginative use of digital technologies could be transformational for teaching and learning, taking us well beyond the incremental value of more accessible lecture presentations. The problem is that transformation is more about the human and organizational aspects of teaching and learning than it is about the use of technology. We have the ambition. We have the technology. What is missing is what connects the two.[11]

After conceding that he enjoys an idyllic job at Virginia University, Caplan comments that if his recommendations were taken seriously, it would end in his dismissal. He asks, "Why promote policies so dreadful to me? A blend of idealism and cynicism. I'm duty-bound to blow the whistle on my industry's vast, ongoing abuse of the taxpayer." But he adds, "Fulfilling my duty is painless because even the most intellectually compelling arguments won't convert the typical voter to distasteful conclusions."[12]

Criticism of Sugata Mitra's vision for education is especially worrying. On the outside wall of his office in Delhi, Mitra put a computer which could be accessed by completely uneducated children. He was amazed to find how much they were able to teach themselves.[13] Consequently, he attempted to apply these principles to mainstream education in India and North East England.[14] Peter Wilby's *Guardian Online Learning* article about Mitra, however, makes for discouraging reading.[15] Whilst clearly impressed with some aspects of Mitra's work, Wilby does not see much future for it and can understand why the profession is not too interested. He gives reasons, such as: Mitra has had no experience of teaching so he does not know what he is talking about; he is an outsider like Ivan Illich, the visionary of the short-lived de-schooling movement of the 1970s; anything exceptional which seems to be happening is due to the effect of novelty, exceptional people, etc. Moreover, Wilby asserts that Mitra's work lacks academically valid evidence produced through properly controlled experimentation, which can screen out effects temporarily created by any new idea, and it has not been published in reputable peer-reviewed journals.[16] See my relevant comment on such kind of research in Chapter 6.

Much reluctance to reform is short-sighted

An obvious reason for radical reform in education is the fact that we now live in a new age – the digital age. The use of digital technology marks how the younger generations are now thinking and behaving. Marc Prensky introduced the term *digital native* in 2001 to describe anyone born after 1979.[17] The education of digital natives must be managed differently.

Neil Selwyn notes a current feeling that conventional schools are no longer appropriate in the digital age; they are outmoded and obsolete. He quotes Seymour Papert, who in 1984 proclaimed:

> The computer will blow up the school. That is, school defined as something where there are classes, teachers running exams, people structured in groups by age, following curriculum – all of that. The system is based on a set of structural concepts that are incompatible with the presence of the computer.

Selwyn also quotes Greg Whitby:

> The current model of schooling has been tweaked long enough. It's time for a new model, and I fear that if we don't move on this, schooling will become increasingly irrelevant in the lives of the young people and the society it serves.[18]

Couch begins his book on rewiring education with a pregnant quote from Dewey: "If we teach today as we taught yesterday, we rob our children of tomorrow." Couch develops the point:

> Much of our educational system is outdated and disconnected, perpetually struggling to meet the needs of the users (students *and* teachers) who depend on it. Repairing

(patching) and replacing (starting over) education is not the answer. What's really needed is the *rewiring* – upgrading our educational operating system so that it better connects students, teachers, parents, and society, and so that our schools can foster creativity and innovative thinking.[19]

Quite apart from such vision at the prospect of what digital technology can do, there is another powerful consideration increasingly to the fore. Reform is needed because of concerns about the future of employment. Even a utilitarian approach to education may render reform necessary. Using schools as a means of preparation for an industrial age is becoming more and more inappropriate. Dewey delivered a warning a century ago:

> [I]ndustry at the present time undergoes rapid and abrupt changes through the evolution of new inventions. New industries spring up, and old ones are revolutionised. Consequently an attempt to train too specific a mode of efficiency defeats its own purpose. When the occupation changes its methods, such individuals are left behind with even less ability to readjust themselves than if they had a less definite training.[20]

The complexity of the real world, and specifically of the digital age, may mean that what schools offer and what the economy needs are no longer aligned. AI is proceeding at an incredible pace; robots are poised to take over many jobs. Take, for example, Marc Benioff's cloud computing company, Salesforce. It produces a robot called Einstein that attends executive meetings, criticises presentations by senior staff and quotes reams of statistics to show where sales projections are unjustified. This undermines and discomfits the human staff who are criticised in front of their peers. Mark Bridge notes, "analysts believe that robo-managers will be supervising millions of people to some degree within the next few years."[21]

Derek Smith, a materials scientist, considers the impact of AI and robotics and what it should mean for education:

> Like it or loathe it, the management structure of virtually all Western corporations depends on promotion of so-called "high flyers" who distinguish themselves from the herd largely by deployment of an enhanced factual base, itself the product of a superior memory. These people are often recipients of the silver spoons of the education system for being successful in examinations which themselves reward enhanced memory of "facts" (i.e. the current beliefs of syllabus writers and teachers). Now that robo-students can succeed better than any human at fulfilling present educational test requirements, it seems at least plausible that the Benioff scenario will gradually become the norm. Successful human executives will no longer be judged on their memory for facts but on other criteria. Their education should therefore have prepared them for their new roles.

We need to bear in mind Seldon's powerful parallel between the arrival of AI and Karl Benz's invention of the internal combustion engine in 1886:

> People had no idea how the invention would take off, or that it would transform human life across the planet. The comparison is wrong though in one respect. AI is far more wide ranging than the car, and will carry humans much further.[22]

Perils of digital technology

In many ways I share Seldon's enthusiasm and excitement at the potential of AI. I agree with what he says about the role of the teacher:

> Because AI technology will remove or reduce much that is humdrum and repetitive in the life of teachers, they can spend more time interacting and inspiring young people, and free them up to do what brought them into the profession. They will be able to read deeply and reflect on their subject, allowing them to be fellow learners alongside their students, dispelling the fiction that the teacher must be the fount of all knowledge. AI will truly usher in a land of plenty for the teacher, and transform the profession forever into what it should always have been, inspiring students with learning and living better lives.[23]

I recognise, however, that AI is a potentially dangerous force and caution is needed. Seldon sees this himself. He notes, for example, how easy it is to forget that the technology is managed by humans – it is not value-neutral:

> When introducing notions of intelligence into machines, we must be careful to make sure that their programming does not similarly reflect our bias ... in selecting the data we feed into machines, we must seriously question the process of its collection, the variables contained within it and what those imply.[24]

Neil Selwyn alerts the reader to some of the problems: "Even the most complex intelligence system is essentially built around closed forms of repetitive training. Despite claims of open-ended and socially-rich learning, these systems are most successful in navigating along rational and repetitive lines."[25]

Selwyn discusses the grave dangers of using physical robots in education, especially when they are associated with technologies designed to form emotional bonds with humans. He asks, "Should we allow children to form emotional attachments with machines that they mistakenly perceive as cognitively sentient?"[26]

Advanced research into monitoring systems, continuous assessment, "personal" robotic tutors and the use of conditioned response alongside the idea of *nudging* people into making certain decisions – all this can suggest an intrusive invasion into people's private space. It could lead to dangers regarding the autonomy of the individual and freedom to choose. Instead of helping people towards thinking for themselves, it could infantilise them. As Selwyn notes:

> Having one's instincts shaped and nudged can be a depowering and infantilizing experience for some people – preventing them from thinking for themselves. In this sense, there is much about having constant monitoring from a lifelong learning agent that could be ultimately unhelpful.[27]

Moreover, there is a serious threat of tyrannical takeover by those in authority who do not care about democracy. Both of the valuable pillars of democracy may be badly served by masterful machinery. This would constitute a form of indoctrination, which is the opposite of education. As Selwyn puts it:

> There is a fine line between being assisted and being supervised ... a technology that records and analyses all conversations that take place between a teacher and their

students *might* be used as a personal tool of reflective practice. However, it might *also* be used as an institutional tool of performance management.[28]

I conclude this section with four points about what the use of digital technology should *not* involve

1 Digital technology should not presume that more and more data leads to better education

In fact, it is quality of judgement that education is about. The use of information and questioning of interpretation – these are all very much human skills. Massive amounts of information, in fact, bring particular problems. Selection of content is essential, but on what grounds? To assume blithely that the more information the better is to ignore the human element of selection, understanding and use. Information by itself does not resolve problems – it is how it is applied, which requires skills, judgement and discernment.

2 Digital technology should not encourage children to relate to robots as though they were human

Anthropomorphising machines would foster extraordinarily dangerous confusion. Children at play in real life know that their teddy bears are not real, so there is no problem. If they are encouraged to think that the robot really is responding to them, then it would be to blur the distinction between things and people.

3 Digital technology should not utilise mechanical means of testing and reaching standards across the board

For very low-level skills tests, mechanical testing systems are legitimate and helpful. However, for marking essays, for example, it disguises the subjective element in presumed standards.

4 Digital technology should not be trusted to learn about children/students and their emotional states

Shades of Orwell's *1984* are an immediate warning. Digital technology *is* about measurement; it is impersonal and mechanical. It aspires to be human-like because it is not! Even in its role as an aid to teachers technology can easily become a mode of dictation and rob teachers of their freedom to educate. This could very easily make education a form of indoctrination.

These four considerations prompt the question: how can the perils of the educational use of AI be guarded against?

Seeking to ensure a human and humane use of AI

Educationalists need to be much more closely involved in the research and production of AI educational materials. It is very easy for commercial and technological enthusiasm to run away with ideas and innovations regardless of their educational value. This is why it is serious that there is not more in-depth debate about the use of AI for education. For, above all, a high concept of education needs to be present.

I find it disturbing, for example, that within the orbit of Dewey studies, David Hansen raises an objection concerning "what has come to be called 'personalised learning,' a pet idea of technology entrepreneurs who dream of discarding schools as we know them in favour of highly individualistic, computer-based activities with teachers hanging around as facilitators in panopticon-like settings."[29] Hansen's understanding of a personalised curriculum is clearly anti-educational and very definitely *not* what I have in mind. It represents what I see as a gross travesty of what a personalised curriculum should be. It can and should operate within schools and form only a part of the educational process. I envisage schools of inspirational value which, nevertheless, encourage all to learn in the way that suits them best.

I also find it worrying that Selwyn appears to be afraid to give the answer "*No*" to the question raised in the title of one of his books, *Should Robots Replace Teachers?* He deliberately contrasts the "should" query with two other questions: *Will* robots replace teachers? and *Can* robots replace teachers? All of his careful discussion in the book leads to the answer "*No.*" Education cannot possibly be carved up into the measurable units of technology. To be human involves far more. Yet, he refrains from saying that and prefers to leave the question open for discussion by as many people as possible, especially in the teaching profession.

Does his reluctance exemplify the secret hold of scientism, the dangers of which I discussed in Chapter 2? Is he seeing education too much through the lens of *social science* alone, rather than seeing it as enabling each generation to see and live by the high ideals which lie behind democracy, respect due to every person and the importance of guarding their freedom from tyranny? I also see the fact/opinion divide lurking in the comment he makes that his arguments in the book "simply reflect my personal take on the topic."[30] This may be standard procedure for safeguarding oneself against criticism, but there is a difference between a personal take and an argument. The many cogent points he makes should not be belittled into just a personal opinion.

We certainly need a good deal more serious debate by educationalists, but it should not reflect the fact/opinion divide. Instead, it should broaden out into a holistic form of reasoning. Selwyn himself expresses the urgency for this.

> All these technologies carry implicit assumptions about what education is, and in whose interest education operates. For example, many of the systems and applications described in this book imply continuous monitoring and measurement, "nudging" decisions and changing individuals' behaviours, and the increased involvement of commercial actors. Is this *really* what we want future forms of education to look like?[31]

Selwyn appreciates that "AI in education is related closely to one of the primary existential challenges of our modern era – what does it mean to be human in a digital age?"[32] Seldon also sees this as the major question facing education: "Will AI infantilise or liberate humanity? Ensuring the right education system that develops our full humanity is more important than anything else we might do."[33] Here I would refer the reader to the discussion in Chapter 3 of Rowan Williams on the difference between a person, an individual and a machine. For our understanding of education at root comes down to how we understand the word *human*.

Such a right education system depends crucially on the role of the teacher. The difference between a teacher and what a piece of technology can teach is huge. Couch very effectively sums up the difference:

> The only thing technology can do effectively in a classroom is supplement good teaching. The best technology on the planet doesn't even come close to being able to do

other things that great teachers can do ... Even the best-designed artificial intelligence in the world will never have the one thing possessed by great teachers – heart. Remember the Tin Man from the *Wizard of Oz*, who spent the entire story in search of a human heart? What happened to him? Every time a piece of the Tin Man got chopped off, it was simply replaced by another piece that fit the role. In technology that's called upgrading. But without a heart, the Tin Man eventually rusted away in the forest, which is where Dorothy found him. Dorothy had a good heart. The Tin Man joins her, along with other key allies, on a highly successful adventure. In our story, the Tin Man is technology. Dorothy is our teacher. Neither are effective substitutes for each other, but they do an excellent job supplementing each other. Together they are better than they could ever be alone. Wired technology certainly has the *potential* to transform both education and students, it takes great teachers to actually unlock it.[34]

Relating Parts I and II of this book

A good education system depends upon a reliable approach to life in general – on assumptions which are, as far as possible, positive and true. Part I discussed four common misunderstandings which have implicated how we tend to understand the word *human*. The seriousness of these challengeable assumptions needs to be weighed. Thus, intellectual doubt concerning free will and consciousness, made possible by the narrow view of reason discussed in Chapter 2, operate against the whole concept of education, for education presumes that we are conscious persons. This fact has been disputed by many intellectuals for over two centuries, and because there is no watertight intellectual proof that it is a fact, it is regarded as doubtful, despite the way in which everyone has conscious experience. We could not be having any discussion or trying to influence anybody were we not conscious persons. Yet, such is the apparent precedence given to the life of the mind over real life, echoing the isolation of the school from the rest of life. We do not listen easily to common sense.

The confusion in thinking here needs to be laid bare. As argued in Chapter 3, without consciousness and freewill human beings are effectively no more than machines obeying orders given to them. They can have no purpose except to serve ends outside themselves, namely, those dictated by the huge evolutionary machine of which they are a part. The phrase *an educated person* implies consciousness, purpose and values which are ethical. Neither machines, nor the whole evolutionary structure that supports them, possess any of these characteristics.

Applied to education, this raises the intriguing question: what is the matter with the industrial model of education? If we are machines, there is nothing wrong with treating the young as machines. The whole notion of the personalised curriculum becomes absurd.

Moreover, other shocking considerations follow. Chapter 4 raised the question of the reality of moral principles. Are they just what people happen to conjure up or feel, or is there something about them such that we do not *make* them, but we need to *relate to* them? We can and do expect all to have commitment to what is good and opposition to what is evil, as in the importance we give to the search for social justice. Michael Young's appeal to social justice in connection with education assumes a moral requirement in everyone to work towards that goal; it is not just a political aim with which many people can quite legitimately disagree.

Yet, such an ethical appeal to work for social justice loses its cogency if, as discussed in Chapter 4, the word *moral* is purely relative to particular settings. Linking this with the uncertainty about human consciousness and freewill, if I am a kingpin and you are a cog, what does that matter? That is what we are. Our role in life is dictated to us. Being efficient and long-lasting is all that education in the AI era is about – the factory model of education brought up to date. Life is little more than a conveyor belt to maturity.

Fortunately, no one lives as though they believe this. We all know from experience that we are conscious persons. However, because we have given the life of the mind an isolated reality distanced from the real world, we have split our personalities into what we are and what we know. We feel one way and think another. Seldon is right that intellectualising everything has been damaging in the Third Education Revolution.

Unlike Seldon, however, I do not put the blame on the over-cognitive approach *per se*, but rather on the poor quality of thinking and false assumptions on which intellectual enquiry has been based. In point of fact, emotions and thinking are always intertwined. They cannot be neatly separated from each other. In Chapter 2, I developed the thesis that the life of the mind has an important part to play in helping to guide feelings. Emotions should not be allowed just to wander off on their own in any direction. They should be controlled by the proper use of the intellect.

Seldon quotes W. B. Yeats, who wrote just over one hundred years ago:

> The best lack all conviction, while the worst
>
> Are full of passionate intensity.[35]

This describes well the state of intellectual limbo in which the West has got stuck. This connects, as discussed in Chapter 5, with the determined refusal by so many intellectuals to engage with anything to do with religion. Has academia thus thrown the baby out with the bathwater? There is a huge amount wrong with religion, which needs constant reform and criticism, and the secularisation process has had many advantages for the health of religion as well as for society. However, the fundamental insight of there being some kind of overall Mind or Transcendence responsible for the physical world of which we are a part makes sense. Take that away, and materialism easily runs rife. If faith in such a Mind or Transcendence is either considered to be pure imagination, as atheists believe, or not taken seriously as a possibility and virtually ignored – as is the case for most of life in the West, including education – then something crucial is missing.

Concluding thoughts

Seldon is optimistic that AI can put things right in education. I am not quite so optimistic because the basic mindset has not changed. Are humans, who have some measure of doubt that they are anything more than machines themselves, perhaps ill-equipped to meet creatively the dangers of the AI age? Trained, rather than educated, by the dominant factory model of education, may they not themselves be in some ways just machines? The distinction between a machine and the person has become hazy. We need to radically and confidently trust the human dimension which we share.

The impact of this lack of clarity concerning what we mean by *human* also affects the practice of democracy. I argue that education should show the way. If the faulty assumptions discussed in Part I are challenged, then there is some real hope that education will help democracy to flourish more securely. Education based on more adequate assumptions is the place to start to turn attitudes around.

I have hopes, however, precisely because there is much to appeal to in people as persons whose intuitions can often be more trustworthy than academic theory. There is a huge capacity for good to be drawn on. If the conditions under which education takes place can be improved in the direction outlined above, then permitting teachers to be a "guide, philosopher and friend" who delights in the progress of every child/student under their care will be the single most important feature driving education which really is fit for democracy and which is due to every person. Such a liberation for teachers can happen if the promise of digital technology is humanly and humanely applied.

We live in exciting times. We have the opportunity to use technology as never before. It matters very much, however, how we use it. As Iain McGilchrist noted about the Left Hemisphere of the brain, it makes a wonderful servant but a dangerous and disastrous master. The West has still to learn this lesson, so deeply distracted as it has been by the inadequate assumptions exposed in Part I of this book. I look forward to the time when, as Dewey envisaged over a hundred years ago, democracy and education can be mutually supportive for the benefit of us all.

Notes

1 L. Starkey. 2012. *Teaching and Learning in the Digital Age*. p. 14.
2 For example, the kind of material broadcast by Lucy Worsley, Chief Curator at Historic Royal Palaces and presenter of BBC Television programmes on historical topics, and David Attenborough, globally known for his marvellous programmes on the natural world. In the UK, educational institutions have access to materials through BoB: On Demand TV and Radio Education from Learning on Screen. https://learningonscreen.ac.uk/ondemand
3 A. Seldon. 2018. *The Fourth Education Revolution*. University of Buckingham Press. p. 174. See especially chapter 7. "The Future of AI in Schools."
4 Ibid. p. 208.
5 M. Bower. 2017. *Design of Technology-Enhanced Learning: Integrating Research and Practice*. Emerald Publishing. p. xi.
6 J. Couch. 2018. *Rewiring Education*. BenBella Books. See especially chapter 14. "Transformative!" pp. 189ff.
7 D. Laurillard. 2007. "Foreword to Rethinking Pedagogy for a Digital Age." In H. Beetham & R. Sharpe (Eds.). *Rethinking Pedagogy for a Digital Age*. pp. xv–xvii. Routledge. p. xvi.
8 K. Sheehy & A. Holliman (Eds.). 2018. *Education and New Technologies: Perils and Promises for Learners*. Routledge. p. 2. The book emerged from a symposium on "The Promises and Perils of Technology in Educational Contexts" at the 28th International Congress of Applied Psychology in Paris in July 2014.
9 G. Thomas. 2013. *Education: A Very Short Introduction*. Harvard University Press. p. 96.
10 L. Cuban. 2001. *Oversold and Underused: Computers in the Classroom*. Harvard University Press.
11 Laurillard. "Foreward." p. xvi.
12 B. Caplan. 2018. *The Case Against Education*. Princeton University Press. p. 287.
13 Mitra's experiment inspired the film *Slumdog Millionaire*.
14 Mitra is a Professor at Newcastle University.
15 P. Wilby. 2016. "Sugata Mitra – The Professor with his Head in the Cloud." *Guardian Online Learning*. June 7.
16 Wilby notes that "the most quoted paper, written jointly by Mitra with a teacher at the Gateshead Primary, was published in a little known journal with a low impact rating. It reported startling results … The authors admit the samples were tiny and, to draw valid conclusions, more rigorous measurements are needed." Ibid.
17 M. Prensky. 2001. "Digital Natives, Digital Immigrants Part 1." *On the Horizon* 9, no. 5. pp. 1–6. Prensky introduced the term *digital native* in this paper.
18 N. Selwyn. 2017. *Education and Technology: Key Issues and Debates*. Bloomsbury. pp. 132–5.

19 Couch. *Rewiring Education*. p. 18.
20 J. Dewey. 1917. *Democracy and Education*. Myers Education Press. 2018. p. 127.
21 M. Bridge. 2018. "Robot Einstein Humiliates Executives in Front of the Boss." *The Times*. January 26. p. 3. Bridge quotes the claims of Marc Benioff, founder of the American software company Salesforce.
22 Seldon. *The Fourth Education Revolution*. p. 105.
23 Ibid. p. 254.
24 Ibid. p. 96.
25 N. Selwyn. 2019. *Should Robots Replace Teachers?* Polity. p. 68.
26 Ibid. p. 46.
27 Ibid. p. 71f.
28 Ibid. p. 121.
29 D. T. Hansen. 2017. "Foreword." In L. J. Waks & A. R. English (Eds.). *John Dewey's Democracy and Education: A Centennial Handbook*. pp. xix–xxii. Cambridge University Press. p. xxi.
30 Selwyn. *Should Robots Replace Teachers?* p. x.
31 Ibid. p. 103.
32 Ibid. p. 23f.
33 Seldon. *The Fourth Education Revolution*. p. 321.
34 Couch. *Rewiring Education*. p. 172f.
35 W. B. Yeats. 1919. "The Second Coming." Quoted in Seldon. *The Fourth Education Revolution*. p. 318f.

Index

Page numbers in italics refer to figures.

3D printing 185

academic/skills dichotomy 108, 154
accountability: of teachers 174; test-based 122, 123, 125
active listening, and debate 58–9
Acton, Lord 12
adaptive learning 185
Allen, R. 161, 164, 174
Allott, Philip 26–7, 95, 96
Aloisi, C. 164–5, 166
amoralism 65, 106
anecdotal evidence 52
anger 14, 29; and debate 56–7; and democracy 16–17; and forgiveness 57–8; management of 76
antagonism 32, 95, 109
anti-elitism 48, 49, 75, 139
antisemitism, falsity of 43, 52-3, 66
anti-social behaviours 70, 183
Artificial Intelligence (AI) 184–5, 188, 189, 193; human and humane use of 190–2; impact on examination 128
arts 49, 149–50; and foundational values 79–80; as subject 151
Ash, Timothy Garton 50, 62n14, 81n9
Ashton, Elizabeth 134
assessment: continuous assessment 134; and discernment 41; mechanical testing systems 190; *see also* examinations
assumptions 1-3, 21, 32, 36, 40, 53-4, 68-9,104,162,179
Asthma, Stephen 74
atheism 93–4; denial of Transcendence 94; irrationality of *90*; and negation of theism 94; negativity of 94; and reason 94; *see also* religion
Athenian democracy 61, 92
Athens, Council of 500 in 13–14

Attenborough, David 194n2
augmented reality 185
Avery, A. 27
Aydon, Sean 80
Ayer, A. J. 33, 34, 69–70, 92

Baggini, Julian 28, 30, 31, 39, 40, 41, 89, 94
Ball, Philip 149, 150
Ball, Stephen J. 162
banking education 105
Barenboim, Daniel 80
Barrett, B. 139–40
Baugh, David E. 159
beauty 49; concern for 75–6, 77, 87, 166, 181; nurturing, and curriculum 141
beliefs 19, 21–2, 40, 43, 89, 151–2; in reality of Transcendence 92, 93, 95; and religion 83, 85, 87; religious and non-religious, public acknowledgement of 96–7
benevolence 75
Benioff, Marc 188
Bennett, Christopher 70, 93
Benz, Karl 188
Bernstein, Basil 110
Bezzina, C. 163, 167
Biggar, Nigel 48
Blackburn, Simon 19–20
Bloom, Paul 75
Blyton, Enid 73
boo-hurrah theory of morality 69–70, 92
Bower, Joe 126, 131, 134
Bower, Matt 185
brain hemispheres, characteristics of 3–4, *5*, 194
Bredo, Eric 112
Brennan, Jason 9–10, 12, 13, 57, 102
Bridge, Mark 188
Bridge International Academies (BIA) 162
Bridges, David 18–19

Printed in Great Britain
by Amazon